I0203134

Always on My Own:
My Life on the Street

By James E. Long & William R. Siebenschuh

red giant
+books

Copyright © 2015 James E. Long & William R. Siebenschuh

Always on My Own: My Life on the Street

Red Giant Books
ISBN: 978-0-9905435-3-4

All rights reserved. No part of this book may be reproduced or transmitted in any
form or by any means, electronic or mechanical, including photocopying, recording
or by information and retrieval systems, without the written permission of the author,
except when permitted by law.

10 9 8 7 6 5 4 3 2 1

Printed in the United States of America.

www.redgiantbooks.com

Acknowledgements

As with any project like this one, I have benefitted from and am grateful for many peoples' help. If Professor Melvyn C. Goldstein had not given me the chance to work with him on two similar autobiographical projects, I don't think I would ever have been able to complete this one. Indeed, I might not even have known how and where to begin. I am similarly grateful to Charles Michener who, while he was at Case Western Reserve read an early draft and made suggestions that helped me make the finished story a great deal better than it would otherwise have been. I am also extremely grateful to friends who read the manuscript at various stages and offered both timely advice and encouragement—in particular I want to thank William Steffee, Henry Adams, John Orlock, Mary Grimm, and my wife, Sandra.

William R. Siebenschuh
Cleveland, Ohio

For Mattie Tellis

Foreword

Detroit, Michigan. The boy hears the grownups talking in the dining room, and he knows they are talking about him. He hears his uncle say, "He's not our responsibility." His grandmother protests, but his other uncle cuts her off: "We can't keep him anymore. The county's going to have to take him, and that's that." The boy backs away and goes up to the roof of the apartment building because he knows no one will look for him there. Tears come as he watches the cars going back and forth on the Ambassador Bridge. He thinks the people in the cars probably know who they are and where they are going. He doesn't have a clue about himself.

Boys Vocational School, Lansing, Michigan. The boy has been warned. He knows they will try to sodomize him in the shower after dinner. All the other boys know it, too. They have all cleared out. He is alone, but he is ready. When the two older boys come to get him, he pulls a homemade knife from his towel and stabs one of them in the shoulder. It's a deep cut. There's blood everywhere and the toughs panic when they see it. They never expected this, and they run away screaming. When the cottage manager comes to find him the boy gives up the knife but won't answer questions about what happened or why he did it. He knows the other kids know. No one bothers him for the rest of his time there. They give him a lot of room, and he likes that.

Cleveland, Ohio. 4:00 AM. The bar at the old Majestic Hotel has shut down. The stage is dark, but Billie Holliday is wide-awake. The performance went well, but she is tired and in fact near the end of her days. You can see the toll the life she's lived has taken. The needle marks in her arms are visible even in the low light. At the moment, she sits quietly in the dark and seems at peace. The tall, good-looking emcee is still around, too, and she is waiting for him. They go to her favorite all night place for breakfast, and she tells him stories about her life till the sun finally comes up and she can get some sleep.

Carson City, California. The punks have come back just like they told the store manager they would. He doesn't pay to be "protected", they're going to work him over. They don't see the big stranger in the expensive suit till it's too late. When they realize he's there, all they see is the .44 magnum. What happens next goes down in a back room. When it's over, there's blood on the walls and the punks are in shock. The big man isn't even breathing hard. Before he lets them go he takes their wallets and pockets their driver's licenses. Now he knows who they are, he says. If he ever has to come back, they'll never know what hit them. They stumble out into the night and when they think they're safe they run for their lives. The big man knows he won't need to come back.

Lakeview Cemetery, Cleveland, Ohio. It is late October and the fall colors are at their peak. It is a peaceful, quiet place full of gnarled trees and larger than life-sized statues: stone angels and haunting cowled figures. There are obelisks, rows of mossy headstones, and mausoleums with Tiffany windows that people make special trips to see. It is the final resting place of, among others, James A. Garfield, John D. Rockefeller, and Eliot Ness. A car is parked at the side of one of the roads that wind among the gravestones and terraced lawns. Not far away a large black man, standing with the aid of a walker, has stopped at a grave. He is alone, and he is smiling. He spends several minutes and at times appears to be talking to someone. Finally, he *smiles, pats the stone affectionately, laughs to himself, walks back to the car and slowly drives away.*

* * *

The above snapshots are moments in the life of James E. "Diz" Long. (He got the nickname "Diz" because he liked Dizzy Gillespie's music so much.) This book is his account of the story of his life. It has been my privilege to help him tell it.

I began interviewing Diz Long regularly in late April 2008. For a little over a calendar year we met once a week most weeks at his apartment in the Abington Arms, which is at 11501 Mayfield Road in Cleveland, Ohio. The Abington, a self-described "senior/disabled community", is just beyond the eastern edge of the Case Western Reserve University Campus and is an easy walk from my office, only a few blocks. In many senses, however, it's a lot further than that.

When I first met and began visiting Diz, I was chairman of the English department at Case Western Reserve, where I had been teaching since 1978. It is a mid-sized research university with approximately 10,000 students about forty percent of whom are undergraduates. There are 2,600 faculty members, almost all of them PhD's. The undergraduates are hardworking and motivated, waiting their turn to become lawyers, doctors, engineers, accountants, and college professors. The faculty work hard, publish a great deal, and have national and international reputations. Some are Nobel Laureates.

The university is an ivory tower in more senses than the obvious. The 155-acre grounds are located in University Circle, the cultural center of Cleveland. The campus is bisected by Euclid Avenue, historically a symbolic barrier, which divides the sciences from the humanities and social sciences and what used to be the campus of Case Institute of Technology from what used to be Western Reserve University. (The two merged in 1967 to form the present university.)

In its heyday, part of Euclid Avenue not far from the campus was known as "Millionaires' Row." In the Gilded Age and the early decades of the twentieth-century the Rockefellers, Wade's, and Hannah's visited one another and rubbed elbows there. When my parents, who were natives of western Pennsylvania and northeast Ohio, were married in the 1930's, they came to Cleveland for their honeymoon. At the time, it was the place to go.

Obviously those days are long gone. Like all the other rust belt cities, Cleveland is struggling to find its way in the twenty-first century. The Rockefellers and Hannahs would now find little to recognize along Millionaires Row. Even after the growth of the Cleveland Clinic and an impressive a recent facelift, Euclid Avenue is now a noisy, distinctly urban thoroughfare with heavy commercial traffic during working hours. Near the university it is crisscrossed several times a day by unruly swarms of students who assault major campus intersections when classes change.

The campus itself, however, is a partially protected little world bounded by Martin Luther King Boulevard to the West and 115th Street to the East. To the north west is the most beautiful part of University Circle boasting Severance Hall, an Art Deco treasure that is home to the world famous Cleveland Orchestra, the beautiful lagoon at the front of the Cleveland Museum of Art near which are the Natural History Museum, Wade Commons, the new Botanical Gardens, the Cleveland Historical Society and the Cleveland Institutes of Art and Music. The southern edge of the campus meets the beginning of the hills that at the top become Shaker, Cleveland, and University Heights. To the east, just beyond 115th street, the campus is partially cut off from the surrounding neighborhoods by the high embankment of the railroad tracks busy all day with both commuter and freight trains. The western side of the campus is buttressed by the immense and sprawling Cleveland Clinic.

The world I live in is, thus, a partially protected world of high culture, humanistic learning, science and medicine. It includes distinguished institutions, venerable classroom buildings, laboratories, libraries and controversial architecture like the Peter B. Lewis Building designed by maverick architect, Frank Gehry. There are faculty dressed like faculty everywhere—a fairly broad sartorial spectrum that includes everything from tweeds and elbow patches to natty three-piece suits to the various forms of the academy's versions of grunge and self-expression. The professors have bulging briefcases and think deep thoughts. They have places to go and things on their minds.

There are students dressed like students everywhere, too. They have backpacks (some with wheels), cell-phones, touch pods, net books, ear buds, mountain bikes, skateboards, pierced ears, navels, and eye brows, and all the optimism and energy of motivated high achievers who are nervous about the future to be sure but who deep down think that if the world isn't their oyster yet, eventually it will be. They are young, idealistic, and usually in motion at a dizzying variety of speeds. At my age I have to keep a sharp eye out to avoid collision with aggressive skateboarders and bicyclists. As is the case with many urban universities, however, outside the perimeter of the campus the transition from Ivory Tower to harsher realities is fairly abrupt.

North of Euclid Avenue and West of Martin Luther King Boulevard between Euclid and St. Clair is Hough, the black neighborhood that was aflame in the riots of the late 1960's. To the east and northeast, especially on the other side of the railway embankment and not far beyond the beautiful, state of the art new dorms, is East Cleveland, much of it now low rent and high crime. Most of it black.

The Abington Arms, where Diz Long lives, is located on Mayfield Road a block or so to the east of the university on the campus side of the railroad tracks at the back of a section called the "Triangle." It is in a kind of No Man's Land. Up the hill on the way to the heights is Little Italy. Down the hill is the campus. Looking over its shoulder is East Cleveland.

The Abington Arms is a respectable, functional facility, a large, square, impressively solid brick building of fourteen stories. Designed for senior citizens, it offers small, manageable, one and two bedroom apartments with patios, air conditioning, and cable. For the residential community there are things like a library, a media room, a community room, a chapel, and 24hr emergency maintenance service. Flyers in the lobby regularly advertise special activities and bus trips to nearby malls. Obviously, it is a world that is completely different from the university. The residents aren't young, and they don't have backpacks and I-Phones and the energy and optimism of youth. The majority of their days are behind them, not ahead. They are people who have lived hard lives, many now facing tough physical challenges and the limitations imposed by modest means. Nobody is speeding anywhere. They move slowly and often with difficulty, not because they want to, but because they have to. They are survivors who know what it means to get old with not much of a safety net. Most but not all of them are black.

The building is secure. You enter a small foyer from the street but the door to the lobby is locked. You find your party's name on a list of residents, punch the number by the name into a call box, and wait to be buzzed in. Inside there's a sign-in sheet for visitors at a desk on your left. To the right there is a waiting room with places to sit and lots of the kinds of plants that don't need a lot of light. Directly ahead, at the far wall there are two elevators, one of them large enough to accommodate a gurney or a mobile hospital bed. In a glass case in the elevator where weekly announcements are posted there is an inspirational message that reads, "In this home you will find joy and good company . . .If you bring them with you." At the bottom of the same page it says, "Make your life a good life with what you have."

When I arrived for my first meeting with James Long—it was a while before I felt comfortable calling him "Diz"--I rode up in the elevator alone. While I waited in the lobby and on the way up, all I could think about was the surprising chain of events that led up to my being there. The way it happened was a complete surprise—like a bolt of lightning out of a clear blue sky.

Around the middle of April 2008, near the end of the spring semester, I was sitting in my office when my department assistant said there was a man on the phone who wanted to talk to the head of the English department. When she put him through the caller got right to the point. He said quickly and with some emotion, "I have lived an amazing life for a black man, and I need somebody to help me tell my story. Can you help me?"

I have been teaching English for well over thirty years, and I have gotten that kind of request a few times before. Even though I regularly teach a course in biography and autobiography, in the past I had always begged off. However, I had recently had the good fortune to participate in several collaborative projects that involved ghost writing or co-ghost writing the lives of some extremely interesting people. If a person had a good story, I now knew how exciting it could be to help them tell it. In addition, the emotion in the caller's voice— the urgency-- struck a chord. Other people who had contacted me had sometimes acted like they were doing me a favor by approaching me. This was different. Getting his story told meant a lot to this man. You could hear it in his voice. I didn't know him from Adam, nor he me, but the request sounded personal. He had asked, "Can you help me?" and the way I heard it, it sounded as if the emphasis was on "*You*". At least I took it that way, and without knowing more than that, I arranged to meet him.

At my suggestion we met at a McDonald's on the Euclid Avenue side of the Triangle. It's an easy walk from my office and near, he said, to where he lived himself. Also, it's a public place. If things weren't what they seemed, I thought it would be easy to get away.

I got there early, and he was a bit late. Figuring it maybe wasn't going to happen, I ordered and was halfway through a Big Mac Meal when I saw him come through the glass doors: a big framed, nicely dressed older black man, moving with difficulty with the aid of a walker and carrying an obviously heavy canvas shopping bag. Lifetime academics like me are pretty easy to spot in a busy urban McDonald's. He took a quick look around and knew immediately that I had to be the one he'd talked to. He came straight over, sat down across the table, and looked at my Big Mac Meal. "Well. Where's mine?" he asked.

That was how it began.

When he finished his Big Mac Meal and started to tell his story he went non-stop. It was easy to listen because it was eventful to say the least and because he was so passionate in the telling: born in rural poverty, a troubled childhood, in and out of social institutions that meant well but only made things worse, eventually becoming a professional-level athlete, a paratrooper in an elite black unit near the end of World War Two, playing semi pro football in a game against a team whose quarterback was John Unitas, working as an emcee at the old Majestic Hotel in Cleveland, taking Billie Holliday out for breakfast after performances, helping Lana Turner get home safely while he was bodyguard for Harold Robbins, meeting Maria Callas and shaking hands with Pablo Picasso on trips while a body guard for Reuben Sturman, enforcer for the numbers people in Cleveland for years—and on it went.

At first I remember thinking that it was fun to listen to, but I wasn't sure I was buying all of it. It sounded over the top to me. I remember I was smiling and trying to look like I was paying close attention but in fact I was two-thirds of the way to finding some way to escape gracefully. I didn't know how sharp he was then, how good at reading people's faces. He saw what I was thinking, suddenly stopped talking, and said, "Hand me that bag." In it was a large album that had to weigh six or seven pounds because it was full to bursting with pictures, clippings, and a lifetime of assorted documents. It was the photographic record of everything he had been telling me about and more.

The pictures were eye popping: Diz in his paratrooper outfit, Diz at dinner with athletes I used to listen to on the radio as a kid—Ollie Matson, Marion Motley, Night Train Lane—Diz at a piano with Nancy Wilson at the Majestic Hotel, glamour photos of Sarah Vaughn signed over to "Diz". The pictures just kept coming: Diz with Frank Sinatra, Diz the enforcer in his prime in front of Lancer's Restaurant on Carnegie Avenue in Cleveland, one foot on the bumper of a Lincoln Continental with a license plate that read DZLONG and looking like a cross between Shaft and Superfly.

Perhaps even more startling to me were some older photos taken, I think, with a Kodak Brownie camera at some of Harold Robbins' big Hollywood parties. On the surface they looked like my own fading Kodak Brownie pictures from the sixties. However, my pictures are of my parents or wife or maybe a fishing trip. These candid shots were of Vince Edwards (Ben Casey), Barbara Eden (Jeannie), Dolly Parton, and so on. By the time I finally gave the album back, I was a believer. I told him I thought he had a story worth telling and that I would try to help him. We agreed to begin meeting at his apartment the following week.

When I knocked on his door that first time he called me to "Come on in." The door was unlocked, as it would always be for my visits. His apartment was small but I thought comfortable looking and sensibly laid out. Just inside and immediately to my right was a small kitchen. To my left were a closet with sliding track doors, and beyond that a very short hallway with doors to a bathroom on the left and a bedroom on the right. The biggest room was the living room, and Diz was sitting in a well broken in, comfortable looking Lazy Boy at the end nearest the door.

Because it's hard for him to get around, the Lazy Boy is his command central. He has his phone and a remote control for the chair next to him on the floor where, with his long arms, he can get to them easily. On a folding TV tray right out of the 1950s were the remotes for the TV and stereo, papers, medications of various kinds, and all the little things he needs to get his business done —pens, pencils, a calculator and magnifying glass. There was a walker folded but near to hand for when he needed to move around.

Although the room wasn't cluttered, there were a lot of things in it: a new, big screen console TV, a large sofa to the right of his chair in front of which was a glass-topped coffee table with papers and photographs on it. (He had prepared for my first visit.) Like me, he likes to have things—physical objects— around him that remind him of people and events in his life. There were paintings on the walls but mainly photographs filled with the people that are or were important to him. I didn't know who any of them were at the time, but I would learn.

He was eighty-three when I began interviewing him, and it was obvious that the years and the life he led had taken their toll physically. What was most obvious was that he could no longer bend his left leg. Old athletic injuries and complications following a hip replacement had left it immobile and straight as a board, and although he never complained, I soon realized that he was sometimes in a lot of pain because of it. He also told me that he had been diagnosed with Parkinson's, and he was self-conscious about the fact that it sometimes slightly affected his speech and movement. As we got to know one another better, he showed me scars where he had been cut and the still visible mark on the left side of his face from when he had been shot. It was a lot to process at the time, but in a few weeks I ceased to notice all but the most obvious impairments—like his leg-- because if he had paid a price for the years and the kind of life he had lived, he by no means came across as an invalid. He was—and still is—a big man who looks, I believe, like exactly what he is: a formidable old warrior of the streets and the clubs, a man who has had his day and knew how to live the good life. He still has the quiet confidence of someone who for years knew that he had things under control.

As the pictures in the album make clear, in his prime he was not simply a big man but an impressive, even commanding physical presence. As I was to learn in the coming months, in his heyday, from the mid-1960s through the 1980s Diz Long was a familiar figure in the black neighborhoods on the east side of Cleveland. In the worlds he moved in—the black clubs, the streets, the old Majestic Hotel, Lancer's Restaurant—most people knew who he was and many feared him. He was strikingly handsome, with an athlete's grace and the physical menace of a heavyweight boxer in training. He dressed with style, flashed expensive jewelry, drove big cars, and often carried a .44 magnum in a shoulder holster. People who owed money did not want to see him coming. In 1976, when he was shot from ambush while standing at the window of his apartment at what is now Lake Park Towers on Superior Road, along with the details of the shooting the reporter for the Cleveland *Call and Post* noted that, "Associates credit Long with being extremely skilled with his fists." One of Diz's friends told the reporter that, "[Diz] is the Muhammed Ali, the champion of any corner he happens to be on."

From our first meeting at McDonald's I could see the outlines not only of the former size and strength but also of the confidence and self-possession, the result of awareness of his physical gifts from an early age and from years of working with and being taken seriously by strong personalities and powerful people. His eyes are sharp and can be disconcertingly piercing but usually have a smile in them. His speaking voice is surprisingly soft and from the beginning his manner to me was almost deferential although there was never any doubt about who was talking and who was listening. I once asked him if he'd ever had to deal with any real problems when he was a bodyguard. He said no. If anyone seemed to be causing a problem, he said, he would quietly take them aside and, for example, tell them that Mrs. Harold Robbins didn't want to talk to them; he would consider it a favor if they would respect her wishes. He said that was all he ever had to say. Even knowing him, as I do, only in his eighties, it's easy to see why. That's all he would have had to say to me.

At our first interview the apartment was dark when I arrived, and the TV was turned up. After we greeted and shook hands I walked around the coffee table and sat down just off his right shoulder on the sofa that, as we would joke later, was a real man-eater. That is, it was easy to sit down in and—because you sank into it—hard to get out of. After I was seated and comfortable there were a few seconds of awkward silence. Then he hit the "mute" button and told me to turn some lights on. After that I got settled in, opened my notebook, and we began.

As I look back, I realize that our first actual interview was a bit stiff and formal. I think in the beginning neither one of us knew exactly what we had just signed on for. For a few weeks I carefully called him "Mr. Long" and he was careful and very much on his manners, too. He had clearly given some thought to how he wanted to tell his story and would often have prepared categories of things to talk about, stories he had thought about for some time, and ways he wanted to phrase things. We proceeded fairly carefully, I think trying to find a style for conducting these interviews that would suit us both. The most important thing that happened at that first meeting was that it broke the ice and didn't change either of our minds about the project. After that, we quickly got into a weekly routine.

There were no marathon sessions. Without either us saying a word we found that a bit over an hour was enough for this first time and with a few exceptions, that's how long each meeting took. We had a little ritual at the end of each session. He had a calendar on the far kitchen wall with his various obligations and medical appointments on it. I would go to it or bring it to him and we would find a time that was good for both of us for next week. We would shake hands and I was soon back in the elevator on the way back to my office and my world, sometimes so excited by the things he had shared with me that I could scarcely sit still in my chair.

When I got back to my office after that first meeting I played the tape of it over and over again in my head. It seemed to go pretty well for a first time—hadn't it? I asked him about the things that were really important--hadn't I? I felt frustrated that I hadn't been as prepared as I thought I was. I was certain there were other questions and follow up questions I should have asked. What I was most certain about, however, was that the opportunity to help James Long tell his story was a chance to tell a story that was interesting and, I believed, important in many ways and on many levels. I wanted to do justice to it. Above all, I didn't want to blow it.

For the first few weeks I just let him talk and took notes as fast as I could. We went where he wanted to go. Pretty soon we got more comfortable with one another and the process itself. We were "Diz" and Bill by that time, and I started asking more questions and then follow-up questions that he was usually happy to answer. The answers sometimes went at right angles to what at the time seemed like the main story, but they often led to whole new sets of memories.

When we were just starting, what he wanted to concentrate on were the amazing things that he—a black man--had done, the celebrities he'd met, the sheer variety of things he'd seen and been a part of. Indeed, it is a remarkable story. Because of his unusual combination of athletic ability, personal charm, and his size, strength, and savvy, he did things and met people that most people would consider amazing for anyone—black or white. However, as we kept talking, an additional story started pushing its way up to the surface.

I had learned from a colleague I collaborated with on earlier projects that you don't just interview once. You keep going back because there are always second and third crops of memories. This was certainly true with Diz. When he started talking about his childhood and early years the second time around, he opened up more than he had before. He wanted to talk about the facts that he was on his own so much as a child, that for whatever reasons his parents weren't there when he needed them, that for years on end he didn't really know where he belonged, that at crucial moments in his life he had to take care of himself, no matter what it meant doing, because no one else was going to do it for him. He kept coming back to the issue of his sense of identity. He would often say, "When I was little and my parents weren't there, I didn't know who I was. Was I a 'Long?' Was I a 'Tellis?' At times I didn't know." He has often told me that he thinks this book's title ought to be, "Who Am I?"

He has told me many times that he wished he and I had met ten or twenty years ago because his memory would have been sharper then. As I have told him, I think his memory is quite good. Moreover, I'm not sure that the story he wanted to tell would have been the same if he had been twenty or thirty years younger. All autobiographers tell their stories in the present, which directly affects how and what they remember about the past. They tell you what's most important to them at the time of writing. At eighty-three Diz clearly wanted to visit the early years and see the later ones in light of them. I believe the result is that the more sensational events in his later life take on new meaning in the context of the way he now sees his childhood. It doesn't make the things he did and saw any less amazing (quite the opposite in some cases) but it does make it clearer how it all could have happened—and to a certain extent why.

Diz has read every line of every draft and has felt free to make corrections whenever I have gotten something wrong as he remembers it. When all is said and done, though, it is certainly fair to ask how accurate his memories are. We both have thought about this a lot, and I think it's fair to say that the story is as accurate as we could make it. I am in my mid-sixties and I have trouble remembering whether this or that happened in the 1970s or '80s. Diz is in his eighties, and of course there were episodes in his life that were hard for him to locate exactly. A fact of life for anyone his age is, also, that many of the people he might have checked with are no longer living. Fortunately we had help from a variety of sources. His shooting, the Brenda Ayers-Jim Brown affair, and several events involving Reuben Sturman were covered by *The Cleveland Plain Dealer* and the *Call & Post*. We also had Diz's divorce papers, which allowed us to locate all six marriages in time and in relation to one another. There are easy-to-find records about the 555th all black parachute infantry division. Sequencing the early childhood events was harder, but we worked at it painstakingly and Diz is convinced that although there may be small gaps in his memory, the main sequence of events is accurate.

Looking at the divorce papers was a part of this process of telling Diz's story that I will remember for a long time. We were still in the early stages of getting a timeline established, what happened before what. He hadn't talked much about his wives till then but suddenly mentioned that he had been married five times. I perked up, because I knew if he could remember the dates of the marriages and the order, it would help us align other events, so I asked about it. He had a little trouble thinking back and then brightened and said, "Wait a minute. I have all my divorce papers. That will tell us what we want to know," and he got up and went to the bedroom to get them. He brought them back, handed them to me, and then made some phone calls while I looked through them. "How many wives did you say you had, Diz?" I asked. "Five," he said decisively. "Look again," I said. "There were six." "No way," he said—so I read the names and dates in order: Martha, Loretta, Joan, Mary, Eleanor, and Delores. Several of these marriages were short lived, but when I read the names, he started to smile. "That's right. Now I remember. After Delores I just had girlfriends. No more wives." In a small way the moment was a breakthrough because, although he had forgotten much, once we had the names, the specific memories started returning. Predictably they in turn triggered more memories, and as I wrote and asked more questions I could see the specific details slowly coming back. As I always told Diz, it was for sure that he forgot things, everybody does. But when he did remember, he had a surprisingly good command of details.

Does he tell all? I have been a student of biography and autobiography for decades, and I think the answer is that nobody tells *all*. People telling their own story talk about the things that are most important to them at the time of the telling. What surprised and impressed me about Diz is how candid he has been about some of the more painful the details of his story. He has lived a life that involved violence, crime, and a lot of personal pain. He makes no bones about it. I spoke with him about it several times, and tried to emphasize that he didn't need to tell me anything he was uncomfortable with me knowing. His answer was immediate and direct. "It's my life," he said. "It's what I did. I don't mind people knowing about it."

The full story of Diz's life covers a lot of ground. He was born in 1925. Considering the pace of change in the twentieth-century, that's a longer time ago than perhaps it sounds. There was, of course, no civil rights movement in 1925. Women had just gotten the vote five years before. In the year Diz was born, Calvin Coolidge uttered the famous phrase, "The business of America is business" and was the first president to have his inauguration broadcast on radio. F. Scott Fitzgerald published *The Great Gatsby* in that year, and Adolf Hitler published *Mein Kampf.* The technology that would make television possible arrived when Charles Francis Jenkins achieved the first synchronized transmission of pictures and sound, which he called "radio vision." *Rin Tin Tin* and *The Phantom of the Opera* opened at the movies. Louis Armstrong and Duke Ellington made their first recordings. A pound of bread cost $.09, a pound of butter $.55, a pound of coffee, $.50, a dozen eggs, $.68, and a half-gallon of milk was $.28. Going to the movies cost $.10. And in Dayton, Tennessee a biology teacher named Scopes was arrested for teaching Darwin's theory of evolution. The famous trial soon followed, as did the Great Depression, which began in 1929.

Obviously, the world Diz Long was born into was changing rapidly and at a pace that would only increase. Anyone's perspective that begins in those years is valuable today, but what we see through Diz's eyes is that world and those changes from the point of view of someone who lived in the black world, not the white. It is a fascinating, perspective. Helping readers see these decades through Diz's eyes became one of my greatest challenges and I believe one of my greatest opportunities.

After we were comfortable with the interview process, I looked forward each session because no matter what we had tentatively planned to talk about, I never knew where the memories of that day would take us. For example, one day Diz mentioned that, during the events he was talking about at the moment, he was carrying a gun.

"What kind of gun?" I wanted to know.

"Do you want to see it?" he asked.

I said of course I did, and then for a moment felt bad because it was an effort for him to get up and get it. But he did, and when he came out of his bedroom, he had one hand on his walker, and in the other he was holding what looked to me like a small cannon. It was a long barreled, blue steel, .44 magnum revolver. In a small apartment like his it seemed to take up half the room. He obviously saw my reaction because he smiled and said, "That's right. Clint Eastwood. Dirty Harry. Go ahead, Make my day!"

He didn't come straight back to his chair. He stayed on his feet and, balancing himself carefully, he took the gun in both big hands and held it, arms extended, in the firing position. I have fired a similar weapon and couldn't help asking him how he could hit anything with it. I told him that when I had tried— out in the woods in Idaho with my brother in law—no matter what I did, when I fired the power of the recoil threw my arm and the gun back over my head. I didn't even come close to what I was aiming at.

"Watch," he said.

Then, letting go of the walker completely, he extended his arms, dropped them so that the gun was pointing at the rug, and then raised the barrel slowly. He appeared to be aiming at a framed picture on the far wall, but when the barrel was at a point between his knees and waist he pretended to pull the hammer back and then, as the gun continued to move slowly upward, he said, "Bang!"

"You start low and fire on the way up," he said.

After the imaginary shot had been fired he looked for a second at the picture he had seemed to be aiming at. It t was as if he was checking to see that he'd hit his target. Then—apparently satisfied that he had done so--he smiled, as if to say, "See. I can still get it done."

When he slid the huge weapon into a leather holster and finally got back into his chair, I was full of questions. "Is that the gun you always carried?" "How could you possibly conceal it?" "Did you have a license to carry it?" And so on. He said that for many years he was licensed to carry a concealed weapon and that he had smaller weapons for when he really needed them to be hidden. What he liked about the .44, he said, was that the size alone got peoples' attention. Usually he just had to let people see that he had it. Problem solved.

That was one side of Diz. As I learned quickly, however, there were others. Not too many weeks after that, as I was getting ready to go back to my office, he suddenly said, "Don't go yet. I want you to taste something." He made his way to the kitchen, got a large spoon from a drawer, and dipped something out of a pot still warm on the stove.

"Try this," he said.

I did, and it was delicious: white beans and chopped onions in a mouth-watering fat-beaded broth that had at some point been on a first-name basis with smoked pork hocks. He beamed when he saw my reaction. "My grandmother taught me that recipe," he said. "Sometimes when I misbehaved, she would make me stay in after school. She was always cooking something then, and I learned how to cook watching her. She was a wonderful cook", he said, and there were tears in his eyes. "My grandmother was the only one," he said. "When I was growing up, nobody wanted me. My grandmother was the only one who loved me and looked out for me. There was nobody else."

Both these episodes and many others like them profoundly affected the way I have approached my part of the shaping of this story. Seeing Diz that day, arms extended full length, sighting down the barrel of the .44 magnum told me what in fact I already knew: That in many ways he had lived a kind of life that ordinary people don't live. He was at times a violent man who had lived in a violent world. On the other hand, when I saw the emotion with which he remembered his early life and his grandmother, when I realized how young he was when he had had to learn to fend for himself, when I learned how uncertain he had been about who he was and where he belonged, I realized, that—as unusual as the some of the events of his life may be--his story is also one that lots of people will understand. From the beginning, therefore, I felt that my task and challenge were to give proper balance to *all* the stories Diz was trying to tell. In doing so, I have tried not to impose my own interpretation on a scene or episode or attempted to give any of them more importance than it was clear they had for Diz himself. It's his story, and from the beginning I have considered that my job was simply to help him tell it. There is one exception: The idea for the Auden poem in the epigraph is mine. The better I got to know Diz, the more appropriate it seemed, and Diz did not disagree.

William R. Siebenschuh, Cleveland, Ohio

I and the public know
What all schoolchildren learn,
Those to whom evil is done
Do evil in return.

September 1, 1939
W. H. Auden

Always On My Own

How I Came to Tell My Story

There were three things that made me want to take a hard look back at where I came from and what I've done and try to make sense of it. The first was getting shot, the second was getting old, and the third was working on this book.

Getting shot came first. It happened in Cleveland on April 26, 1976, and except for the fact that I was shot from ambush that evening, it was pretty much like any other day at that period of my life.

I was working as an enforcer for the black numbers rackets at the time, and since I sometimes made enemies and there were always other people who wanted to muscle in, I took sensible precautions. That night I went back to my apartment like I always did. The Forest Park Towers (it's called the Lake Park Towers now) is at 13855 Superior Road in East Cleveland. My apartment was on the fourth floor and faced south, towards the Lake. The fence around the eastern edge of Lakeview Cemetery is across Superior to the left. Down the hill from my window, you can see Euclid Avenue and beyond it the neighborhoods of East Cleveland.

I was always careful. Each night when came home I varied my routine. Sometimes I parked in the parking lot and sometimes on the street. Sometimes I parked in the back and sometimes in the front. Sometimes inside in the underground parking lot and sometimes outside. Sometimes I took the elevator and sometimes I took the stairs. Occasionally I rode up to the fifth or sixth floor and walked back down. I didn't do these things because I knew for sure I was a target. I did them because the numbers was a rough business with a lot of competition in those years. It just made sense to take steps.

That night I got to my apartment with no trouble, and when I was inside I did what I always did. I walked in, locked the door behind me and turned on the TV. It was a big console model to the right of the door where I came in. There was a couch in front of it, and behind that to the left a table, right in front of the window. I remember the program that came on was the movie, *Helter Skelter*.[1]

The shooter must have been stalking me for some time. He knew my routines and obviously was counting on my next move, which was to walk around the couch and empty my pockets onto the table. It was what I always did when I was done for the day. I put down my gun (a snub-nosed Smith & Wesson .38), my money (in a clip), my jewelry (a diamond ring and a gold chain with a diamond on it), and a cellophane bag with $100 worth of cocaine in it. After that I always went to the window.

I didn't suspect a thing. The venetian blinds were down, but they were open, and I remember I could see the lights of the cars on Euclid Avenue. The sound was up on the TV, but I just heard it in the background. My engine was switched off, and I was enjoying the calm. I let my guard down the way you do when you feel you've made it home free. I learned later from the police that the shooter was on the ground over a hundred yards away. He used a 30.06 with a telescopic sight. It was a quiet night and the shot sounded like a cannon. By the time I heard it, I was hit and there was blood everywhere.

The bullet caught me in the neck, glanced off my shoulder

or collarbone, went tearing through the left side of my face, and put a hole in the wall behind me. It must have been a steel jacketed bullet and not the kind that explodes on impact, which is probably why it didn't kill me. It went right through, and fortunately it didn't hit the carotid artery, the big artery in the neck. (It must have broken up a little, though, years later my dentist showed me an x-ray of small fragments that are still in my jaw.)

I don't know why, but the impact of the bullet didn't knock me out. I must have had some kind of adrenaline rush because I knew immediately what was happening. I grabbed my gun from the dining room table and, bleeding on everything, I ran down the stairs to the lobby.

When I got there I screamed at the desk clerk that I had been shot and he said they knew; they had heard it, too, and had called the police. I of course wasn't thinking too clearly, but I remember feeling like I couldn't wait for the police. For all I knew the guy that shot me was coming to finish the job. But the police had apparently been making regular rounds in the area and were there in less than five minutes, which was a good thing. The adrenalin wore off quickly, and the blood I had lost took its toll. Before I knew it I was going in and out of consciousness and was soon on my way in an ambulance to nearby Huron Road Hospital.

What I remember of the next few days gets a little sketchy. Only bits and pieces. I do remember that a policeman who rode with me in the ambulance kept trying to get me to tell him who shot me. "You gotta tell us," he kept saying. "You gotta tell us because it looks like you may not make it!"

The *Call & Post's* headline the next day read "**Who Shot Diz Long, He Won't Tell.**" They had it right. I didn't know who shot me, but if I had I wouldn't have told. In the world I lived in, we took care of our own problems. However, as the article went on to say, I was operated on that night, and again, the memories are just fragments. I remember they had to take an X-ray before they operated, and while they were wheeling me to the X-ray room they kept after me to tell them who had done it. I remember a doctor at some point saying urgently, "You've got to hold on. You've got to fight going to sleep. You've got to help us." But I don't remember at what point he was saying this or what else was happening, which is probably just as well. The next thing I remember was waking up in Intensive Care.

It was maybe on the second or third day, after they started cutting back on the morphine, that I woke up and saw the cocaine on the bedside table. My head ached badly and my neck and the left side of my face were on fire. I didn't feel like moving much, but when I looked to my left I could see the moveable tray on a stand next to the bed. On it were a plastic water pitcher, one of those liver shaped containers that hold pills, some straws, a ballpoint pen, and a box of Kleenex. And right in the middle of all that clutter was a little cellophane bag of cocaine worth about $100. I recognized it because it was my cocaine, and it brought me all the way awake.

I had already learned from friends who were looking after my things that by the time they got to my apartment there was nothing on the dining room table. The jewelry (worth $4-5K) the cash (close to $1,000), everything was gone. When I thought back about it, I realized that when the police who were questioning me got up to leave the last time they visited, they must have been the ones who left the cocaine. It had to have been them, and the bag of cocaine on my table was a message that I understood perfectly. The message was: "You don't want to tell us anything, that's fine. Just remember, we can bust you for cocaine possession any time we want, so don't be asking questions about where your money is."

I was in the hospital for a month because they had to repair what the bullet had done to the whole left side of my face. When I was finally able to come home, the people I worked for sent me to Las Vegas for several weeks, all expenses paid. They even gave me some money to gamble with. I spent a lot of time in the casinos and by the pool just resting and getting my strength back. It also allowed for some time for things to cool off back home and gave me time to think. I didn't realize it then, but some of the things that went through my head at the time of the shooting and also what I thought about during time I spent recovering were the beginnings of the process that eventually led to my wanting to tell my story in this book. During that time I started remembering some things that had been going through my mind in the ambulance on the way to the hospital. I knew enough to know that I had lost a lot of blood, and although I remember being fairly calm about it, I started wondering for the first time if this was it. Was I really going to die? Like this? There was so much I wanted to do. How had I gotten to this point? If I died—right then—what would people say about me? About my life? It's not like I brooded on it or that my life changed from that moment on. As I got my health and strength back, I began to go back to all the old ways of thinking. But when I was shot I was in my early fifties. I wasn't a kid anymore, and those questions never entirely went away.

Getting old snuck up on me, the way it does on most people. Till I was into my sixties I thought I was thirty-five. However, like everyone who lives long enough eventually I was forced to accept the truth. I think when you're a person like me, and you have done some pretty exciting things in your time, the more you have to realize that you can't do the things you were accustomed to any more, the more you start to think about the past—when you could. At any rate that's what I did. I started thinking that if you considered where I came from and the fact that I was a black man in a white man's world, my life had been pretty amazing.

I was born in a mining town in West Virginia that was scarcely a town at all. When I was two years old my parents sent me to live with my grandmother in Detroit, and I lived there till I was a teenager. I was happy as a small boy, but my parents never really came back into my life, and the older I got, the more it bothered me. One of the results was that as a teenager I had a tough time. I got into a lot of trouble. In time, though, I found there were things I was good at. I was an athlete. I could box, and when I got older I played football, even for a short time in the pros. Some years later I won regional boxing championships. I could run like the wind, and when I was in the service I was fast enough to get sent to the Olympic tryouts.

It wasn't easy in the beginning, though. By the time I was fifteen or sixteen, I was out of control, having brushes with the law. The family I was living with didn't want me around anymore, and I kept being moved from one special school or social institution to another. When I was old enough, or almost, the service seemed like a way to get out from under things. World War Two was still going on, and I enlisted in three different branches of the service: the marines, the army, and the paratroopers. I lied about my age the first time I enlisted; I was only sixteen at the time. I kept getting into trouble in the service, too; that's why I ended up trying three different branches. But my athletic ability helped me a lot, and I served briefly in the famous all-black parachute unit, the 555th—the Triple Nickels.

After I left the service I played some professional football in both the U.S. and Canada and eventually came to Cleveland. I worked for the city and for Carl Stokes, the first black mayor, and I got involved in the numbers. I was mainly in collections and the muscle end of things. It was a good time for me. I was still young. I had money. I had clothes. I had Rollex watches. I had big cars. Over a period of years I had six different wives. And it seemed like I was always around famous people. When I worked for a while as an emcee at the Majestic Hotel and the Chatterbox in Cleveland, I got to meet people like Billie Holliday, Ray Charles, Dinah Washington, and Dizzy Gillespie. (I liked Dizzy Gillespie's music so much my friends started calling me "Diz," and the nickname stuck.) Any way you looked at it, I thought I had lived quite a life. But at the time that's about as far as I got with it. The memories helped make up for the physical limitations I was starting to feel.

Deciding to try to write it all down happened almost by accident. When I started living in the Abington Arms, I started meeting a lot of new people. Sooner or later we would end up telling each other the stories of our lives, and I found that people were really impressed with mine. They kept telling me I ought to write it down, and finally I decided they were right and that's when I decided to get some help. It was that simple. What wasn't simple was actually doing it.

At first I thought it was going to be cut and dried. I was going to remember the events of my life and make a record of them. I knew I would need some help writing them up, but I thought my story would tell itself, and after that, what could be simpler? What I worried most about at first was whether my memory was still good enough. Would I be able to remember all the things that were important? What I discovered after we got started and I began having to answer a lot of questions, was that the questions helped jog my memory, and I remembered a lot more than I thought I would. During the course of the process of creating a first version of my story my ideas about what was most important started to change.

In the beginning mainly what I thought about were the sensational things: the high living, the athletics, the money, the glamour cars and expensive clothes, the celebrities I met and worked for, the violence, the danger, the living on the edge. But a lot of the questions I found myself answering had to do with things I hadn't thought about in years: my childhood, what it was like growing up black during the depression, the fact that my parents didn't seem to care whether I was with them or not for most of the early part of my life. I hadn't realized how much of the time in those early years I was on my own or what it meant that I had to take care of myself as much as I did. I hadn't given much thought to what kind of difference it might have made in my life if my parents had been there with me and for me from the beginning. If you live long enough and have a decent memory, you get a perspective on the events of your early life that isn't possible (at least it wasn't for me) while you're busy living it. That was the real discovery for me while I was working on this book. My idea at first had been that I would tell somebody my story. What happened in the process was that I learned what my story was.

My First Two Years

For obvious reasons I don't remember much about my first two years. What I do remember probably either came from later or from hearing my relatives talk about it.

I know I was born in Meadowbrook, West Virginia, on June 16, 1925.

If you were to drive down Interstate 79 south from Pittsburgh towards Morgantown and Clarksburg today, you could still see the kind of country it was: steep wooded hills and mountains with narrow valleys in between. Here and there you would see a small farm perched on the hillside. The woods are heavy, a lot of hardwoods, and the leaves are beautiful in the fall. A lot of country but not a lot of people.

If you were to get off the interstate and onto back roads, it might look something closer to what it did then: the heavy woods broken up by small farms here and there, a few cattle in a fenced field, a tumbledown barn (maybe with a faded sign that says, "Chew Mail Pouch Tobacco") and houses that badly need paint. There are a few small towns with short main streets, and then you're past them. But you wouldn't find Meadowbrook, because it isn't there anymore. It lived and eventually died with the coalmines.

My memories of Meadowbrook at that time in my life are, of course, sketchy, but because I was there later for a short while when I was older I do remember some things about it. There was something that passed for a main street with rows of shacks on both sides. There was a one-room school, a post office and a general store. That was about it. My parents lived in the black section but up on a hill, and so we were better off than some. We looked down on the rest of the town, and that was something. The whites lived across the highway.

Nobody in Meadowbrook had cars in those days. The mines were about an hour away and buses came to pick up the men in the morning and brought them back at night. There were no phones in the houses and no electricity. If you wanted to make a call, you had to walk to the post office or the general store. Like everyone else, my parents used oil lamps to light the house at night. Nobody had indoor plumbing; we all used outhouses. Some people had small gardens, and my family kept pigs in a pen behind the house. I remember there was a stream. And the Greyhound bus sometimes made a stop in Meadowbrook. That's about what I remember.

My father's name was Eddie Long, my mother was Cora Lee Tellis, and I was apparently a surprise to both of them. However, when my mother became pregnant with me, her family saw to it that my father did the right thing, and they were married in that same year.

Our immediate family consisted of my father and mother and me. My sister didn't come along for a while. My mother's mother, my grandmother Tellis, and my father's parents, my grandfather and grandmother Long, also lived in Meadowbrook but in their own house. I had a lot of uncles, but none of them lived in West Virginia. My mother's brothers—my uncles Chris, Allen, and Claude—all lived in Detroit. So did my uncle Hosea, who was the butler in the Fishers [2] house in Grosse Pointe, and his wife—my aunt—was the maid.

Like most people, I don't remember much about my first year except I have a general sense that I was happy. At any rate

33

I have no bad memories. What I have learned since is that when I was about a year old, maybe a little older, the mines went down. Families had to make decisions about what to do and where to go. When my uncle Hosea in Detroit learned about our situation, he sent for my grandmother Tellis to come up and live closer to him in Detroit. Her brothers Chris and Allen were also there. I'm told my grandmother agreed to go and said, "I'll take Jim," and she did.

The idea was that my parents would follow my grandmother to Detroit as soon as they could. But they didn't. The way I have heard it told, the mines started up again and my father didn't want to make the move to Detroit, so they wrote to my grandmother and asked her to bring me back. She told them she would bring me back to Meadowbrook in the spring, but that never happened. I don't know why my parents didn't make more of an issue of it, why they didn't insist that she bring me back or come and get me themselves. All I know is that I spent the next six years living in Detroit. It was the beginning of a sequence of events that as I think now affected me in one way or another for the rest of my life.

Early Childhood in Detroit

"Come on James. It's time to go to school."

There was a pause.

"*Come* on. Nothing bad is going to happen to you. I'll walk you there myself".

That's what my grandmother Tellis said on my first day of kindergarten. I was five years old, really didn't want to go, and I was crying. It's one of my earliest detailed memories from Detroit.

At first I thought maybe I could talk my way out of it or maybe the crying would help. But I saw right away that it wasn't going to work, so I just let myself be pulled along. My grandmother made me a huge breakfast, pancakes and lots of butter and syrup, everything she knew I liked. I knew she was doing it to make me feel better, and it did a little bit. Then when it was time she took my hand and said, "Ok James, we've got to go now". And off we went.

The school was Columbia Elementary. It was a two-story brick building, like all the big city public schools were in those days, and it was, I think, at the intersection of McKinley Street and Warren Avenue right in the middle of a residential neighborhood although there were stores across the street on one side. It was about four or five blocks from our apartment. I tried to stall by walking slow, but my grandmother had my hand the whole way and we got there in what seemed like no time at all.

We went to the principal's office first, and there were kids all over the place, and I didn't know anyone. I thought they were all looking at me, and I started crying again. But there was no going back. We talked to an assistant principal who seemed nice enough, and after my grandmother had registered me and finished the paperwork, he said, "Well, Mrs. Tellis, we all three can walk over to the kindergarten where James is going to start."

The classroom was full of kids, both black and white. Some of them were sitting on the floor, some were playing games at a table. They all stopped what they were doing and looked at me when we walked in.

The teacher, Mrs. Goetz, was a white woman and one of the first white people I got to know. She had a nice smile and was kind to me from day one. "Boys and girls," she said, "this is James Long, and he's going to be part of our class." At that point the assistant principal told my grandmother it was time for them to leave. My grandmother told me to be a good boy, and then they were gone.

When the actual class started, I just sat still and didn't look at anybody and the morning seemed to go on forever. The afternoon was better. The kids in kindergarten didn't go home for lunch. We had graham crackers and milk and Mrs. Goetz was nice to me, and after lunch I started to feel a little better. I remember I started playing with some of the kids and fell down but nobody made fun of me. I started to look around a little bit and recognized another boy my age who lived on our block. We started to talk and ended up walking home from school together. When I got home my grandmother asked, "How'd you do, James?" and I said, "It was ok." And it was. For a while I had trouble getting used to the idea that I had to get up and go to school every day, but after that first day the worst was over.

Eventually I started liking school, at least in those early grades. I remember I liked the routines once I got used to them. After I made more friends, I would run out of the house in the morning and meet other kids I knew, and we would walk together. For a while my grandmother would still ask if I wanted her to walk with me. I would say, no. I'm going to go with Aaron." We would usually pop out of our front doors at the same time and head off together,

I liked the walk to school most days. It wasn't too long, but it was long enough that the closer you got to school the more friends you picked up on the way. We would usually gather at the neighborhood stores across from the school. If I had a few pennies I might get some pumpkin seeds to eat (but you had to be careful and not get caught with them in class). If we got to school early, we would line up at the door and wait for the bell. I remember when I was standing there in line, I would look at the big boys and think, someday I'm going to be big like them.

Kindergarten met in the same room all day, but from first grade on we would line up at the end of the class period and, when the bell rang, march to our next class. The grades were kindergarten through 8th, and the higher classes were on the upper floors—you worked your way up. I remember that when we had fire drills, the kids on the lower floors would line up and march out the door but the older kids on the second floor would get to slide down a chute that took them into the gravel playground. Sliding down the chute really looked like fun, and when I got older and when the school was closed, usually on weekends, we learned a way to get into the building and we used to sneak inside and slide down the chute over and over again till somebody saw us and we had run. Sometimes there would be an assembly, usually because the principal needed to make announcements, and we would march into the assembly hall while one of the teachers played the piano. In the third or fourth grade I was in a Christmas play. It wasn't a speaking part. I was just one of a number of elves who stood around Santa Claus. But my grandmother made me an elf costume with bells on it that I was excited about. And I still remember how proud she was of me.

When I think back, school in the early grades was a good time for me. When I was going to school all day, my grandmother would make me a big pancake breakfast most mornings. As I got into the higher grades I used to come home for lunch, which was usually soup or leftovers from the night before. I got in my first harmless little fights with other boys in the first grade, usually over a girl or something somebody said. Nobody ever really got hurt. The teacher always broke things up and made everyone who had been fighting stand and face the wall for the rest of the class. When I got into trouble at school I had to tell my grandmother about it when I got home. But even if she got mad or punished me, I always knew she was on my side.

I lived with my grandmother Tellis, my two uncles Chris and Allen, and Allen's wife Verna in a nice working class integrated neighborhood on the West Side of Detroit. Uncle Allen was a common laborer and Uncle Chris worked for Hudson Cleaners. Between them they split the household expenses, my grandmother Tellis did most of the cooking, and Uncle Hosea, who was a lot better off, sometimes helped us out. It's true that we moved around—changed apartments—a couple of times in the period, but we always stayed in the same neighborhood, and my memories are that it was a friendly place.

We lived near what would now be the intersection of the Jeffries and Edsel Ford Freeways. But they weren't there then, and the area I knew best was bounded by West Grand Boulevard, Warren Avenue West, the Grand River Parkway, and West 30th

Street. The church we attended, the Hartford Avenue Baptist Church, was at the corner of Hartford and Milford; my school was at McKinley and Warren; there was a nice city playground (now called Ames Park) at the corner of McGraw and Vinewood, and the old Olympia Stadium[3] —at Grand River Parkway and McGraw--was in easy walking distance.

Of course I don't remember much about things that were going on when I was a baby of only two or three years old. I'm sure that some of the memories I have are of things the grownups told me about years later. What I can see now that I think back, though, is that one of the reasons I remember being so happy must have been that for the first couple of years I was the only child in the house. I got all the attention and fussing over. Eventually, of course, Uncle Allen and Aunt Verna started to have children of their own. First there was Allen Jr. and then Delores, and my days as the center of attention were over. But by then I didn't need the attention quite so much. When I was a bit older I even used to take care of my little cousins.

It was mainly a happy time. Except for the fact that my parents weren't there, we were kind of like a normal family. We had sit down meals together. We went to church on Sunday. We had turkey at Thanksgiving and a tree at Christmas. Usually I just got clothes for Christmas, but I remember one year I got a little toy gun. It was the best present I ever got. It was black and made a loud click when you pulled the trigger. I played all sorts of fantasy games with it. Sometimes I was a cowboy shooting the Indians. Sometimes I was a detective taking down gangsters. I wasn't left alone at home very often, but every once in a while my grandmother would be at church for something and my uncles out at the same time. When I was alone I would always hear noises in the basement and think there was somebody down there that was going to get me. I used to take my little gun and go to the head of the basement stairs and click it a lot and say, loudly, "If you come up here, I've got a gun, and I'll shoot you." That little gun was my protector. I felt safe when I had it. It wasn't practical like clothes, and I don't think I ever realized at the time what a nice thing it was for my grandmother or my uncles to get it for me when clothes for school would have made more sense.

Our building was like most of the buildings in the neighborhood. It had two stories and four separate apartments. There was a hallway leading up to our door and at the door rugs or newspapers to wipe your feet if it was wet or snowy. There was a living room and dining room, two bedrooms and a kitchen. I slept with my grandmother in one of the bedrooms, and, before they started having children, Allen and Verna slept in the other. We used oil lamps till we could afford electricity. Nobody that we knew had cars. We all walked places or took the trolley. Very few people I knew had telephones but it didn't seem like you needed phones that much then. You could almost always get what you wanted in the neighborhood. We had a radio, an Atwater Kent, and Uncle Allen liked to listen to H. V. Kaltenborn [4] in the evenings, but when he was done I got to listen to things like the *Lone Ranger*, *Jack Armstrong: All American Boy*, and sometimes even *The Shadow*. Uncle Allen used to give me and later my little cousins a hard time about it. He knew we wanted to listen to our own programs and he would sit there listening to Kaltenborn for what seemed forever. He would drag out the process of finishing up, fuss in his chair, fold his newspaper, and then finally get up and tell us it was our turn.

In general we got along pretty well, but as Uncle Allen and Aunt Verna's family grew, there was tension from time to time, as I think there is in most houses. When you're little you know when there's trouble among the grownups, but most of the time you don't know exactly what's going on. The first argument I remember where I knew what was going on started in the kitchen.

As I have learned since, two strong women and one kitchen is a recipe for trouble. My Aunt Verna and my grandmother got into an argument about how to cook something or other. My grandmother was a much better cook than Aunt Verna, but Aunt Verna was Uncle Allen's wife and more or less the lady of the house. She had her authority to uphold, and so the battle grew to include questions about who was supposed to do what in general. I don't know what the men's roles were in all this. If it had been me, I would have stayed as far away from the women as I could have. At some point, however, it seemed to get decided that my grandmother would be responsible for most of the cooking, and Aunt Verna would do most of the cleaning. I don't know how happy Aunt Verna was about it, but things seemed to quiet down after that.

Lots of people have pointed out to me that I grew up during the depression. That's true enough, but I don't really have painful depression memories the way some people do. For one thing, we weren't living that high on the hog to begin with, and so if we had a little less it wasn't that noticeable, at least to me as a child. And God knows nobody in our neighborhood jumped out of a window because they lost it all in the stock market. I suppose it did affect us to an extent, though. We certainly didn't have anything extra.

My Uncle Allen worked for the WPA digging ditches. I think it was probably the only work he could get at the time. He made $25 a week and we had to pay the rent out of that and some of the food and clothing. Some of the older teenage boys in our neighborhood went away to government Civilian Conservation Camps (the CCC)[5] and sometimes they were sent to other states. Most sent the money they made back home. But that was for the older kids.

We always seemed to have enough to eat, but, as I found out early, if you didn't like what you got, you got nothing. I'll never forget what happened one night when I complained about what we were having for dinner. For whatever reason, we had beans two nights in a row. When I saw my plate coming I said, "Beans again?" and made a face. I was sitting next to my Uncle Allen, and before I knew what was happening he took a sweeping swing with his arm extended, knocked me head over heels out of my chair and onto the floor, and said, "Boy, you don't have to eat what I put on this table, but don't you *ever* turn your nose up at it." I was stunned. My grandmother got up to help me and Uncle Allen, who was still angry, said, "Momma, don't you get up. That boy's got to learn that hard work put those beans on this table. If he doesn't want to eat what's served, he doesn't have to. But he's got to learn not to belittle it." What do you know about life as a little kid? As I look back, I think my Uncle Allen was under a lot more pressure than I knew. I also know that we made what we had go as far as we could.

In our neighborhood we had routines that organized the week. Monday was washday. When the weather permitted, everybody hung out their wash in the backyards on the same day. It smelled good going and coming home from school. Wednesday was bath night, and my grandmother would give me a bath in big metal tub on the floor in the kitchen. If it was cold, she would light the stove and open the oven door to warm the room. The other bath time was either Saturday night or Sunday morning, so you would be clean for church.

There was a routine for meals, too. Sunday was always the big meal, after church. On most Sundays we would usually have chicken with stuffing and mashed potatoes and for dessert Jello with fruit in it if we were lucky. On Mondays we would have leftovers from Sunday. The next day we might have greens, sometimes with fat back, which I hated. My grandmother got the fat back from the butcher in big chunks. (Some people called it salt pork, but we called it fat back.) It was really greasy and I couldn't stand it, so when we had it, my grandmother would cut it into big chunks that were easy to spot so I could avoid them. Maybe the next day we would have beans, maybe bread and gravy.

Friday was fish night in every house on the block. A guy would drive around through the neighborhoods in the morning in an old truck or a Model T. The fish were on crushed ice in boxes in the bed of the truck, and he would drive slowly through each neighborhood stopping often and calling out, "Fish Man. Fish Man," and people would come out and snap things up, sometimes fresh perch, sometimes catfish, and once in a while a blue pike [6]. My Uncle Allen was a good customer and often got "deals". He would ask the fish man ahead of time to get him a nice pike, and when the truck came around, the fish man would give him a nod and slip him his pike on the sly so it wouldn't look like Uncle Allen was getting special treatment.

There weren't any vacant lots in our neighborhood and not many people had gardens. There were big markets, though, bigger even than Cleveland's Westside Market, where my grandmother and Aunt Verna would go and buy basic foods in large quantities. We didn't have refrigerators, but we had iceboxes to keep things fresh. The Ice Man came around regularly and sold big blocks of ice that kept for a surprisingly long time—25 cents for a 25lb block. And we had chickens!

It wasn't hard to raise chickens in our backyards, and a lot of people did. When it was time to kill one, my grandmother would grab it by the neck and wring its neck by holding its head and whirling its flapping body around and around in a circle, like a cowboy with a lasso. Even after it was dead, the chicken would still flop around for a while, maybe even run around the yard. My grandmother always had a tub of boiling water ready, and when the chicken had stopped running or flopping, she would cut it open to clean it out and look for the giblets, then she would grab it by the feet and dunk it in the hot water, which loosened the feathers. When the time was right she would pull it out and start plucking, and sometimes she would let me help.

Chickens were an important part of our economy. We ate just about every part of them but the beaks. Besides the usual ways to eat chicken, my grandmother would sometimes fry up the feet. I loved it when she did that. I remember I used to stand right by the stove, and when they were done, she would give me a few and I would take them out into the backyard and eat them still hot from the skillet.

In our household economies, pigs were even more important than chickens. Nobody that I knew tried to raise pigs in the city, but they were one of the most important staples in the black community. As people in our neighborhood used to say, "You eat everything on a hog from its snout to its tail." When I was seven or eight, I remember getting up in the morning and having a piece of fried pork with biscuits and syrup. On a good day, the syrup was mixed with some bacon grease or butter. The syrup was Alaga brand (stands for Alabama-Georgia) with a heavy molasses tang. You can still get it today in stores that cater to the black community, and I still buy it. In those years it didn't get any better than that, and I'm not joking when I say that we ate every inch of the pig.

In the late 1920's and early 1930's there used to be slaughterhouses in the city of Detroit, and there was one close enough to our neighborhood that you could walk to it fairly easily. As part of the butchering process they used to throw away the parts of the pig they couldn't sell to the markets and restaurants, and we ate practically everything they threw away. The 8, 9, and 10 year-old kids from the neighborhood (and other neighborhoods) used to haul wagons carrying big pots and buckets to the slaughterhouse. The slaughterhouse workers would bring baskets of pigs' snouts, feet, tails, and chitlins (intestines), out to the loading docks to throw them away, and the kids would fill up every container and get it back home as fast as they could. The workers there obviously knew that the kids were from relatively poor families, and sometimes they would sneak a really nice ham out or some good bacon, and the kids would wrap it up quickly and take off running. But mainly it was just the stuff that nobody else wanted.

My grandmother cooked these pig parts all sorts of ways, but what I remember the best was the chitlins. When we got a good quantity, we used to throw what we called a "Chitlin Strut." It was always exciting. The women would start the day before cleaning the chitlins, which was a lengthy and for obvious reasons an extremely important process. Then on the night of the "Strut" they would cook them in big pots. When the customers started coming, they would take the chitlins out of the pots in long strips and cut them to just the right size. We would sell them on a plate with a small salad and a glass of beer (either home brew or something we bought and then resold). We sold the whole meal for .10 or .15 cents, and on a good night we might make enough to help with the rent that month or help buy coal for the furnace.

Getting coal was an adventure, too. We all used coal to heat the water in our radiators in the fall and winter, and each family had to buy its own coal. Each apartment in our building had a coal bin assigned to it with a chute so it could be filled with coal from outside. When the man with the coal truck came around, you would buy your coal and he would dump it down the chute into your bin. Coal wasn't that expensive, but in the winter when you used a lot, the bills could run up, so we were always happy to find ways to get it cheap. One of the things people in the neighborhood used to do was get some from the coal cars as they rumbled through the city.

The railroad tracks went right through some of the nearby neighborhoods. There were places where the grade was steep enough that the big coal trains with a hundred cars full of coal had to slow down enough that people could jump on safely while the train was moving, and that's exactly what people in our neighborhood did. The older kids, teenage boys, would hop the cars, sit down on their butts on the piled up coal, and start kicking it out onto the ground with both feet as fast as they could. When the grade evened out and the train picked up speed they had to get off in a hurry. Meanwhile, people from the neighborhoods—men, women, and smaller kids--would be along the tracks with baskets, boxes, bags, anything they could use to haul the coal, picking it up as fast as they could.

There was a system to it and even unwritten rules. One understood rule was that each street had a section of the track. Everything they picked up in that section was theirs but they couldn't horn in on some other street's section. Another rule was about the boys who kicked the coal off the cars. It was a job that had some danger to it (jumping on and off) and was certainly dirty. When they came off the cars they were covered with coal dust. So as the younger kids got older—old enough— the older boys who had been doing it would come up and say, "Ok. You're old enough now. Get you ass up here (on the moving railroad cars) and we'll show you how to do it." People took it seriously enough that if a boy wasn't willing to do his part when he was old enough, they would say to his family, "If your boy's too good to do it like all the others, then don't expect to get any coal."

It certainly wasn't legal to be getting our coal this way, and sometimes the railroad police would come around and we would have to run. But I think the police understood how badly some people needed the coal. They never chased us very far or very hard, and sometimes you would realize that they were there, but they would just turn their backs and walk away.

I guess the long and the short of it is that we did all sorts of things to help us get by in those years and stretch a dollar or a meal as far as it would go. We were near enough to the old Olympia Stadium that sometimes, when the crowds for a hockey game or a championship fight were big enough, we could "sell" parking spaces, usually in our driveways, for 50 cents a car. If we got just two cars and made $1.00 you could maybe get a whole chicken and a loaf of Silvercup bread! But I don't mean to suggest that because we had to take steps like these, the experience of day-to-day living was somehow dark or gloomy. People in our neighborhood—my uncles included—knew how to have fun.

Every neighborhood around where we lived had a local grocery store, a poolroom, and a beer garden. But if you really wanted to get dressed up and do something special, you went to a place like the Graystone Ballroom [7] over on Woodward Avenue. All the big bands—Count Basie, Duke Ellington—came there, and there was dancing outside in the summer and inside in the winter. My uncles Chris and Allen loved to get dressed up and go dancing, and on a good night, that's where they went.

For a little kid, there's something magic about watching

grownups get all dressed up and go out. They're the same people you see every day but something is different, too. There's a grownup world they're going out into that you don't know anything about, and you can tell by the way they look and act that it's special. My uncles loved to go dancing, and on the nights when they went out, they would come home from work, take special pains to clean up, and get into their fancy clothes. They even put on spats! I used to sit perfectly still and watch every move they made. The way they cared about how they looked and the pains they took about their clothes made a big impression on me. I remember one time my Uncle Chris bought himself a beautiful pair of soft, white leather gloves with black ornamental stitching down the side. He bought them to wear when he went dancing, and Aunt Verna and my grandmother really gave it to him. There were all sorts of things they could have used the money for instead—what was he thinking? But Uncle Chris kept the gloves and I kind of admired him for it. I still have them and get them out to look at every once in a while.

No matter how hard their life was, my uncles knew how to have a good time, and I have to say I had a pretty good time in those years, too. At my age now, it's hard to be exact, to pinpoint what I remember about which year. But as I got a bit older, in the third, fourth, and fifth grades, the two things I remember most fondly are what it was like living day-to-day in the neighborhood itself and going to the playground after dinner and on the weekends.

I had friends, like the Hortons, who lived next door. Eddie's mother, Mrs. Horton, was the matriarch of our block, and she kept an eye on all of us. Eddie Horton was my age and my best friend. We did everything together. He had two sisters, Helen and Hazel. Hazel was a bit older and a really good-looking girl, and she taught Eddie and me to dance. Eddie also had two older brothers named Skeet and Fox. They were cool, and Eddie and I learned how to dress—how to have some style—by watching and imitating them.

It wasn't just the Hortons, though. Everybody knew everybody in our neighborhood. Everyone trusted everyone. Other parents could scold you if you were acting up, and my family could scold anyone else's kids. For example, let's say I finished drinking a coke and just threw the bottle down in the street. Mrs. Johnson might be sitting on her front steps two doors down and she'd say, "Hey. James Long. What do you think you're doing? Pick that up right now." And I would. If I didn't or if I sassed her, Mrs. Johnson might come to our house and tell my grandmother. If she did, I couldn't deny it. If I tried to, my grandmother would have said something like, "Are you calling Mrs. Johnson a liar?" and that would have been that.

People looked out for each other's kids then. If you came home from school for lunch and for some reason no one was home, you could go to a neighbor's and they would either feed you themselves or let you into your own house and feed you there. Most of the families left keys under the mats or above the doorsills. Close friends and neighbors knew how to get in if they needed to. The little neighborhood stores let you buy things on credit, too. I remember we lived down the street from a store owned by Mr. White (the father of Berry Gordy [8], who would grow up to become the founder of first Hitsville [9] and then Motown Records). At Mr. White's store, everyone in the neighborhood ran a tab. Mr. White had a big book he kept under the counter, and when you bought something he recorded how much you owed and put it down under your name. On payday, or when you had the money, you went around and settled accounts. Nobody stole anything. I never heard that anybody cheated or skipped out. It wasn't just a black thing, either. While our neighborhood was mostly black, it was in fact integrated. There were some Polish and Italian families, and they acted the same as everyone else. One of our neighbors was Italian, and I remember going to her house at lunchtime sometimes when my grandmother just didn't get home in time. If that happened she would take me in and give me lunch, and my grandmother would do the same for her kids if the situation was reversed.

Even the relationship with the police was different than it is now. Policemen worked a beat. They walked their beat every day, and they got to know everyone and we all knew them. If the beat policeman caught one of us kids doing something we shouldn't, he might give us a whack across the butt and tell our parents. But it was usually over then and there. Maybe the beat policeman would talk things over with your family. If there was nothing really serious involved, the people most directly involved would work it out. When there was a serious crime and police came in from outside the neighborhood, the first person they would talk with was the policeman on the beat, and we trusted him to be fair and tell it like it was.

By the time I left Detroit the second time, when I was fourteen, this situation had begun to change. The 1930s saw the first waves of the migration of poor blacks from the South to the big cities of the North. That's where the jobs were, in places like Pittsburgh, Cleveland, and Detroit, but especially in Detroit because of the auto industry and later the war effort.

A lot of things started changing in our neighborhood after the migrations began. The blacks coming from the south were poor, and they were mainly rural people. They didn't understand much about how we lived, and it seemed like they didn't share our values. For example they didn't care about keeping the neighborhood nice. We didn't like or trust them, and they didn't like or trust us. We didn't want them to know where we kept the spare keys to our houses. The kids didn't play together. We kept away from them, and they stuck together and kept away from us. By the time we were teenagers, this kind of distrust was the beginning of rival gangs, and as we all got older, the rivalries grew more serious.

The whites in the neighborhood didn't like any of this, and in a few years they had simply moved out. The worst of it came later, though, with the bigger migrations during the war when there were so many jobs in the northern cities. In my first stay in Detroit, till was about eight years old, though, my neighborhood was mainly like I have described it above. And one of the things I liked most about it and that I remember most fondly was the fun we all used to have in the evenings, especially in summer and early fall.

As old as I am, I can remember it as if it was yesterday. It stayed light outside for a long time in Detroit in the summer, and our parents allowed us to stay up late and play outside after dinner. The excitement would start to build as we were finishing the meal. I remember that on those summer evenings I'm talking about, when I had finished eating I would fly out of the house and head for one of the city parks or recreation areas to meet up with my friends and playmates.

There was always something fun going on. The grown men might be playing horseshoes or just smoking and talking. The older kids might be in the middle of a pick-up softball game. (We used the big, sixteen-inch softballs, the kind you could all chip in and buy at a drugstore and catch without having to have baseball gloves.) And sometimes there was boxing.

In the early 1930s there were no black football or baseball players. The Jim Browns, Jackie Robinsons and Hank Aarons came later. In Detroit in the 1930s and 40s our sports heroes were boxers like Joe Louis and Sugar Ray Robinson and even Detroit black fighters like my cousin Jimmy Edgar, who fought Jake Lamotta to a draw in the old stadium.

The Kronk Recreation Center [10], one of the oldest in Detroit, was a ten-minute walk from my house. In the 1970s it became Kronk's Gym and would be made famous by Emmanuel Steward and associated with names like Tommy Hearns and Evander Holyfield. Even Lennox Lewis and Oscar De La Hoya trained there. But a lot of boxing went on there even in my day, too. It went on in all the playgrounds.

The way it worked when I was there was that Mr. Futch, a young man who worked at the McGraw playground near our house, used to give us boxing lessons. We knew him then only as Mr. Futch. His name was Eddie Futch [11], and years later he would become a boxing legend, working in the corners of fighters like Joe Frazier, Alexis Arguello, Michael Spinks, and Riddick Bowe. He trained my cousin, Jimmy Edgar, and later he trained Berry Gordy as an amateur. But we didn't know who he was going to be at the time. He was just a nice guy who knew a lot about boxing and was happy to teach it to us kids.

To be honest, I didn't like boxing much, but I learned right away that I was good at it, and so I stayed with it. We would take our lessons and work at it, and every now and then Mr. Futch would set up a ring in the playground. Then, when he had us all gathered around he would pick a couple of us to have a match. For example, he might say, "All right, Jim, let's see what you've learned. You're going to box tonight." And he would call out another boy in the same way, and we would fight. The ring was a small area bordered by a rope that was lying on the ground. The two boys who were fighting would step inside and go at it. Mr. Futch knew us all and what we could do, and he was always careful to make the matches even.

If you got pushed backwards and went across the rope, it was considered a knock out.

It was scary but it was exciting, too. On these boxing nights, sometimes crowds would gather. You'd hear people who were playing ball or just lounging around stop and say, "Hey, look. They're boxing tonight." You could feel the crowd gathering. The girls would be there in pretty dresses. If they were older, they were really dressed to the nines.

If it wasn't boxing, there was always something going on in the evenings in summer. Sometimes there would be street dances, even with some pretty good bands. Sometimes somebody would set up a record player, maybe an old Victrola. The hot dances were the jitterbug, the shag, and the lindy hop. I was too little to do that kind of dancing at the time, but I loved to watch the older kids and the grownups go at it. On really warm nights it seemed like the whole neighborhood came out. Parents and young families would sit on their porch steps and watch. Older people would come out, too, because they knew it was safe.

I hated to have to come in at night, and so I stayed out as late as I could. My grandmother's rule was that I had to be home by the time the street lights came on, which in Detroit in the summer was between 9:00 and 9:30. I used to stay out all the way till they came on and then, wherever I was I would start running as fast as I could to get back to my house. I remember I would sometimes hear people sitting out on their porch steps laughing and saying, "Look at Mattie Tellis' boy running to get home. He's gonna get it tonight." And sure enough, I would run up to the house and there would be my grandmother, arms folded sternly across her chest, waiting for me on the porch.

If I was only a few minutes late, I might get a look, but nothing bad happened. If I was a lot later than I should have been, my grandmother would sometimes punish me by making me stay in the house and watch her as she worked in the kitchen. For example, the next night when I was getting ready to go out she might say something like, "Where do you think you're going? You can just stay in and watch me work tonight." I'm sure I was frustrated enough at the time, but I never minded punishment if I knew in my heart I deserved it. And I liked to watch my grandmother cook, which is what she did most of the time when she kept me in. I didn't realize it then, but I learned a lot about cooking that way. There are dishes I make for myself today that I learned to make staying in watching my grandmother.

What I realize now is that during those years what was happening was that my grandmother was becoming my mother. She was both strong and beautiful. She was small, with bronze skin and high cheekbones. (She had some American Indian in her background.) I remember she had beautiful hair, and she was proud. But what I remember most is that she was the only one I got physical affection from, from the time I was a baby. She was the only one who was watching out for me all the time. My parents weren't there—in Detroit. My uncles were busy with their own lives, and my Uncle Allen had his own growing family. It was my grandmother who gave me warmth and affection, who looked out for me, stood up for me, let me know when she was proud of me, and did everything she knew how to do to discipline me and keep me under control. I think that's why it was such a disaster when I finally got sent back to Meadowbrook.

I Don't Know Where I Belong

"Jimbo, is that you?

There were two women looking at me. One of them took a step forward and said, "Over here, Jimbo. I'm your mother, Cora Lee Tellis."

I had just gotten off the Greyhound bus in Clarksburg, West Virginia. I had had a lot of time to think about what was going to happen to me on the bus ride from Detroit. What I had been afraid of most was that I wouldn't recognize my mother, and that's what had just happened.

I looked at the woman, but I couldn't think of anything to say. I was two years old when I left Meadowbrook sometime in 1927. It was 1933. I hadn't seen my mother for six years, and nobody we knew had cameras or sent pictures. If my parents sent letters to my uncles and grandmother, they hadn't sent any to me. They hadn't sent me anything on Christmases and birthdays while I had been in Detroit. I had no memory of a voice or image of a face, or a person, no handwriting to encourage me to try to imagine what the writer looked like.

The woman was nervous and kept talking. She was tall and dark-skinned and she was trying to be nice. I could see that the nervousness was real. She introduced me to a friend who had come with her and, whom she said had been there when I was born. What are you supposed to say when grownups tell you things like that? It means something to them, not you. I tried to be polite and smiled.

The tall woman was very anxious. She was watching my face carefully, and she could see when I decided I believed her. In the way kids can have strong instincts about things even if they can't explain them, I knew she was my mother. She had to be. Why would anyone else say they were? And besides, what else was I going to do? In the past six years, my grandmother had become my mother, but she wasn't there. Just when I'd come to depend on my grandmother, it seemed like suddenly she was out of the picture. This tall stranger was what I had now. I needed her to be my mother. Where else would I have gone if not with her?

There was an awkward silence for a few minutes, but the worst was over, and we both could feel it. Now we had to go the rest of the way home because Meadowbrook was the last stop on the bus's route, and it didn't always go there. It made its last regular stop in Clarksburg, and if there were people who had tickets for Meadowbrook (or if there was somebody in Meadowbrook who had a ticket out) they would go there, and if not they wouldn't. My mother had had to take a bus to Clarksburg, and wait till the bus from Detroit dropped me off. She explained that this was why we didn't need to take my bag off the bus. She looked at her friend and then me and said we would all go back to Meadowbrook together. When she offered her hand, I took it and we got back on the bus.

When you're little, the grown-ups don't tell you everything. I don't know exactly why I got sent back to Meadowbrook when I did. I don't know what role my parents played or didn't play in the decision. I know some of the reasons my Detroit family wanted to send me back, though, and they make a lot more sense to me now than they did then.

I think what was happening in Detroit was that as I got older and physically bigger, stronger, and more active, I was simply getting too hard for the family to handle. Nobody had the time or the attention to spare. Uncle Allen had his own growing family and not a lot of extra time or money for me. Uncle Chris was taking care of my grandmother Tellis and me. The older and bigger I got, the harder it was for my grandmother to handle me by herself. Uncle Chris worked hard and couldn't pay the kind of attention to me that a parent should have, and of course he wasn't my parent. I remember my uncles actually had a meeting about it—about me—and I heard my Uncle Chris say, "We don't need this problem." Whatever the specifics were, "the problem" was obviously me. I think nobody except my grandmother wanted me to stay there. My uncles agreed that it was time to send me back, and it wasn't long before I found myself on the bus. As we rode along from Clarksburg to Meadowbrook, I looked out the window but kept sneaking looks at my mother. I kept looking for things I remembered, but it was no use. The memories would have to start now.

It was early evening by the time we arrived. The hills in West Virginia were a lot bigger than anything I had ever seen in Detroit, and the dark was a lot darker. The hills seemed to be closing in. I looked around and didn't see anything or anyone that looked familiar. I was as far away from what I had learned to consider home as an eight-year-old boy could be. Young as I was, I was already a city kid. The world I knew and had been living in had apartment buildings and paved streets with streetlights at night. There were trolleys, and you would see people driving cars. The "outdoors" for me there meant the city parks, the Kronk Recreation Center. On this dark road in rural West Virginia I might as well have been on Mars. If I could have thought of anywhere to run to get away, I would have done it. But there was nowhere I could think of to go.

When we got my bags off the bus in front of the post office

in Meadowbrook the first thing I saw was Turkey Mountain, which was rose steeply behind the town. As the dusk settled it seemed to get bigger and bigger. The heavy woods didn't seem inviting. They looked dark and foreign. They made me feel as alone and isolated as I in fact was. But there was nothing to be done about it. There we were, and when the bus pulled away, my mother picked up my suitcase and we started walking.

In about a quarter of a mile we came to a row of shacks on either side of a road that wound slowly up a hill. There were people in the shacks who must have known we were coming. (It was a very small town and of course the Longs' baby boy coming back home would have been big news.) People I didn't know would come out of the shacks as we passed and smile and yell, "Hey, Jimbo." "How are you, Jimbo?" It was dark by then and so mainly I just saw shapes and heard voices. Once in a while an oil lamp would give me a glimpse inside a house but not for long. I didn't say anything. My mother would respond to the voices, sometimes wave back, but we kept going. Soon we passed a little pond or pool on the left, and all of a sudden there was our house. My grandmother Long, Grandmother Julie, was sitting on the porch, and when she saw us, she said, "Oh, Jimbo. Praise the Lord, it's Jimbo."

The house was strange and didn't look like anything I had seen in my neighborhood in Detroit. To put it bluntly, it was a shack. It was clean; my grandparents were particular about that. It was nicer than most of the other houses for blacks in Meadowbrook, but compared to where I had been living it was a shack. Inside there were a small front room, two small bedrooms (one for my grandparents, one for my mother and me), and a tiny kitchen. There were stoves that burned both wood and coal in the living room and kitchen. They lit the oil lamps when we went in because by then it was almost dark.

My grandfather was in the living room—the central room—when I went in. He had only one good eye and no patch over the one that didn't work, and when he stepped forward to greet me, I was terrified. He said, "I'm your grampa Long. How you been, boy?" I said, "All right", and he said, "Well, you're home now." While he went on talking I looked out the back door and saw the hog pens, the chickens pecking around in the backyard, and the outhouse.

I realized even at the time that they were all a little fussed. Everybody was trying to be too nice, and the voices were a little high. My mother was talking a lot faster than I learned she normally did. My grandmother Long kept saying, "You must be hungry. I'll fry you up some chicken," which she did, but it didn't help much. We only had one oil lamp in the front room, and I wanted so badly to be back in Detroit with my grandmother Tellis that I started crying. My mother said all the right things, but she didn't hug me. My grandmother Julie was more physically affectionate.

Over the next few weeks I got to know the place better—the town, the people, and my new home--but it didn't help much. A day or so after I arrived, my grandfather Long took me out back to show me what my chores would be. "Everybody's got a job around here," he said, "You need to know yours." My duties turned out to be slopping the hogs and raking up the yard around the house, and I hated it. In Detroit I had been going out to the park, watching the older kids dancing and imagining when I would be like them. Now I would be slopping the hogs. The hogs and the slop I had to give them almost made me sick.

Then there was getting used to the outhouse. What we did was use buckets in the house at night, and then every morning we would go out and empty them in the outhouse. I hated going near it and looking down that hole. Our chickens would sometimes fly down inside and then fly out when someone opened the door, and it used to terrify and disgust me.

To help try to get me acquainted with people and them with me, my mother used to take me with her when she would go visiting friends and neighbors. One day when we were going out visiting, I was putting my shoes on and she told me to take them off. She said lots of the kids here didn't have shoes that they wear all the time, and it would make them feel bad. I told her I wanted to go home, meaning home to my grandmother Tellis' in Detroit, and she said, "Hush up, boy. You *are* home. Those Tellises have spoiled you rotten."

I've sometimes thought that it might have made a difference if my father had been there. But he wasn't. I got a letter from him telling me that he was working in Pittsburgh and that he would try to come and see me. But I wasn't there that long, and while I was there he never came. Although there were other kids in the town, I didn't make much effort to get to know them. For one thing I felt badly out of place. For another I think trying to make new friends quickly would have been admitting that I felt like I was there to stay, and I didn't.

When September rolled around, it was time to go to school. The older kids in junior high and high school were bused to Clarksburg. Those of us in the lower grades were taken to the local school building in an open, horse-drawn wagon. We took our lunches with us and ate them outside at recess, and we used an outhouse at school just like we did at home.

I didn't get along too well with the other kids at school, and I'm sure part of the reason was that they thought I was stuck up. I can see why they thought that if they did. Even though I had had the summer to get used to things I couldn't get over the differences between my life in Detroit and my life there. As I think back on it, I did act as if I was better than the Meadowbrook kids. I think it was probably defensive. I didn't want anyone to think that I looked like I belonged there.

My first fight didn't help matters. It happened in the second week of classes, and I don't remember what it was that started it. Somebody said something. I pushed someone or they pushed me. It doesn't take much more than that for boys that age. What I remember is that I realized right away that these kids didn't know much about fighting. They knew about pushing and wrestling, but they didn't know how to use their hands. I did know how to use my hands. I knew how to get my punches in first. I bloodied my opponent's nose pretty quickly before the teachers came out and broke us up. I had to go stand in the corner and they sent a note home with me, but that wasn't the bad part. The bad part was that the boy I hit lived in the shacks near our house, so the word about the fight got around right away, and it certainly didn't make anybody like me better.

I lasted in Meadowbrook for a total of about four months. What happened to end my stay was this. One day I didn't do one of the chores I was supposed to. My grandfather Long ruled this house with an iron hand, and when he found out what I had done he said he was going to whip me. He had used a razor strop on me before, and he went to get it. When I saw him do that, I took off running, but before I got twenty yards, he was at the door with a shotgun in his hand. He told me to stop or he would blow my brains out, and I believed him. I came back to the house and he whipped me till I was bleeding. My mother and grandmother Long were there—right in the same room—but they just sat by the stove and didn't do anything. I know now how hard—maybe impossible—it would have been for them to try to intervene. Women just didn't do that in small town West Virginia in those years. But at the time, I couldn't believe they would do nothing to help me. That was when I started hating my mother. It was also when I decided I had to get out of there.

It was pretty easy to get away. My grandmother got sent regular checks, and one of my chores was also to go and pick them up at the post office, and sometimes I was allowed to cash them at the general store. One day not long after my grandfather whipped me, I went to get my grandmother's check, but instead of cashing it and taking the money home, I cashed the check, walked back across the road to the post office and bought a one-way ticket to Detroit for fifty cents. As soon as the bus came through, I was gone. I didn't think about what my mother would think. I didn't think about what my family in Detroit would think. All I knew was that I couldn't do this. I had to get out of there.

When the bus pulled into the station in Detroit, there was nobody there to meet me because nobody knew I was coming. I had thought a lot more about how I would get away from Meadowbrook than about what would happen when I got back to Detroit. However, I had the money from my grandmother Long's check, and I knew how to take the trolley, so I took the trolley home. I don't know the specifics, but I know that the Tellises let the Longs in Meadowbrook know I was there and safe. They sent grandmother Long a check for the money I had taken, and they told the Longs that they weren't going to send me back right then. It wasn't exactly a happy homecoming, though.

There was some real debate about what to do with me, which surprised me. As young as I was, I had thought it would be easy. I didn't want to live in Meadowbrook. I wanted to come back to the only thing I had known as home and live there. Of course I can see now that it was never going to be that simple.

Uncle Chris and Uncle Allen were concerned that I was or was going to be too much for my grandmother to handle. I obviously hated Meadowbrook, and so apparently sending me back to live with my mother and grandfather Long wasn't an option. What they decided to do instead was try sending me to live with my father and his two brothers in Braddock, Pennsylvania, just outside of Pittsburgh. Whether rightly or wrongly, what I took this to mean was that they didn't want me, and before I knew it I was on a bus again, this time heading for Braddock, Pa.

The bus ride was like a rerun of the trip to Meadowbrook. I had the same fears I had had when I was going to meet my mother. I had no idea what my father looked like and wasn't sure that he would recognize me. It wasn't quite as bad this time, though. I think having done it once before made a difference, and my father was a different person from my mother.

My father spotted me right away. When I got off the bus, he said, "Jimbo? Are you Jimbo?"

"Yes, sir," I said quickly.

"Well (smiling) I'm your father, Eddie, and I haven't seen you since you were a year old."

The man who was speaking was short and well built. I still remember staring at the muscles in his arms. He was a light-skinned black man with freckles across his face. (His nickname was "Red" because of the freckles.) He was good looking and had a ready smile, and I liked him right away. His brother Richard was with him, and he turned to him and said, "This is my son, Jimbo." He said it like he was proud of me.

Uncle Richard drove us from the bus stop in Pittsburgh to their home in Braddock, a steel town near Pittsburgh that in those days it was doing pretty well. My father was living with his brother Richard and Richard's wife, and the family I was now joining was like the one I had left in Detroit. Richard and his wife had no children yet. I was instantly the center of attention, and I was still young enough to like all the fussing over I got when I arrived. We lived in a fairly large apartment complex with a courtyard in the center. There were lots of young families and lots of kids to play with, and except for an incident that happened soon after I got there, I got along fine with the other kids. There were no porches and so people who lived in the apartments there used to sit out on the front steps a lot, especially on warm summer evenings. The people there liked my father, and because I was Eddie Long's son, they liked me, too.

The incident that happened right after I got there brought me especially close to my dad. I was the new kid on the block, and one day three or four of the neighborhood boys jumped me and roughed me up. When I came home, my father asked me what had happened. When I told him, he said, "Come on, Jimbo. Let's go on back there and see about this."

We walked back down the street to where it happened. The kids who had picked on me were still there at the corner, just standing around. My father asked whether those were the ones, and I said yes, and we walked right up to them.

"Who's the toughest one of you?" he asked.

Nobody said anything for a minute, and then he asked again and one of the boys stepped forward. My father said, "All right. You're going to fight Jim but it's going to be one at a time, not four on one."

We started fighting with my father watching, and when I started winning the kid backed away and said he didn't want to fight any more. But my father just smiled and said, "I think you need to know a little more about Jim," and we kept at it. I was landing punches pretty much whenever I wanted to, and soon I knocked the kid down. My father said, "That's enough," and it was all over, and that was the end of trouble for me in the neighborhood. But what really mattered was that my father had stuck up for me, and it made me proud. I felt like I knew he loved me and that being with him was going to be completely different than being with my mother in Meadowbrook. It wasn't. Like all the attempts to find a home for me at this period of my life, my situation in Braddock didn't last, and it was my mother who was the problem again.

My father had gone to the Pittsburgh area when the mines kept closing in Meadowbrook. He had hoped to find steadier work in the steel mills, and he had done so. His job in the mills looked secure and so he thought it was safe to bring my mother and sisters to Braddock so the family could be together. Of course it made sense, but it was an idea that sounded a lot better than it turned out, at least for me. When my mother and sisters arrived and moved in, they brought with them all the tensions I had felt when I was in Meadowbrook and a whole lot more.

Honestly, the minute my mother walked in the door I knew it wasn't going to work. There was no warmth there, no indication that she was glad to see me. And things changed right away between me and my father. He may have been the breadwinner and respected in the neighborhood for his toughness, but my parents' relationship was very different from the household in Meadowbrook. There, the man of the house was like a god or a king. His word was the law; nobody questioned it. In our new family, my mother was the head of the household and the children now. I would ask my father if I could go here or there, if I could have some money to go to a movie. He would say, "You have to ask your mother. Go ask Cora Lee." It wasn't what I wanted to hear. I felt like not only was she not on my side, but she was against me most of the time. She would say to my father, "You spoiled him enough. They spoiled him in Detroit." It was like she could sense my dislike for her and my preference for my grandmother Tellis and she seemed to want to take it out on me.

My sisters Delores and Lucille being there didn't make things any better. I didn't get along with Delores. She would always tell on me, and my mother would believe her and take her part. For example, sometimes I would hustle a little money on my own. An old man in the neighborhood would give me some money to go buy him some beer, and when I brought it back he would let me keep the change. Things like that. When I had my own money, I would buy things for myself—usually something extra to eat. If Delores found out she would tell Cora Lee and my mother would make me give some to my sisters. It didn't work the other way around, though. When I took similar complaints about my sisters to my mother she would just wave her hand and dismiss me. She always took their parts, not mine, and my father never intervened. "You gotta ask Cora Lee." That's all I would get from him.

This may not sound like earth-shaking stuff, but it was a symptom of a bigger problem. We were finally together as a family, but we weren't together. It never worked for me. I distrusted my mother because she hadn't taken my part in Meadowbrook when my grandfather was whipping me. Moreover, she had never been separated from my sisters. She was their mother from day one, but she didn't know me. She hadn't had any hand in shaping how I grew up, and I think it bothered her and put distance between us. She knew how I felt about my grandmother Tellis and had resented my affection for her. Though the physical circumstances were somewhat different now, it was Meadowbrook all over again. I felt like I had to get out of there. I had already run away once, so it wasn't hard to imagine doing it again.

I planned it carefully. I had taken the bus to Detroit once before, and so I wasn't intimidated and knew what to do. I kept hustling up small amounts of money and saving it. I hid it, so my sisters wouldn't know. When I had enough, I left the house one afternoon and got on the train to Pittsburgh. It wasn't a long trip, and when I got there it was easy to find the bus station. I was careful, too. I felt like it might cause someone to ask questions if I went up alone to the ticket window—an eight-year-old boy—buying a ticket to Detroit. What if they asked me where my parents were? So I paid an old guy fifty cents to buy the ticket for me. (The ticket cost twenty-five cents.) Then I had about four hours to kill before the bus left.

I was afraid to hang around the bus station alone because I knew my parents would be missing me by now, and I was afraid they would figure out what I had done and catch me before I got on the bus. There was a telephone in the Braddock house and they could call the train and bus stations. Also, there were sometimes policemen in the bus station, and I didn't want them wondering why a kid seemed to be wandering around by himself. There were theaters near the station, and so I went to a movie. It was Dorothy Lamour in *Jungle Princess*, and it took up most of the time I needed to kill. When it was over, I walked back to the bus station, terrified that my family would be there. But they weren't, and I got safely on the bus, and was headed for Detroit once again.

It was nighttime when I got there, and I remember as I left the bus station I could see the Michigan Theater lit up brilliantly. The marquee said *Light Must Fall—Starring Robert Montgomery*. I got on the trolley once again, and made my way back to what I considered home.

I can only imagine what must have been going through my

Uncles Chris' and Allen's minds when I showed up on their doorstep again, but my grandmother Tellis was glad to see me and full of hugs. I don't know how they worked it out with my real family in Braddock, or why my parents didn't come and get me. All I knew was that I was staying in Detroit, which was what I wanted. In a short time I got settled back in my old place in the household, and I went back to Columbia elementary School. I thought it would be just like it was before I left. I thought I could just pick up where I had left off when I was happy—weekly routines, summers in the parks, all my old friends in the neighborhood. It didn't happen that way, though, and as I got older, this time became one of the most confusing and difficult periods in my life.

Things Start To Go Bad

I can see it in my mind's eye. It is very early on a Sunday morning, not long after sun up. I am standing under my grandmother's bedroom window, and I am crying. My grandmother hears me, as I know she will. She puts up the shade, opens the window more fully and says, "James, what are you doing out there? Where have you been? You scared us all to death!"

My uncles are still asleep. Tearfully I tell my grandmother what I have done, how I went to the movies all night, how I walked home by myself and slept out in one of the neighbor's cars. While I am talking, I hear one of my uncles get up. He takes a look into grandmother's room, sees me, and goes to get his belt to give me a whipping. By the time he returns I am inside and in my grandmother's room. He takes me by the arm, holds me at arm's length so he can get a better swing at me, and starts to let me have it. Unlike my mother, however, my grandmother Tellis sticks up for me. She watches me getting it and when she thinks I've gotten what I deserve, she says, "That's enough," and my uncle stops. I go and take a bath, get dressed up, and go with the family to church. Next weekend or the weekend after that I do the same thing again. I learn later that sometimes because our houses are so close together, Eddy Horton's sisters can hear when I am getting a whipping, and it makes them cry when they hear me yelling.

How did it come to this? The simple answer is that I don't know. However, it's easier for me to understand now than it was then why things got so hard for me.

Now I can see that when I got back to Detroit I was home, but I wasn't home. My grandmother Tellis loved me; I was sure of that. But Uncles Chris and Allen had their own lives and families. I wasn't one of their own, and they used to have discussions about what to do with me. Of course they wouldn't talk about it in front of me, but it was a small apartment, and sometimes I heard them through the walls. If I knew they were talking about what to do with me I would get very quiet and try to hear everything. I still remember listening to my uncles discussing the possibility of letting the county take care of me and crying because I couldn't believe they would want to just get rid of me and send me to some home or state school. I knew my grandmother wanted to keep me, but even then I knew that she wasn't the boss of the house, and it wasn't going to be her decision.

It was in these years that I started acting out and causing even more trouble for my uncles, and although it came across mainly as confusion or anger, what I realize now is that what bothered me most was that I didn't know where I belonged. It upset me far more than I was aware of at the time. With the exception of my grandmother Tellis, nobody seemed to want me, but it was even more confusing than that. I was sure my father liked me, even was proud of me. But if that was so, why wouldn't he stick up for me with my mother? It wasn't even clear what my name was. The kids in the neighborhood called me Jim Tellis, but at school the teachers called me Jim Long. The kids in the neighborhood knew who they were, and they were called by the same name at home and at school. The home they went to had their parents in it, not their uncles and aunts. It didn't seem to me like I really belonged anywhere. Sometimes in those years, I used to go to the top floor of our apartment building, climb up a ladder, and go out onto the roof where I knew no one could see me and cry. From the rooftop you could see the Ambassador Bridge, the one that went to Canada. I used to sit and watch the cars going across. I was sure all the people in the cars knew who they were and exactly where they were going. I didn't have a clue about myself.

It was at about that time that I learned how to escape by going to the movies. My grandmother and my uncles didn't go to movies, but they let me go on Sunday if somebody else would take me. Church was a big thing in my grandmother's life. She went regularly to The Church of God in Christ. As one of my uncles put it, "there was a lot of whooping and hollerin'" in that church and there was just plain a lot of "church." There was a service on Sunday morning, another service on Sunday night, and then another meeting on Wednesday. My grandmother used to take me to all these services, till one of my uncles finally said, "That's a little too much church for James." After that they started taking me with them to the Baptist Church on Hartford Avenue, where I only had to go to Sunday school and then church. After church and after Sunday dinner, I was allowed to go to the movies with other kids and their parents or, more often, friends of mine and their older sisters or brothers. Eddie Horton's older brothers went to the movies all the time. They were old enough to look after younger kids, and so Eddie and I often went with them. It didn't take long. When I fell in love with the movies, I really fell hard.

I loved the films of the 1930s, the westerns, the musicals, the gangster movies, the horror pictures. I loved the stars: Buck Jones, Tim McCoy, Shirley Temple, Nelson Eddy and Jeanette MacDonald, James Cagney, Edward G. Robinson, Lon Chaney, Boris Karloff, Rin Tin Tin, Gene Autry, and Richard Dix--not a big star, but I can still hear him saying, "Remember the Alamo!"

I knew all about the big studios then. Warner Brothers made the gangster movies. Paramount made the big westerns, and Alan Ladd and Robert Taylor were the stars. Universal made the comedies; they had Fred Astaire and Ginger Rogers. I knew all the gossip back then. If you gave me the names of the biggest stars, I could tell you what studio they worked for. If you gave me the names of the studios, I could rattle off the names of their biggest stars. Just like that!

As I realize now, going to the movies helped me handle all the things that were scaring me in the real world. I needed that kind of escape pretty badly, and it wasn't long before it wasn't enough for me just to go to the movies on Sunday afternoon if there was somebody who would take me. I wanted more, and I knew what I had to do to get it.

If you went to the eight o'clock show on Saturday nights, you could watch not only the double feature for that week, but late at night they'd show the double feature for the coming week as well. You saw four movies in a row, and they lasted into the early hours of the next day. At the time seeing all those shows would have been my idea of heaven. But there was no way my grandmother and my uncles were going to let me do something like that. Not in a million years. So I had to think of something.

I thought it out carefully. I had to go to church and dinner on Sundays, but I had Saturdays to myself. When the weather was nice, I could go out and play all day, and as long as I didn't get into any trouble and was back home when I was supposed to be, they didn't need to know where I was, and so what I did was this: instead of asking if I could go to the movies, I asked my grandmother if I could go over to my friend Eddy's for the day. She said it was all right, but I had to be back on time in the evening. I knew I could get away with it that far because Eddy's family didn't have a phone. Therefore, even if she used a public phone my grandmother couldn't call to check on me, so I knew I was going to be all right till it was time to come home. I didn't know exactly what I was going to do then, but I didn't care. I was so excited that I didn't even think about things that could go wrong.

In those days it cost ten cents to go to the movies. I went to the eight o'clock showing and stayed right through into early Sunday morning. I loved every minute of it. I didn't care what happened as long as the pictures kept moving on the big screen. I was Tim McCoy shooting the gun out of somebody's hand. I was a gangster: tough and self-confident. People were afraid of me and not the other way around. The Boris Karloff Frankenstein came out in 1931, when I was seven or eight. I loved that movie then and still do. I remember when I first saw it I got upset when the people chased the monster after he killed the little child. He didn't mean to do it. I could see that he didn't mean to do it. I wanted to tell the people who were chasing him to stop. I was completely inside the world of the movie.

It was a different story when the movies were finally over and I was out on the street at two or three in the morning, though. It was scary. It was scary just being alone on the streets at that time of night. Sometimes I could walk home with Eddie's older brothers, but sometimes I was on my own.

It was even scarier thinking about what I was going to say when I got home. The only thing I knew for sure was that I couldn't hang around in front of the theater all night, so I would start walking. There were Coney Island hot dog places in Detroit in those years and they stayed open all night. I found one, and with the change I had left I got a hot dog and a cup of coffee and stayed for a while around the little lighted shanty. Finally, of course, I had to move on, but the closer I got to home the more frightened I got at the thought of having to wake the family up and tell them what I'd done. In fact, when it came right down to it, I couldn't face it in the middle of the night, so I started looking for a place where I could sleep till the sun came up. I tried the doors of a few cars on my street and finally found one that was open. I crawled in and went to sleep till the sun woke me up around six thirty or seven. Then I had to pay the piper.

You would think the whippings I got and the fact that I knew I had upset my grandmother would have made me stop staying out all night like that, but it didn't. If anything, I was more hooked than before. For a while I kept doing the Saturday thing—going in the evening and coming home in the wee hours of the morning on Sunday, even though I knew I would get a whipping every time. Sometimes I was able to find a car to sleep in. Sometimes I slept in the lobbies of apartment buildings in the neighborhood—the room where all the doorbells and mailboxes were. It was fairly safe and out of sight and the weather, and at that time of night there was a pretty good chance that no one would even know that I had been there. After a while, though, I went to another plan. Instead of staying out all night on Saturday night and sneaking home Sunday morning, I started skipping school and going downtown during the week. That raised the ante, and things got more serious then.

I didn't do it every day. I didn't leave for school with the intention of skipping out. But once I started doing it, once I saw that it would work, I started doing it more often. I would go to a few classes in the morning, and then sometimes I'd just take off. Usually I would wait till after lunch because they gave us our lunch at school and I didn't like to miss that.

I didn't always go to the movies. Sometimes I would go home. I knew nobody would be there in the middle of the day, and I knew where the key was to let myself in. On those days I would leave school after lunch, go back to the house, turn the radio on, and listen to the daytime soaps: *Our Gal Sunday, One Man's Family, Backstage Wife*, and sometimes *The Shadow*. Even though I was just a kid, it was surprising how wrapped up in those things I could get.

On other days, I went to the movies, which wasn't as easy. The theaters in our neighborhood didn't show movies in the afternoons, and so I had to go downtown. I almost never had enough carfare, at least not to go both ways, and so lots of times I hitched a ride, and sometimes I was able to sneak onto the trolley. The way I would do that—when it worked—was that I would wait at a crowded stop, and when the bus driver was busy making change for a whole line of people, I could sometimes sneak right between the grownups and he wouldn't see me. Or maybe he would see me and just wouldn't care. When that didn't work, I walked.

The theaters I went to weren't the fancy ones that showed the best movies. They were much smaller theaters mostly on Michigan or Gratiot Street. They were open all day and all-night and there were always a lot of bums in them, people who looked like they had maybe slept there overnight. I didn't find that scary, though, and nothing ever happened to me. They never seemed to want any trouble. I think that like me they were there because they just wanted to get away from something. The movies they showed in those theaters were B movies, and I knew it: second rate westerns and gangster films. But it didn't matter. I was just glad to be there and living in whatever fantasy world was playing on the big screen at the time.

I've asked myself many times what it was that made me do these things. It isn't fair to say that I hated school. I didn't love it, but I didn't mind it. I didn't hate living with my uncles, either.

And I wasn't crazy about spending time alone. The thing was, though, when I was at school or at my uncles', I was always reminded one way or another that it wasn't really my home. No matter how loving my grandmother was, I knew she was not my mother or father, and I knew they were somewhere else and that it was all right with them that I wasn't with them. I think I went to the movies—even the worst of the B movies—because when I got lost in them I stopped thinking about the things that upset me. After I got used to the escape, I started to depend on it.

My system worked pretty well for a while. The city public schools didn't go to a lot of trouble to let families know if their kids were missing classes. As I've said, my uncles didn't have a phone. There was no easy way for the school to call them if they had wanted to. I usually got to the movies downtown around one o'clock and I was almost always able to get back to our apartment by between four and five. At the worst, it just looked like maybe I had gone to somebody's house to play after school. The trouble didn't begin till the police got into it.

The police got into it because when you were an eleven or twelve-year-old kid running around downtown Detroit when you were supposed to be in school, you were pretty easy to spot. After I started going to the movies during the day it was just a matter of time. Sooner or later a cruiser would spot me. They would pick me up, find out right away that I was skipping school, and take me to the station. Because they couldn't call my family, eventually they would have to take me home in a squad car. Then they would talk with my uncles and grandmother, and then my uncles and grandmother would get together and talk about me. Eventually this happened one too many times, and my uncles and grandmother decided that something had to be done about my behavior. I don't know exactly how it went down; I wasn't in on that discussion. But the end result was that I was taken out of the public schools and sent to the Moore School, where they thought I would be under closer control.

The Moore School was known to be a school for "bad boys." Everyone who was sent there was in some way like me. They had been acting up. They had become a problem for their families or their neighborhood—or for the police. Because the students were tough and difficult, the school was run strictly. They allowed corporal punishment, and if you got caught breaking rules or became a discipline problem, you could expect to get slapped down pretty hard. It wasn't a live-in school. I continued to live with my uncles while I went there, and because it was on the east side and we lived on the west side, I was given bus tickets for each school day. I gave it a try. I had no choice. But I only lasted a few months there.

I only lasted a few months there because even though they watched you pretty carefully and punished you when you broke rules, I still kept sneaking away and going to the movies. I still kept getting caught and hauled back home by the police. And I was getting into trouble at the school, too. I remember there was this kid named Roy Jenkins. He was bigger and stronger than me, and he got on my case one day and gave me a real beating. The next day, we got into it again at lunch, and he beat me again, but it was a closer fight. Not long after that I got into it with him for a third time, and it was a draw. When we quit fighting, we looked at one another, and I said, "I'll quit if you'll quit" and we agreed. And I didn't have any more trouble with Roy Jenkins, but after those fights and with all the sneaking away to the movies I was doing, the Moore School had had enough of me.

The biggest problem for me was that I didn't have a real home they could send me to with parents who could promise to keep an eye on me. My uncles worked and had their own families, and my grandmother couldn't do it any more, or at least whoever it was that made decisions about these things didn't think she could, and it finally got to the point where when the police caught me when I should have been in school they didn't take me home. They took me to a juvenile detention house. That's when I went into the system.

By now I was between eleven and twelve years old, and the juvenile detention house was the scariest place I had ever seen up to that time. It was like a prison. You couldn't leave till the court decided what to do with you. They were the ones in charge now. You couldn't get out to go to school, either. You couldn't get out at all, and the kids inside were tough. Many of them were considerably older and in detention for things like robbery, auto theft, and assault. There was danger everywhere, especially the older kids, and from the staff, who could be a lot more physical than the teachers at the Moore School. I still remember Mr. Vandenberg at the house of detention. He had a mean voice, and if he caught you doing something you weren't supposed to, he would say, "Come here" and believe me, you came. Next he would say, "What did I tell you about" whatever it was you were doing. And the next thing you knew you were on the ground and your head was ringing like a bell.

The detention house was a big operation. Although it was all in one big building, and the kids who had been sent there couldn't leave it, it was like a campus. If I remember correctly, there were three floors. We had rooms where we slept on one of them, and we took our meals on another. There were business offices, classrooms so you could keep going to school, rooms where the counselors and the visiting nurse could see you, and there was the gym, where all of us kids who were sent there spent quite a bit of the day together. The gym was where you got into trouble if you were going to because there were a lot of kids milling around and it was hard for the people who were watching us to keep an eye on everybody. The gym was where the fights started and occasionally people got hurt.

I wanted out of there in the worst way. I knew that other kids would be there for a while and then get back home to try to work things out. That's not what happened to me. Those kids had parents, but in my case it was up to the court to decide what to do with me, and that was especially hard on my grandmother. When she came for visits and was about to leave, I would start crying and asking, "When are you going to take me home?" She would get upset, too, because she knew there was nothing she could do by herself.

I don't know any of the particulars of the decision making process about what to do with me because I wasn't part of it. All I know is that the courts finally decided that something fairly drastic had to be done. I know there was a social worker who talked with my uncles, and a judge who made the final decision, and the final decision was that it wouldn't be a good idea to send me back to my uncles' house because my grandmother was the only one there who could really look after me, and they felt she couldn't control me. So the judge decided to send me to Boys Vocational School in Lansing [12]. It was a turning point in my life.

I Go Into the System

When you're as young as I was and the system gets a hold of you, they can do pretty much whatever they want. They didn't let me go home. I wasn't allowed to go back to my uncles' house or say good-bye to anyone. They sent me to Boys' Vocational in a county car.

I still remember the trip. Another kid and I were driven straight from the detention home to Lansing. There were just the two of us and two staff people to keep an eye on us. It was a very quiet, very lonely ride. I sat there with plenty of time to think, and I remember wondering why this was happening to me. While I had been in the detention home, I had seen all sorts of kids who were in for auto theft or assault get sent home, given another chance. What had I done? I had just skipped school, and I was being sent away. I understood that I was acting out and not doing what I was supposed to do. I understood that I deserved some kind of punishment for my behavior. But not being taken out of the only real home I had known up to that point and sent to an institution. I had had no idea that the stakes were going to be that high.

I started to get angry, but there was nowhere to go with it with the staff people right there in the car, and there wasn't really any way to talk with the other kid. One of the adults was a social worker, though, and I did try to ask her some questions like, what was it going to be like at Boys Vocational? Did she think I would like it? What kinds of things did they do there?

Not surprisingly she tried to calm me down, picture things in the best possible light. She meant well, and even at that age, I knew why she would want to say the kinds of things she was saying: "The campus is very nice. I think you'll like the classes you'll take." And so on. I tried to look like I was listening politely, but I tuned out after a few sentences.

I got a different picture when we stopped for a bite of lunch. It was the first time that the other kid and I had a chance to talk privately. I remember we were at a gas station and had a moment to ourselves. He grabbed my arm and said he had heard what the social worker had been telling me, and it was bullshit. He knew kids at the detention home who had been to Boys Vocational, and they said it was a really tough place. He wanted us to run away right then. He said this was our chance. Nobody was watching closely. They'd never be able to catch us, and we could worry about the rest later.

I had to decide quickly, and I decided I wouldn't do it. I didn't know this kid very well. I didn't know how much he really knew about the school. I thought I would at least give it a chance. He wasn't willing to try to run away on his own, and so we both got back into the car, and before too long we were there.

Maybe because I had been expecting the worst, my first impression pf Boys' Vocational was a pretty good one. The first thing I saw was the campus, the buildings and grounds. It certainly looked a lot better than the detention home. I saw boys marching from one class to another in blue uniforms with a black stripe down the leg and neat military caps. I started thinking maybe this wasn't going to be so bad after all. When we got out of the car I said so, and the kid I was with looked at me and said, "You just wait!"

The campus was good sized. There were the main classroom

buildings, fairly nice grounds, and cottages where the boys all stayed. The cottages held between fifteen and twenty boys each and two adults, usually a couple, in residence. We lived and took our meals in the cottages and marched to classes and church in the blue uniforms. We had time outside for recreation, and in summer when classes were over we worked in the fields.

After a couple of weeks, my impression of the place was not as bad as the kid's I drove out with, but it wasn't sunshine and roses, either. The Boys Vocational School was a serious place. Nobody who got sent there mistook it for a vacation. There were no walls or fences. It wasn't literally a prison like the juvenile detention home. But the appearance of openness and apparent freedom was deceiving. The school and cottages were run strictly. There were tough kids there, and you had to be on your guard all the time with the other kids as much as with the staff and teachers. Besides that, it was at or close to the end of the line so far as Michigan's social services were concerned. If the vocational school didn't work out for you, you were not many years or steps away from the adult criminal justice system.

Not surprisingly, there was a lot of structure to the average day and not much unsupervised time. We slept on cots in the basement of our cottage. The day started at around 6:30. We got up, washed up in the basement, and then came upstairs to the dining room to take our breakfast. Everyone had chores to do, and if you had morning chores like doing the breakfast dishes or cleaning and dusting, you did them then.

The classes were basically just like the ones in the public schools for the same grades: reading, writing, and math. They were held in separate buildings, began after breakfast, and went till the noon break. We had our lunch in the cottages, and then after lunch it was back to class till about 4:00, at which time we went back to our cottage and stayed down in the basement living and sleeping quarters till dinner time at 5:00. When dinner was ready we marched upstairs and took our meal—then it was back downstairs till bedtime at 8:00.

Between dinner and bedtime we could talk and listen to the radio, but we had to be quiet, and we couldn't act up. The adult cottage manager—Mr. Getz--was sneaky. He would sometimes tiptoe downstairs very quietly so we didn't realize he was there. If people were cursing or starting to get loud, he would all of a sudden step out and pounce on the troublemakers. "Come here, you," he would say, and when you did he would slap you down. Sometimes he even brought a paddle. He wasn't as bad as Mr. Vandenberg at the juvenile detention home, but it wasn't pleasant. You always had to look out for him.

When I got used to the routine, it really wasn't so bad. I accepted it for what it was and never thought about running away. I knew nothing about Lansing, and have no idea where I would have gone if I had tried to get out. Mainly I just did what I was told and stayed out of trouble. When the weather was nice and we had free time on the weekends, we would play baseball or football out in the yard, and I liked that. Honestly, I think the school might have done me some good if it hadn't been for what happened after I'd been there for about three months. That was when I learned that a couple of the older, tougher boys in our cottage—real bullies—were planning to catch me in the shower and sodomize me.

I found out because there were a couple of guys from Detroit who had I recognized from the detention house. We got together because there were kids of all races from all over the state of Michigan at the school, and the black kids from Detroit felt like it was a good idea to stick together.

We were talking one day during some free time, and they pointed out two of the older guys in our cottage, tough looking black guys who were almost sixteen (the age at which they took you out of Boys Vocational and moved you to an institution for older boys). They told me to watch out for them, that they would do anything they could to hurt me if they got the chance. They pointed out a small, fairly weak white kid from somewhere on the Upper Peninsula. They said, "Those guys are fucking that kid. If they go after you and get you alone, they'll make you suck them or they'll fuck you in the ass." They told me that if they heard anything about when these guys might be going after me, they'd tell me so I could at least be on my guard.

The school grew its own vegetables in good-sized fields that were part of the campus. We grew corn, potatoes, beans, cabbages, that kind of thing, and it was sometimes the boys' job to work in the fields—picking or weeding, generally helping tend the garden. Some of the rows of crops were fairly high, and there weren't many people watching us when we worked there. They kept moving around so that sometimes there was nobody watching you closely at all. My Detroit friends and I were out there at one of those times, and they said, in a whisper, "Come here." When I did, they said, "Look over there, between the rows." There I saw that poor white kid down on his knees doing one of the guys I had been warned about. The other one was just standing there waiting his turn. "That's what they do," they said, "And he won't report it. He wouldn't dare." They looked at me and said, "Niggers from Detroit don't take shit like that. If we hear anything in time to warn you, we will."

Now I knew that what they had been talking about was real. It could happen. I knew I was on my own, too. My friends were right. The white kid wasn't going to snitch. If you did that here, your life was not worth living. I'd heard of kids here who had been being picked on and had asked to move to a different cottage. If you did that, everyone assumed you had ratted out the guys who were bothering you, and you were hazed and beaten up everywhere you went. As I learned before I left, a lot of stuff went on here, but people kept their mouths shut. The only one who could take care of me was me, so what I did was make myself a knife.

I snuck a common stainless steel table knife out of the dining room one night, and when I was alone I started sharpening it on a brick. It was crude, but I kept working at it, and pretty soon I had an edge and a pretty good point on it. It was a good thing, too, because it wasn't very long before I had to use it.

Not long after I had the knife ready, my Detroit friends told me this was it. They had overheard the mean guys talking about it the night before. They were going to get me in the shower either tonight or tomorrow night. I had been thinking about it, and I knew exactly what I was going to do. I had a plan.

I had been hiding the knife under my mattress. When it was time to shower, I took it out and hid it in my towel. When I hung the towel up in the shower room, I tied it in a loose knot and hid the knife in the knot. Then I went into the shower.

There were three other boys showering with me. All of a sudden I noticed it was quiet. I looked around and the other three had disappeared. The next minute, in came the two mean guys. I knew this was it, but I just went on washing myself. Then one of them said, "Come here. It's your turn now." I said, "What turn?" and he said, "It's your turn to come over here and put this dick in your mouth. And if you make any noise, we'll kick your ass."

I think they expected me to protest, or plead or at least act surprised. That's why when I broke straight for my towel and the knife, they were taken aback for just a second, and it was all the time I needed. They both came after me, and one of them—I learned later that his name was Wilson—grabbed me by the shoulder. But I had the knife by then, and I whirled around and stabbed and cut him in the shoulder and upper chest. He was really surprised and started screaming when he saw the blood, which flew all over the place. His buddy had frozen when the knife came out, and now I went after him. I was on pure adrenalin, and I started shouting, "You're next, motherfucker." He took one look at me and at all the blood and started running out of the shower and up the stairs.

I started after him. I had completely forgotten about the guy I stabbed, and he nearly knocked me over when he ran right by me, up and out, too. It was all over in I'll bet no more than a minute and a half, if that, and suddenly I was standing in the shower, naked, with a homemade knife in my hand, and blood everywhere. I knew the fighting was over now, and so I went and got my towel, wrapped it around my waist, went and sat down on a bench in the shower, and waited to see what was going to happen next.

It was quiet where I was, but I could hear that upstairs they were going crazy. I could hear people running around all over the place. I heard them call an ambulance for Wilson, and then more running around, and then talking in loud voices but not loud enough for me to understand. And then Mr. Getz, the cottage manager, came down the stairs and started asking questions:

"What the hell has been going on here? Did you stab Wilson?"

"Yes, Sir."

"Why did you stab him?

I said nothing.

"Where is the knife?"

I held it up and showed him.

"Hand it over right now."

I did, and then he asked me again, "Why did you stab Wilson?" and I said, "Ain't nobody gonna make a punk outta me." "What do you mean?" he said. And I said nothing—and I said nothing more to them about it, ever.

I saw the other boys in my cottage all looking at me as they led me out. They had called security, and the guards took me straight to the discipline cottage and started asking questions.

They asked me what happened, and I told them the same thing I had told Mr. Getz: "Ain't nobody gonna make a punk outta me." That just made them angry and one of the guards got up in my face and said, "I just asked you what happened." When I said nothing he slapped me but at that point the other guard pulled him away and they let me alone after that.

After I was taken to the discipline cottage I wasn't allowed to leave. They brought me my books, and I did my schoolwork there. They kept me for a week, and while I was there the school psychiatrist talked with me. He was nice enough—certainly he wasn't mean—but I didn't tell him anything. I tried to be honest with him. I told him straight out that I didn't know how long I was going to have to live here, and I didn't want problems. He talked a lot of psychiatrist talk, but I knew what the reality of the place I had to live in was. If I felt I had learned anything by now it was that I had to look out for myself because nobody else was going to do it for me. The social workers, and the psychiatrist, and even most of the staff meant well. But they didn't go into the showers with you. They weren't there out in the fields. *After* something happened they maybe could do something, but they couldn't stop them. So at these sessions we would sit there. He would ask me questions, and I would say nothing, and afterwards he would write up reports on me. I saw one of them in which he wrote, "James is a very strong minded young man."

After about a week, they let me out of the discipline cottage and moved me to a different cottage from where I had been staying. It was supposed to be a fresh start, and basically that's what it was. Word got around fast among the kids, and I soon learned that because the two guys who had attacked me were so close to sixteen, they shipped them out to a different institution. They were gone by the time I was out of the discipline cottage. In my new cottage, everyone had already heard of me, and I found I had something of a reputation. "Man," I heard one of them say. "He stabbed Wilson. He's a tough nigger from Detroit." I didn't have any more problems with tough kids at Boys Vocational after that.

I don't know how things would have gone over the long haul if I had stayed at Boys Vocational School. But I didn't stay there much longer. As I found out later, even though my grandmother hadn't heard about the attack on me and about the stabbing, she was worried. Apparently they did tell her that I was getting in a lot of trouble and that if it kept up they were going to have to use stricter measures with me. At that point apparently she went to the courts to try to get their permission to let me come back and live with her. The court didn't believe she could control me, so she got my Uncle Claude, married, respectable, and a lot younger, to agree to try to take me. He came to Detroit and talked with the judge and the social worker in charge of my case, and convinced them to let him try it. And so I was on the move again, this time to West Virginia State University in Institute, West Virginia.

West Virginia State University is still there. It is, according to a current on-line advertisement, "a historically black university, which has evolved into a fully accessible, racially diverse, and multi-generational institution offering baccalaureate, associate, and graduate degrees...located in Institute, West Virginia, eight miles from downtown Charleston."(http//www.wvstateu. edu) When I went there, my Uncle Claude was an agricultural extension worker for the university. He helped black farmers in the region by showing them better and more efficient farming techniques. He was doing well in the world and had a pretty good life.

When the people at Boys Vocational called me in to tell me what was going to happen to me, I didn't know exactly what I thought. I knew I had an Uncle Claude, but I didn't know him anywhere near as well as I knew my Uncles Chris and Allen. I remember wondering what kind of life this was going to be for me now. Was Uncle Claude going to be good to me, or was there going to be trouble? I didn't have any answers. But I didn't exactly love Boys Vocational, and more important, I knew I was just a kid and didn't have much of a choice. So I hoped for the best and off I went.

I left Boys Vocational a little after Christmas, just into the new-year. It was 1937 and I was twelve years old. My Uncle Claude brought his wife Margaret with him to pick me up. We stayed overnight in Detroit, so I got to see my grandmother Tellis again. Not for long, though. The next day we were on our way to West Virginia.

Uncle Claude drove, and I worried all the way on the ride. What was it going to be like living with him and Aunt Margaret? What would their house be like? What about the school I would have to go to? I just didn't know what to expect, and I was nervous. But when we pulled up at Uncle Claude's, I was pretty impressed. He had a nice house in a nice neighborhood—right on the edge of the campus. I remember there was a garage under the house, and the football coach lived across the street. Everything looked clean and the whole place seemed well off.

When I got settled in I found that I liked Uncle Claude and

Aunt Margaret, and I liked everything about my new home. The campus was pretty—trees, nice lawns, a lot of open space. I used to walk to baseball games there and sometimes to see a movie. I liked the school and especially the other kids.

This was a whole different ball game from Boys Vocational. The kids my age were faculty kids. They weren't "troubled" or tough and streetwise. They were friendly and polite. A lot of them shook my hand when they met me. Uncle Claude enrolled me in the junior high there and some of my classes were held on the campus. I think I could have been really happy there, but I didn't get a chance to find out.

Sometime during the spring or early summer Uncle Claude got the offer of a better job at Delaware State. It was apparently an offer he felt he couldn't refuse. And when he and Aunt Margaret made their plans to move there, the plans didn't include me. As I look back, I can certainly see why; I don't blame them. That's just the way it was. The result was that I was going to be on the move once again.

It was all over by the end of the summer (I think probably because Uncle Claude had to be settled in by the beginning of fall semester). He went on ahead to Delaware State, and Aunt Margaret went to her parents' home in Lansing to wait till it was time to join Uncle Claude. On the way, she dropped me off at my Uncles Chris and Allen's home in Detroit—my old home—and in some ways I was back to square one.

It was back to square one in the sense that I was back in Detroit in the old neighborhood. I wasn't in the Juvenile Detention Home anymore, and for that I was grateful. But there were a lot of things that were different now. I was older and had had a lot of things happen to me. I was in junior high now—McMichael Junior High. I was big for my age and I wanted to be like all the bigger kids, and I still cut school. Sometimes it was to go to the movies, and sometimes it was to go downtown with Eddie Horton and some of the other kids and shoplift things. (The first thing I ever stole was a pocketknife from Hudson's Department Store.) Why did we do that? I don't know. Why do teenage kids without much supervision do any of the things they do? I remember we all got kind of a kick out of shoplifting. Maybe it was the thrill of getting away with something, doing something you knew you weren't supposed to do but that didn't seem to hurt anybody? We were getting something for nothing. I don't know. We just did it, and we liked doing it.

I had my first sexual experience in those years. It was with Mrs. Jones, who lived in our neighborhood. Her husband was the iceman. He delivered ice and coal all over the city and he was gone a lot of the time. I used to go over to the Jones' to do simple chores, picking up the yard, running errands, that kind of thing. One day when I was there Mrs. Jones started paying attention to me. She got kind of close and said, "Don't you have a girlfriend, Jim?" I said no, and she got a little closer and started touching me. I was between twelve and thirteen years old. I don't say I didn't like it; but I don't think I knew what I would have done if I hadn't. I was flattered and a little nervous. She said, "I'll show you how to do it, Jim", and then she did and we started doing it.

After a while, it got to be every weekend. (That was when her husband was sure to be away.) She told me when she wanted to see me, and at first I sort of dragged my feet about it. But it wasn't long after the sex started that I started liking it, and I would start getting ready early on Saturday. That's what tipped my grandmother off, I think. When she saw me getting all spruced up for no apparent reason, she figured things out right away. (I guess Mrs. Jones had something of a reputation in the neighborhood.) I remember I was combing my hair and washing and I had even made sure to put on clean underwear. My grandmother took one look at this and asked me right out where I was going. I said to Mrs. Jones', and she said, "No you're not." I said, "Mrs. Jones is expecting me." "No," she said, "Mrs. Jones knows you're not coming over there." And that was that for Mrs. Jones.

My grandmother was a smart woman, but that wasn't the end of the troubles I kept getting into. When I think back about it, I feel bad for all the worry I must have caused her. At the time I just did what I wanted to do, which meant that besides all these other things I started skipping school again and going downtown to the movies.

I don't like to be always blaming people. We are responsible for what we do, and I know that. But I can't help wondering what might have happened if I'd been growing up with my real father to keep an eye on me, or if I had been able to grow up with my Uncle Claude and Aunt Margaret. I suppose questions like that are pointless. It didn't happen. The police eventually started catching me skipping school. When they took me downtown to the Detention Center, the juvenile court had a file on me by now, and it included the stabbing incident at Boys Vocational. I wasn't little kid anymore, and I was a repeat offender, and so it wasn't long before I found myself in court and standing in front of Judge Baxter.

I liked Judge Baxter. I remember him fondly. He was a white man (there were no black judges in Detroit at that time—at least not that I knew about), but he seemed genuinely to take an interest in me and to have my best interests at heart. That's not what I thought at first, though.

I remember watching him looking through my file. He didn't look at me, just down art all my records, and I kept wondering what he was thinking. How did I look compared to all the other kids he saw? Was he going to throw the book at me? Because I was afraid, I assumed the worst and started getting angry at him in advance. He didn't really know me. What right did he have to treat me the way I was sure he was going to? He was going to send me back to Boy's Vocational. I just knew it.

He did nothing of the kind. When he was finished looking carefully through my records, he looked up and said, "Jim, I don't think you're a bad person. I think I can see some good in you. So I'm not going to send you back to Boys Vocational. I'm going to send you to a place I think you'll really like." He then went on to tell me about Boys Republic. "It's like the movie— Boys Town [13]—Spencer Tracy," he said. And up to a point it was.

Boys Republic was and still is in Farmington, Michigan. In their on-line description they say that, "The residential program is designed for at-risk youth whose problems at home, school, or in the community deem placement necessary to bring about change. Youth are engaged in individual and group counseling, family counseling, year-round academic education, pre-vocational training, on-site job placement, therapeutic recreation, and aftercare. Young people are taught how to make good choices and sound decisions. A major program goal is the child's return to family and community as a healthy productive citizen." (oakgov.com/circuit/assets/docs/guide/b/boy-girl-republic.pdf) It was something like that when I went there, not as much of the counseling stuff but basically the same. I was driven to Farmington in a county car, with a social worker to help get me installed properly. It was the same as when I was taken to Boys Vocational, except by now I was getting used to the routine.

In some ways the setup was like Boys Vocational in that it was a campus-like facility. The boys all lived in cottages, and each cottage was supervised by a husband and wife team who lived there and kept an eye on things. I remember that on that first day we got there around noon. The social worker took me to what was going to be my cottage and the first thing we did was have lunch upstairs in the dining area with the other boys. After lunch we went to the administration building to get all the paperwork taken care of, and then to a sort of store or commissary where I was given new clothing. It wasn't uniforms this time, just regular, sturdy clothes. Then it was back to the cottage by suppertime, and after that I was on my own.

To my surprise, being on my own wasn't so bad there. To begin with, I think I was genuinely influenced by Judge Baxter's saying that I was going to like it. I had it in my head that I was going to like it (I knew Spencer Tracy movie, Boys Town) and I did. Right off the bat, I realized the kids there were different from the ones at Boys Vocational. I never met any tough, hardened street kids of the kind I had known plenty of at BVS. There were no Wilsons at Boys Republic—at least that I was aware of. The kids here seemed not to be delinquents but rather kids from broken homes or family situations that were unworkable. They didn't challenge you; they would come up and introduce themselves.

In a lot of ways the daily routines were the same as BVS, though. We got up early for breakfast in the cottage. The food was prepared in a separate building and brought hot to each of the cottages. We all had chores we had to do, and the boys who had breakfast set and cleared the table and did the dishes.

After breakfast and clean up, we went to classes in a separate classroom building. We went back to our cottages for lunch and then back to school till three o'clock. Dinner was at about five-thirty or six back at the cottage, and after cleanup we could play outside till dark. Then were allowed to listen to the radio till it was time for bed. Sometimes we got movies, but mainly it was the radio, serials like the Lone Ranger or the Shadow!

I got there near the end of the spring term. When classes were over, I think in late June, we all got to work in the school's gardens. Like BVS, the Boys Republic grew a lot of its own vegetables, and we got to tend the gardens and sometimes help store the vegetables in the root cellar. In the evenings after dinner we played baseball till it was dark. Judge Baxter was right. I really liked Boys Republic. It was just my bad luck that I wasn't able to stay.

This is what they told me. Apparently there was a high demand for places at Boys Republic. More kids wanted in than they had room for. I was one of the older boys there and in somebody's judgment I was a good candidate for a foster home to free up a place for a needy younger boy. Somebody whose decision mattered felt that "Jim would be able to handle it." So I and a number of other kids they felt could handle it were sent to foster homes in Ypsilanti to make room for the others. That's what they told me.

I lived in my foster home for several years. My Foster mother's name was Wilhemina. She took three boys from the county, Fred, Milton, and me. She got more money from the state because she took all three of us. [14]

Wilhemina lived with her grandfather and her boyfriend, Harold. It was quite a household. Wilhemina ran poker games once a week that were famous in the neighborhood. Sometimes even "Big John," the mayor of Ypsilanti, used to play in them. And Wilhemina "cut" the games. That is, she took a percent of every pot for the house, just like the casinos. Grampa was a character, too. He was a big man who had been a bartender when he was younger, and he drank quite a bit still. He was a good cook, though, and he did most of the cooking for Wilhemina.

I kind of liked him. He said he actually met Jesse James, and for all I know, he did. He was old enough. Harold was another story, but more of that later.

We foster boys slept in the same room, and I was the only one who was still going to school. While I was there I finished junior high. When I went to high school, I went to the Ypsilanti public high school and two of my schoolmates were Preston and Rosemary Tucker, the children of Preston Tucker, the famous automaker. I remember Preston and Rosemary were really nice kids. They were rich, but you would never have known it from the way they acted. Everybody liked them.

For the first year or two I liked my foster home and everything about Ypsilanti. Partly it was because nothing bad happened during that time, but partly I think it was just my age. I was getting into the teens. I was big and athletic and people thought I was good looking. I had a lot of girlfriends, and there was always something going on. There wasn't a cloud in my little sky until I found out I couldn't play high school football.

Besides being able to box, I was finding out that I was a good athlete in general. Better than just good. I was really excited at the thought that I was going to be able to play football for the high school, and then somebody checked my records and found out I wasn't quite old enough. I was big for my age and had gotten my strength early. And because I had been moved around from one institution to another so much, it wasn't always clear exactly how old I was. It turned out that when they finally got it straight, I was too young yet to play high school football, and so they didn't let me. I was so discouraged (because my hopes had been so high) that I told Wilhemina I didn't want to go to school any more. I wanted to go to work like Fred and Milton, and she said that would be all right. If I had it to do over again, I'm not sure I would do the same thing, but at thirteen or fourteen and big for my age, it looked like a good decision, and nobody from the county objected.

I got a job in a shoe store, and besides my regular salary, I found another easy way to make some money. The owner of the shoe store was an alcoholic and didn't pay much attention to details. I hadn't worked there too long before people in the neighborhood found out about it, and some of them would come up to me and say, "If you can get me a pair of shoes like this or that, I'll pay you for them" (always a good deal less than they really cost). I knew how easy it would be for me to do it, and I didn't even think once about it. The word got around. I had a lot of customers, and was getting three and sometimes four dollars a pair. Eventually, of course, I got caught, but while it lasted, I felt like I was living pretty high on the hog. I used some of the money to buy myself nice clothes. I started going to dances and met a lot of really cute girls. And I started hanging around with some pretty wild older guys.

Wilhemina had a nephew named Bill Guthrie. He was in his late twenties and really a wild man. He had a fast car, he drank, and he ran around with all sorts of women. I was fascinated by him. He had a couple of friends named James and Fritz who were the same age and they were "running buddies." They all hung out and did things together. When they started letting me hang out with them—as much older as they were and as much cooler (or so I thought)—I was excited and flattered. I liked their confidence and what seemed their freedom to do whatever they wanted. At that age, I wanted to be like them and for them to like me.

Some of the things they did were harmless enough. For example, they would sometimes go skating at a roller rink nearby in Jackson, Michigan. I would ask if I could go with them. Wilhemnia would say no, but then Bill would say, "Oh, come on. We'll look out for him," and she would let me go. When I was out with those guys I felt ten feet tall.

Sometimes it got serious, though. One night when I was hanging out with Bill and Fritz and James, they decided to go to a whorehouse. I went with them but I stayed in the car while they went inside. Then the police came and they all got busted, and so did I. The police found me in the car and asked me if I had been inside, and I said yes, because I didn't want to seem like I was ratting on Bill and his friends or trying to weasel out. I think the police must have had their doubts, because they brought me inside and asked the whores if I had been there. They all said I wasn't involved, but I said yes I was. I insisted. I know it may seem crazy, but I didn't want to seem disloyal. So the police hauled me in right along with them, and we all got thirty days in jail.

When Wilhemina found out, she was really angry. She came to see me in jail and told me I was a fool to do what I had done. She was especially concerned because if the state found out that something like this had happened to a boy under her care, she was afraid she would lose her license. The county sent a social worker around once a month to check on the kids in their foster homes. The problem, obviously, was how to explain me not being there. Wilhemina found a way to get around it, though. When I got out I learned that when the social worker came that month, Wilhemina said something like, "Oh, Jim just went out for the day. I'm so sorry you missed him. He's doin' fine. You can talk with him next time you come." The social worker bought it, and by the time she came again, I was out and able to talk with her.

After I got out of jail, though, things started to go bad between me and Wilhemina's boyfriend Harold. Harold liked to be the man in the house. He liked to tell Wilhemina's county boys what to do. He would tell me to run errands for him and sometimes order me around in the house. I was getting too old to take that kind of crap anymore. I didn't like being treated like a boy. I had friends like Bill Guthrie and his buddies. Harold wasn't my father, and I felt like I didn't have to jump whenever he wanted me to. This thing between Harold and me simmered for quite a while, and then one day it finally boiled over.

I don't remember whether it was Thanksgiving or Christmas, but I know it was during one of the big holidays. I was with Bill Guthrie and his buddies Fritz and James. We had been at a neighbor's house and they had been drinking pretty hard. These guys didn't give a damn about Harold, and one or the other made a joke about him, and we were all laughing at it. What we didn't know was that Harold had seen us and had heard enough to understand what was going on. He walked over and got in my face. He said, "You little motherfucker, what are you laughing at?" I said nothing. But he wasn't in a mood to let it go. "Did you think that was funny?" he asked. I said yes, and there it went.

Everyone knew that Harold carried a knife, and he was good with it. It wasn't a switchblade. It was what they call a flick knife. People who knew what they were doing could flick the blade open with their thumb in the blink of an eye, and that's what Harold did. One minute I was feeling kind of bad that I got caught laughing at him and the next minute the knife was out and I saw the blade coming right at me.

Instinctively I put my arm up to protect my face and in a fraction of a second I could feel the blade slicing through my wrist and lower forearm. Harold was mad. It was a deep cut, and in seconds there was blood all over the place. When I started bleeding, the fighting was over. I have no idea what happened to Harold. But he wasn't coming after me anymore, and everybody was crowding around me to try to stop the bleeding. Nobody called the police. Somebody wrapped my arm in a towel, and then Bill Guthrie drove me to a hospital emergency room. They sewed me up, but they didn't do a very good job. I was cut deep and they just stitched it up quickly. I'm still numb in the fingers on the hand on that side.

A lot of things were happening all at once. The hospital called the police, and when they arrived they wanted to know what had happened. Before they got around to me, though, Wilhemina got there and she came and sat right down beside me. "Please, Jim," she said, "Don't tell them who did it. If you do I'll lose my license."

I went along with it. I told the police that we were all horsing around and it was an accident. I don't know if they believed me, but nobody told them anything different, and what were they going to do? So nothing legal came of it. But the doctor wanted to have me lie quietly on a gurney for a while before they would let Wilhemina take me home. While I was lying there I had a lot of time to think, and what I was thinking was about Harold. He had pulled a knife on me, and I had to do something about that. I felt like what I had learned at Boys Vocational was pretty simple and basic: If someone was threatening you, you had to strike first or strike back hard if you wanted to protect yourself. Harold and I weren't ever going to patch things up. After the knife thing, there wasn't room in that house for both of us. So I decided I was going to kill him. I remember that's exactly what I said to myself, "I'm going to kill that sonofabitch." It wasn't a matter of "if". It was a matter of how and when. It made me feel a lot better to think that I wasn't going to take that from him. I was going to get even.

I thought for a long time about how I could do it and get away with it. When hunting season came, I thought I saw my chance. Harold liked to go pheasant hunting in the fall, and he would sometimes take us boys. We worked the cornfields after the corn had been harvested, and for safety's sake we walked in a straight across line, nobody ahead or behind the other. We all had guns. I had a .410 gauge shotgun and was using fairly heavy shot. As we worked our way through one field after another, I kept looking for my chance. I thought I had found it when we came to a fence we all had to cross to get into the next field.

I knew exactly what I wanted to do. I worked it so that I got to the fence last. Everybody else crossed ahead of me. Nobody was looking back. They just assumed I would catch up. That was my moment.

As a rule, you had to be careful crossing fences with a gun. You put the gun over or through the fence, climbed it and then picked it up, or you leaned it against the fence before you started climbing and reached back over for it when you were on the other side. You were never supposed to start climbing with the gun in your hands, but that's exactly what I did.

The fence was made of a few rickety strands of wire. I climbed up on it with my gun, set my feet as steady as I could on the wire, and aimed right for Harold's head. Nobody was watching. I could claim it was an accident. That was my plan, but things didn't work out the way I imagined. Just as I went to pull the trigger, the wire I was teetering on gave way. I lost my balance, fell forward, and shot low. I hit Harold in the back of the legs with a full load of shot, and he started to scream bloody murder.

It was bad for a while. We had to get Harold to a hospital. The police were called because it was a gunshot wound. They asked a lot of questions, of course, but the fact was nobody really knew what had happened but me. Everyone else, including Harold, was looking the other way, and my story made sense. Of course

I shouldn't have been climbing the fence with a gun in my hand, but for all anyone knew it was nothing more than that: a stupid accident that could have been prevented. Certainly no one could prove different, and even the police were finally satisfied.

I don't know exactly what Harold thought, but I know that it was really bad around the house for a long time after that. What saved things from blowing up was Wilhemina. I overheard her say to Harold one night, "I don't want you to cause any more trouble. You cut Jim. If he tells, I'll lose my license, and so I don't want you to cause any more trouble around here."

It worked for a while, but I knew it wasn't going to solve things between Harold and me, and so I had a talk with the social worker the next time he came around to check on things. I pointed out that I was sixteen years old now, and asked if there would be any problem with me going to work full-time. He thought that was a good idea, and it wasn't long before I was working for Ford at the huge River Rouge plant in Dearborn. It got me out of the house, but that was about all.

It was an exciting time, though, and for the first time maybe ever I felt like there was something I could do that would give me some independence and get me out of the system. It wasn't long after Pearl Harbor. The whole country was gearing up for war. They were making bombers at the Kaiser plant at Willow Run near Ypsilanti. A lot of the guys at the River Rouge plant transferred over there because they wanted to help the war effort. Even though President Truman didn't integrate the military till 1948, there was a lot of patriotism and excitement among the young black men I worked with, and I picked up the fever myself. I was sixteen; I was sweeping floors at River Rouge, and I wanted to do something a lot more important than that. So I went to a recruiting office, lied about my age (I was sixteen but big and physically mature). There was a big troop build-up at the time. I was eager to enlist, and the recruiters didn't ask a lot of questions. Before I knew it, I was in the army.

Out of the System into the Service

Except for what I had seen in the movies, I had no idea exactly what I was getting into when I decided to enlist. My experience in the service over the next few years showed me a lot of things about myself that it was important for me to learn, some of them good, some I needed to figure out how to deal with. On balance, I think the things I learned changed my life for the better. Some of the lessons were hard, though, and if I hadn't had three different shots at it, I don't know what might have happened. But I did have three shots at it because, before I was finished, I had enlisted—under slightly different names—in the army, the marines, and the air force. It was like I kept trying until I finally got it right.

I tried the army first. I was a year or so younger than you were supposed to be, but I was big for my age and athletic, and there were no careful records kept like there are today. Nobody in Meadowbrook had birth certificates in 1925. Most people were born at home, and a note in a family bible was the most elaborate record anyone I knew had. The Social Security System had begun in 1935, but it was just beginning to be implemented. People in the black community were certainly not all "numbered up" yet, and at local recruiting stations they had no easy way of checking. And it was wartime. They needed young men. They eyeballed the enlistees and used common sense. If the story sounded good and you looked old enough to be a soldier, then you could be a soldier.

I had no trouble enlisting. I was young and strong and a good athlete. They signed me right up, and I even enjoyed boot camp and basic training, which I took at Fort Jackson in South Carolina. The physical stuff was easy for me, and I liked the fact that I was better at things than a lot of the other guys. There was a lot of anticipation, too. The level of America's participation in the war on both fronts was heating up fast, and instead of waiting around, it looked like we might be going right into combat in Europe. My unit was sent to Maryland to a staging area from which we were going to be shipped out—sent to where the action was. But we weren't going to leave till all the units and equipment arrived, and in the meantime my unit was assigned to guard duty at a compound for German war prisoners. That's where I ran into trouble the first time.

When we had guard duty, we had to patrol an area close to a stockade where just a tall fence with coils of barbed wire at the top separated us from the prisoners. I don't know where these German prisoners were from, what rank they were, or what they were doing in a prison in America, but there was one prisoner who really got under my skin. Every time I was on duty he would come to the fence and start calling me "nigger" and any other racial epithets he could think of. I would walk right over to him but he wouldn't back down. He would call me this stuff right to my face.

Finally there came a time when I couldn't take it from this guy anymore. One night while he was mocking me, his face pressed right up against the fence, I lost my temper and hit him in the face with the butt of my rifle. I don't know what I was thinking—something along the lines of I didn't have to take shit like that from him. It was street thinking, not army thinking, and it was a big mistake. He started yelling and really made a stink about it, and it was me who took the heat. They put me in the stockade, gave me some psychological evaluation, but the worst part was that the incident brought me to their attention. You don't want that kind of attention in the military. I went from being a promising new recruit to a possible discipline problem. Evidently my behavior crossed some kind of line and they didn't want to take a chance on me anymore and decided to give me a general discharge.

Strike one.

It was a blow. One minute I had been part of a unit that was about to be sent into combat. I had an immediate future that seemed glamorous and exciting. The next minute I was out on the street. I didn't have anything like a home I wanted to or could go back to, just a place I had lived recently. Because I did know people in Ypsilanti, I went back there, but it wasn't the same. People had moved on, and I couldn't pick up with my old life, and I didn't want to. Most of my friends there were either in the service themselves or for some other reason they were gone. I liked the little taste I had gotten of the service, and I didn't want to hang around Ypsilanti doing nothing, and so I decided I would try to join the marines. What did I have to lose?

I had surprisingly little trouble. When I went to enlist again I told them my name was James Lang. I liked the idea of making it something very close to my real name, Long, because I thought that way I wasn't as likely to be surprised and not know that somebody was talking to me. I didn't think I could get into much trouble if I got caught, and I didn't think they would catch me. And they didn't. I didn't have to have elaborate proofs of identity. Not many black men my age had drivers' licenses and they didn't assume I should. They looked me over, took my word for things, handed me the papers to sign, and before long I was on my way to Camp Le Jeune, North Carolina.

I liked the marines. I did my basic training at Camp Le Jeune in an all- black unit. The drill instructors were tough and really strict, but they made you feel proud of yourself. I remember that day in, day out after working us nearly to death and breaking us down, they did a great job of building us back up. "You are tough," they would tell us over and over again. "You are a marine. You are special." I remember a sergeant telling us, "The guys in the army tuck their ties into their shirts like a dog tucks its tail between its legs. *Marines* wear their ties outside." We got a lot of stuff like that, and I have to say it really made me feel good. I was proud when I finished basic training. I was a marine. It felt great, but it didn't last. I hadn't learned my lesson yet.

It was my temper again. It was that same old street mentality, and it blew up on me when I least expected it. Marine basic training was over. I was a marine, not a recruit anymore. I was walking across the parade ground when I saw a busload of new recruits arriving, and I recognized one of them, an old friend named Charley Athens, who was just arriving.

All the officers in my unit were white, but there were two black sergeants—Sergeant Johnson and Sergeant Hough—and while I was watching my friend Charley coming off the bus, I decided to walk over and say hello to him. Sergeant Johnson was really giving it to the new recruits the way marine drill sergeants are famous for doing, and when I got close I stopped to wait till he was done so I could have a chance to talk with my friend. Sergeant Johnson didn't like me being there and told me to leave, and I argued with him.

Big mistake.

He told me to get out of there and I said something like, "Oh, come on Sergeant. I just want to talk to my friend." He looked at me for a minute, and his eyes narrowed, and then he said,

"Come over here." I thought he just wanted to talk, so I walked right over. When I got close he didn't say a word. He just hit me really hard and knocked me flat on my back in front of my friend and the whole busload of new recruits. I didn't see the punch coming, and when my head cleared I went a little crazy. One minute I had been as proud as I could be about being a marine and the next Sergeant Johnson made a fool out of me in front of a crowd. Everything I had learned about life so far was telling me I couldn't let something like that go. If you let yourself look weak or vulnerable on the street, bad things happen. You don't last long. It's a hard lesson to unlearn.

I jumped to my feet and ran as fast as I could back to my barracks. Charley told me later that Sergeant Johnson made a big deal about my getting up and running. Apparently he tried to make an example of me to the recruits. He said things like, "He thinks he's a marine, but he's not a marine. Look at him run away. Marines don't turn tail and run like that." Charley said he told the sergeant that he was mistaken. "I know Jim," he said, "and it's not going to end like this, believe me." And it didn't.

I was in such a rage when I ran back to the barracks that I couldn't think of anything but revenge. I felt I had been publicly humiliated. I didn't run away because I was frightened. I ran away because I felt I had to prove myself. I had to get even. What I ran for was to get my bayonet, which was in my footlocker, and when I came running back towards the parade ground with my bayonet in my hand, Sergeant Johnson sang a different tune.

He wasn't stupid. I'll give him that. When he saw me come roaring out of the barracks with the bayonet in my hand, he didn't hang around and try anything heroic. He took off running himself, and I went after him as fast as I could go. But by then the MPs had been alerted to what was happening, and all of sudden the guns were out, and it was all over for me. They put me in the stockade and then sent me to Cherry Point Naval Hospital, which is part of the complex at Camp Le Jeune. Apparently they decided I needed psychological observation, so from Cherry Point they sent me to St. Elizabeth's Hospital in Washington, D.C, the place they sent John Hinckley [15] after he tried to kill President Reagan. When they were done observing me, they brought me before a board. By that time they had found out that I had been underage when I enlisted, and they discharged me for fraudulent enlistment.

Strike two.

When I went back home the same thing happened as before. I was at loose ends. None of my friends were around. Moreover, I had been a marine. I had felt proud wearing the uniform. I didn't want to go back to sweeping floors at the River Rouge plant in Dearborn. So I thought about enlisting in yet another branch of the service. It had worked for me once. Why, I wondered, wouldn't it work again? If it did, I knew I had to be really careful. I wasn't going to get beyond strike three.

It went just like it did the other two times. Apparently the different branches of the service didn't share or coordinate records. At least not quickly. The year was either late 1943 or very early 1944. At the time it wasn't clear how long the war in Europe was going to go on, but they still needed fighting men for both the war against the Germans and the war against Japan. I went to the recruiting station for the 82nd Airborne and gave my name this time as James Law, and before I knew it I was on my way to basic training at Fort Bragg. I was hoping that the third time would be the charm, and in a lot of senses it was.

My time in the 82nd Airborne was the best experience I had in the service for a lot of reasons. For one thing I was grateful.

I had not only had a second chance in the service, I now had a third chance. For another, I knew what kinds of things I had to be careful not to do. I knew I had to think and act like the 82nd Airborne wanted me to think and not just lash out when I was angry or threatened. Above all, it was the time when both and the military and I became aware of what I could do as an athlete. I learned how much ability and potential I had and how it could sometimes open doors for me. And, as if that weren't enough, while I was there, I had one of the most exciting experiences of my life as a paratrooper in the famous all black unit, the 555th—the Triple Nickles.

The 555th [16] was something special. A friend of mine recently showed me an article about it on the internet. There was a paragraph in it that I especially liked. It reads:

> *In the frosty Georgia winter of 1943-44, soldiers and officer candidates traveling to and from Fort Benning often saw the sky filled with white parachutes. Most of them assumed that the faces beneath the chutes were also white. The black soldiers they knew drove their trucks, waited on them in mess halls, or hauled their ammunition; they rode in the back of the bus to and from Columbus; they gathered at their own separate clubs on the fort. Some of the faces beneath those chutes, however, were black. As such they were also pioneers, blazing new trails for countless black soldiers to follow. (www.triplenickle.com/history.htm)*

That was my outfit. It was an honor to be part of it. For once in my life I was in the right place at the right time. The famous Battle of the Bulge went on from December 1944 till into January 1945. There were an estimated 77,000 casualties, and a great many of them were paratroopers in the 82nd Airborne.

Replacements were badly needed, and that's when the idea of an elite all black paratrooper unit was born. That's exactly when I enlisted in the 82nd.

Thinking back, I imagine one of the reasons I was picked for this unit was that I was big, strong, and athletic. Whatever the case, I was allowed to try to make the elite squad, and it wasn't easy. The training was some of the hardest I had experienced, but it was also some of the most exciting.

Jump School was at Fort Benning. What you learned there was exactly what the name implies: along with some pretty tough physical training we learned to jump out of airplanes without getting hurt. In the beginning we would get up and run four or five miles every morning and then do what seemed like hours of killer calisthenics. When they thought we were in shape for it, the parachute training started.

They were very particular about the training for the obvious reason that if you made a mistake in a jump that was going to be it for you. They took it in stages. They wanted to teach us how to land properly, and so after quite a bit of preparation on the ground, we were taken to the forty-foot tower.

Forty feet is not the same as jumping from a plane, but if you've ever been up that high and looked down you know that it's a long way up in the air. It's a long way to fall, too. Honestly, this was one of the scariest tests we had to pass. They took you up to the top of the tower, and they hooked the top of your parachute to a strong wire that was anchored on the ground and helped you glide down at about a forty-five degree angle. The idea was to simulate the conditions you would face when coming down from a real jump—from a plane. It was to teach you how to land properly. The thing about landing was to hit the ground and roll, to hit the ground first not with bones and joints but with big muscle masses that could absorb the shock.

They wanted you to learn to hit with your thighs, your butt, and your shoulders—not your feet or your ankles or your wrists.

The reason it was so frightening was that the hook-up—parachute to wire—was above your head. You couldn't see it or even really feel it when it was time to jump. You were looking down forty feet. There was no safety net, nothing but the ground. You had to have faith that the wire would help break your fall and guide you and that the system would work. There were people who just couldn't do it and were sent home at that point. I did it, but I understand why some people couldn't. It was just stepping off into space, and the worst thing was that you had too much time to think about things. We all went up to the top single file, and you saw all the others going down ahead of you. When it was time to jump from a plane, everything went much faster. The jump master gave commands, the wind was whipping past the open door. You just jumped. At the top of the forty-foot tower, you had time to look down and think about what it would be like to fall all that way.

One of the next big exercises was a much higher tower. It was high enough that when you got to the top and they dropped you, you could actually come down using your chute. The idea here was to learn how to guide your descent, control where you were going to land, and then quickly get your chute under control. In those days paratroopers were often dropped fairly close to enemy lines. If you didn't know how to control where you landed, you could lose touch with your unit in combat and get into a lot of trouble.

They spent a lot of time having us practice on the ground before they sent us up there. We learned quickly that there were two kinds of cords on your chute. The smaller ones helped connect you to the chute itself. The larger ones were called the "risers" and they were the cords you got firm hold of once your chute had opened. When you learned how to do it, you could control the direction of your flight down by pulling and twisting on the risers.

The moment when we all had to go up to the top of the really high tower got everyone's attention. They hooked you up and then raised you slowly straight up to the jumping height. When you reached it, they had some way to automatically cut you loose. When you got all the way to the top, you would hear a click, and suddenly you were free floating and had to remember all of the things you were supposed to do—or else. We had to take several of these practice jumps, and then we had to put it all together and jump from a plane.

To get certified—to complete the program—you had to make three successful jumps from a plane. I did that, but the jump I'll never forget was the first. We had been taught over and over again how to pack our chutes properly, and we were very quiet as we packed them for this jump. If you didn't do it right all sorts of bad things could happen. The chute might not open properly or it might not open it all, and if that happened the only thing that would break your fall was the ground.

It was really quiet aboard the plane once we were in the air. There wasn't any joking or horsing around. I remember we flew across the Chattahoochee River and for a brief time were over Alabama. But then the plane turned and headed back. When we jumped we were going to land in Georgia.

As we got near the point where the jump would begin, the jump master began walking up and down the aisle, checking everyone's equipment. Then all of a sudden he began to give commands, "Get ready. Stand up. Hook up." Hook up meant that you clipped your chute to a wire that ran the length of the plane. When you jumped, that's what opened your chute.

"First man in the door" was the next command, and the first

in line stepped up. Then the Jump Master said, "Stand in the door." And when he said that, if you were up, you knew it was time to get ready to jump.

They gave us a lot of practice on the ground before they let us take that big first step from a plane. The big thing was not to just jump like you were jumping off a diving board into a lake. You weren't supposed to squat before you jumped, either, although for me that was the natural thing to do. You were supposed to "kick out" with the leg that was on the outside and let the wind turn your body as you got into a crouch and got your head in and down. Getting your head down was important because we were jumping from the old C-47 cargo planes. The door we jumped from was right in from of the tail. You didn't have to be a genius to see what would happen if your head was sticking up right after you jumped. The tail would likely take it right off. If you kicked out properly and let the wind turn you, you were facing the tail, could see it coming, and get out of the way.

Once you were out of the plane and the tail had whizzed by above you, you counted, "One thousand. Two thousand," and if everything had gone as it was supposed to, your chute would snap open. Usually when you jumped it would seem for a second like your chute was below you, but then you would quickly fall past it and then Wham, it would jerk you up hard when the wind caught it and it snapped open. If that didn't happen, you weren't supposed to panic. In the first seconds of the jump, your hands weren't supposed to be on the risers. They were on the ripcord of an emergency chute. If the main chute didn't open, you pulled that ripcord. That's how it was supposed to work, but it didn't always. One of the things that I'll never forget about that night was the jump itself, the tension and excitement I could feel in the plane, the strong wind in my face, stepping out into space, thousands of feet up, the chute opening, thank God. The other thing I'll never forget is the man whose chute failed to open.

On that first jump we had one guy whose chute didn't open. It must have been packed wrong. They called it a streamer because when the chute didn't open all the way it didn't catch the wind and fill out. It stayed partly together and streamed out behind the jumper—all the way down. It was horrible. The man whose chute didn't open screamed all the way down and apparently died instantly when he hit. When they got to him, they found that he had broken some fingers trying to pull the ripcord for the emergency chute. In his panic he had been pulling in the wrong place.

This was wartime, and in spite of the accident, training continued on schedule. We went up for another jump the night after our buddy had died. You can be sure we were all thinking about it when we packed our chutes for the jump. The rest of us in this group made all three jumps from the planes successfully and completed our training. We were officially paratroopers, and that meant that we got to wear the distinctive high-topped boots. We thought we were getting ready to be shipped out for combat in Europe. But there was an unexpected change of plans.

By 1945 the war was beginning to take a turn for the better in Europe. The Normandy landing, D-Day, was in June 1944. By the new-year things seemed more under control there than they had. In fact, there appeared to be a greater need for the paratroopers on the northwest coast of America, because the Japanese had figured out a way to float air balloons across the Pacific and rig them so that they were capable of dropping incendiary bombs on the coastal forests of the Pacific Northwest.

My unit became part of Operation Firefly. We were sent to Oregon, and I made one jump there. We didn't stay there too long, but it was exciting—and it was different because what we were supposed to do when we hit the ground was different than what we had been training for. We weren't going into combat; we were going in to help fight fires. The packs we wore were much heavier than the ones we had been training with. Therefore, we didn't jump in the regular way—kick out, turn, etc. We fell forward out of the airplane and let the weight of the pack take us down and away. We also were jumping from the famous Flying Boxcar, which made a difference, too. In the Flying Boxcar, the door we jumped out of was located in the rear and already below the tail, not by the wing on the body of the plane like in the C-47. It was much more efficient for jumping. The other thing that was different was that we all wore something that resembled a football helmet with a strong wire mask in front of our faces. That was to protect us from the branches in case we came down in the trees.

When we hit the ground, of course, our tasks were different, too. When we all landed, we rendezvoused with other fire fighters, set up camp, and then did all the things regular firefighters do: cut fire lanes, set back fires, tried to put the fires out or at least slow their progress. I only made one jump for real, and it was pretty hot hard work when you got to the ground. But I was proud I was part of the operation, and especially proud when, a bit later, General James Gavin officially recognized our unit by formally and officially making the 555th a part of the 82nd Airborne. For an all-black outfit in those days before the military was officially integrated, that was a very big deal and we were extremely proud.

Making it in the 82nd Airborne and becoming part of an elite unit was one of the best things that happened to me in the early part of my life. As I look back I can see that, growing up as I had, I badly needed to find somewhere where I could feel I belonged. Being a member of an elite paratrooper unit in the 82nd gave me that feeling. It was also there that I came into my own as an athlete, so much so that by the time I left the service, I was starting to get known as a sprinter, as a boxer, and as a football player good enough to have been scouted by the Detroit Lions.

It was boxing that really brought me to people's attention, and it wasn't something I planned. The main reason I started getting involved in athletics at the base was because I realized that if I was good enough, it would get me out of a lot of regular duties and maybe even get me some special treatment. I thought I saw a chance for myself as a boxer because I already had some experience and some confidence. It also looked like there was an opportunity for me to make a name for myself. There was a big heavyweight who drove a truck, boxed for the army, and was a sort of the king of the hill. Nobody in our unit wanted to fight him. I said I was willing to try.

The brass in the 82nd tried to talk me out of it. At first my they simply said, "No." I kept after them, though. I kept saying I thought I had a chance. I was willing to take the risk. Finally they agreed. It was my funeral, they said.

The fight became a major event, and the night it came off was electric. I still remember it clearly. The fight took place in the base's big field house. There was a lot of hype ahead of time because someone was willing to take on the big trucker. There were women there. General Gavin was there. You could feel the excitement.

This guy—the trucker—*was* big. He had long arms and, by reputation, a big punch. It was a good thing I knew how to box. I knew I had to keep moving and stay inside on him. Even so, he got me good—knocked me down—in the first round. He did it the way Max Schmeling got to Joe Louis. [17] I was using a left jab to try to keep him off balance and away from me. I tried following the jab (which seemed to be working) with a right cross, but after I threw the punch I let my right arm stay down and didn't pull it back fast enough. He came right over the top of it with a left hook, caught me on the chin, and down I went.

There's a point on your chin where, if someone hits it hard it doesn't matter who you are, you are going down. It isn't a question of "if." It's a question of "for how long?" I was lucky. He hit me hard, but it wasn't lights out. I knew by the count of four that my head was clear and I was going to be OK. I stayed down till the count was eight, though, and made it through the rest of the round by hanging on and punching just enough to keep the ref from calling it. When the bell rang for the second round, my head was clear, and I knew exactly what I was going to have to do to stay in the fight.

The bouts were three rounds each. I came out in the second round and ran right at him, punching as I went. I stuck to him like a burr, keeping inside so that he couldn't get those big arms extended and let me have it. I landed a lot of punches, hung on, got him into a clinch when I thought I was about to get in trouble, and I think got him extremely frustrated. He won the first round, but two more rounds wasn't enough time for him to figure out what to do about my new style. I hung on a lot, but the punches I kept landing added up. After three rounds I got the decision, two rounds to one. It was a huge victory, and it got me a lot of attention!

What got me even more attention was my foot speed. When it was time for track season, the 82nd Airborne and I discovered how fast I could run. I became the sprint champion of the 82nd Airborne. My best distances were the 100 and the 220, and after I had established myself in the 82nd they started sending me to major competitions. I competed in the track meet for the entire

Third Army, and not long after that, although the 1948 Summer Olympics were several years away, they sent me to an airbase in San Antonio, Texas, for preliminary Olympic tryouts.

It was exciting. There were athletes there from all over the country. I was in pretty good company. I remember there were four of us who were considered the best sprinters at these tryouts. There was a Japanese American sprinter named Watanabe; an army lifer, Lieutenant Carter; Billy Anderson, who was the son of Eddie Anderson—Jack Benny's Rochester. And me. We none of us made it all the way to the 1948 Olympics, but I was nearly put on a relay team that went to the Penn Relays. The reason I wasn't on it finally was because I made a mistake. They wanted me back at Fort Bragg to run in the Third Army relay again. They gave me a choice, and I decided to go back to Fort Bragg. The result was that I became the Third Army Sprint Champ, but back in San Antonio they replaced me on the relay team and that guy went with the team to the Penn Relays instead of me—and they won. I always felt bad at having missed out on that.

Because I was both fast and big, it was almost inevitable that I would play football as well as everything else. For a while the 555th—the Triple Nickels—had its own football team, and I especially liked that. I played halfback and corner back, and I was good if I do say so myself. My specialty was defense. I played in a championship game, and there were pro scouts who came to see us. I don't think in my life up to that time I had ever felt as good about myself and my future as I did then. However, my time in the 82nd Airborne and the military didn't last too long after the events I've just described. It was my dislike of the routine stuff that finally got me into trouble. But it really didn't matter. I wasn't going to be career military, and I had learned what I was good at and how I could use those things to make my life a lot easier—and better. I liked the way people noticed me and treated me after I out boxed the big trucker. I liked the sometimes special treatment I got as a member or the sprint and relay teams. What eventually was my undoing was the fact that I didn't like the day-to-day routine stuff—the ordinary things you have to be willing to do if you're going to make it in any branch of the service.

More than anything else, I didn't like maneuvers. The truth be told, I didn't like anything about the outdoors. I hated when we had field exercises and went into the woods. I hated the cold, bitter coffee and the bugs and snakes. Sometimes we were actually instructed to dig shallow trenches around our tents because supposedly that would discourage the snakes from coming inside. When I heard that I thought, "You've got to be kidding!" Whenever we had to go on one of these exercises I tried everything I could think of to get out of them. I dragged my feet as hard as I could, and finally one time I crossed some kind of line, and it got serious.

We were scheduled for one of those exercises I hated, and we were supposed to be at the rendezvous point with all our gear and loaded onto the trucks by such and such a time, and I just didn't get there. I got there just after the trucks had pulled out. They told me I should try to catch up with them, but I didn't do it. I was hoping they would be willing to let it slide, maybe let me do something else instead. But that wasn't what happened. Insubordination was what they called it, and all of a sudden I was in big trouble. I was called in front of a board again. I remember one of the examiners asked, "Do you mean to tell me that you're the Third Army sprint champ, the fastest man in the Third Army, and you couldn't catch those trucks?" I knew how the wind was blowing then, and I was right. They didn't buy it, and eventually I was discharged and out of the paratroopers and the 82nd. I didn't see this as "strike three", though. I didn't leave with my head hanging down. I was on my own again, but this time I had had some successes. There were things I knew for a fact I was good at. I just had to find a way to use them to my advantage.

Professional Football: Close, but No Cigar

When I left the 82nd, I kicked around for a while. It was, I think 1947 or 1948. I went back to Ypsilanti because at the time it was the place I knew best and where I felt the most at home. But I didn't go back to Wilhemina's. For one thing, I wasn't a kid any more. For better or worse, I was now legally on my own. For another thing, after being treated like I was responsible for myself the way I was in all the branches of the service, there was no way I was going back into somebody else's home. I had just entered my twenties. I was old enough to know that I had to figure out something to do with my life. I had to go forward because I couldn't go back. But at the moment, I didn't know where to go.

I had a little money saved up from my pay when I left the 82nd, and till I got a job, I signed up for unemployment and started getting a check every two weeks. For a while I lived in Ypsilanti in a little community of prefab houses. Each unit had two separate very small apartments and could hold two people. The kitchen and showers were communal and in another place. It wasn't a great way to live, but it was a way to tread water, and I was grateful for it. It gave me a place to live on my own and time to think. I thought about working for one of the auto companies in Detroit again, but I didn't like the idea of cleaning up some shop and sweeping floors. What I did best at the time was run, box, and play football. I had been a star in the 82nd Airborne. I had heard that pro scouts had come to take a look at me. So took a bus into Detroit, went to talk to the Detroit Lions management, and asked for and got a tryout.

The time was right for a couple of reasons. For one thing, these were the years when black athletes were beginning to make it into professional sports in America. Around the turn of the century, in the early part of boxer Jack Johnson's career, a black man couldn't be the heavyweight champion of the world. He could be the *black* heavyweight champion of the world. It was different now. Joe Louis had been the undisputed champ since 1937 and would be till 1949. In baseball, Jackie Robinson had made it to the major leagues with the Dodgers in 1947, and in the same year Larry Doby made it to the bigs with the Cleveland Indians. And Sugar Ray Robinson held the world welterweight title from 1946 t0 1951. There still weren't many blacks in professional sports, but the ones that were there were making it big time. The tide was turning; you could feel it.

The situation of the Detroit Lions was also a factor. Almost the whole decade of the 1940's had ranged from disappointment to disaster for them. They went 0-11 in 1942 and 1-10 in 1946, and most of the years before, after, and in between weren't any great shakes either. They had just hired a new coach, "Bo" McMillin, a football star in college and a highly successful college coach, who they hoped would turn things around. [18] They had also just drafted a young quarterback named Bobby Layne, [19] who looked like he was going to be a good one, and Heisman Trophy winner and All American, Doak Walker, [20] perhaps the classic "triple threat" back. So it looked like a good time to be hooking up with the Detroit Lions, and, given their record, it also looked like they could use all the help they could get. I really thought I had a chance.

By coincidence, the Lion's training camp was held on the campus of Eastern Michigan University that year—in Yipsilanti. I remember showing up with a lot of confidence but quickly finding myself feeling cut down to size. The Lions may have had a poor record over the last several years, but almost all the players were experienced and established NFL players. It wasn't that I was intimidated by them. But I realized right away that this was a whole different ballgame than football in the service. I knew how I stacked up in the 82nd, but I didn't know how I was going to measure up against these guys.

When you're new and untested like I was, you need a chance to show your stuff. You need some way to get noticed. I got my chance when I got a lot of playing time in a charity game sponsored by the *Detroit Free Press*. I thought I did all right. I held my own, and I knew I was as fast as anybody on the field. I guess I must have made some kind of impression, because they put me on the reserve squad for a while after that. It meant I was somewhere in the middle: not on the team but not off it, either. But finally one day Coach McMillin called me over. He told me to come see him and bring my playbook with me, and of course I knew what that meant.

The first thing Coach McMillin said was, "We gotta let some people go." As I handed him my playbook, I'm sure he could see that I was disappointed. He wasn't a bad guy and he was also a bit of a talker. "Look, Kid", he said. "If you weren't good you wouldn't even be in camp. Everyone who's here is good. To make it here you have to be 'damn good', and even then sometimes that's not enough. Sometimes we just don't have the time to develop all the players we see. Sometimes they're great, but they just don't fit into our system. Some players that we cut loose go on to become big stars for other teams." He paused a minute and then said, "For speed, Jim, no one in camp can touch you. But speed alone isn't enough. There are other factors, and the most important one is experience. You just don't have the experience right now."

He was trying to be nice, and I appreciated it, but I also got another version of the story from the scuttlebutt around the camp. They let me go and kept a kid named Johnny Pennelli, who had played at Notre Dame. The way I heard it, their thinking was that there were hundreds of Notre Dame fans and alumni in the area. If they kept Pennelli, he'd put more people in the seats. Coach McMillin said as much, but of course without any reference to Penelli. He said, "You may think of football as a sport, but believe me it's a business." I don't think I ever heard truer words spoken.

The Lions didn't let me go outright. They sent me to their farm club in Wilkes-Barre, Pennsylvania. It did mean that I still had a connection with the club that I could possibly be called back, but when I got to the camp at Wilkes-Barre, I was a little lost at first and more than a little disappointed. The Lions camp in Ypsilanti had had the feel of big time football, and the Wilkes-Barre club sounded like exactly what it was, a farm club. However, I decided I would rather live there better than in the prefab houses back in in Ypsilanti. It was all I had at the moment, and I was taking it one step at a time.

I found a place to live in Wilkes-Barre at a rooming house for athletes. I made two friends quickly: Harry "Suitcase" Simpson and Al Smith [21], who would go on to become big stars with the Cleveland Indians, but who at that time were pretty much just like me. We were young, black athletes, about the same age, with, we felt, a lot of ability, and with high hopes because black athletes had a chance now. They were playing for an Indians minor league team and hoping against hope to make it up to the big leagues just like I was trying to catch on with Detroit or somebody else. We were waiting for our chance, for the big break, and we hit it off right away. Of course we had different schedules. The baseball season was different from football, and they were on the road a lot. But when we were all there at the same time, we hung out and did a lot of things together. It was the one of the bright spots in my brief stay in Wilkes-Barre.

I remember we used to have a lot of fun playing cards. We played Bid Whist, Spades, and a game called "Tonk" which is still popular in the black community. It's a draw/discard game. Everybody gets five cards and the object is to "go down" with the lowest number of total points in your hand. You discard the cards you don't want to keep and draw hoping to get better. There was some strategy to it, too. You could lay down (and therefore get rid of) three cards at once if you had three in a series—10-Jack-Queen, say, or three of a kind) but if you didn't get all three and you got caught with them in your hand when someone went down, you were sure to lose. It was a game played for money, but the money was whatever amount the players agreed to at the start of the game. We none of us had a lot of money at the time and so we played for small stakes—but enough to make it interesting. I don't know why it was so much fun, but we used to spend hours at it, playing, talking about what was going on, who was dating who, and so forth.

Al Smith and Suitcase Simpson went on to have real careers in the big leagues. They played for a lot of different major league teams, especially suitcase. Both of them played in World Series and had pretty impressive lifetime stats. Their old baseball cards are worth something now. For me it was different. When that particular season was over, I wasn't sure I was going to make it beyond the farm team at Wilkes-Barre, and I knew I didn't want to stay there. In fact, when the football season ended, I left Wilkes-Barre and went back to Detroit, but I had a plan. I had heard talk about a semi-pro football team in Erie, Pennsylvania called the Vets that was trying to take itself up a notch or two by hiring professional quality players. I had come pretty close to making the Detroit Lions. Erie was on my way back to Detroit. So I decided to stop over and talk with the Vets management and see what might happen. What happened was a contract for 1949—1950 with the Erie Vets.

For the next few years I tried to make it in professional football in several different places, and for most of that time I used Erie as a sort of home base. Because their seasons ran at different times, I was able to try Canadian professional football while I was still connected with the Vets. I liked Canadian football. It paid better than what I had been getting--$125 per game for the Toronto Argonauts as opposed to the $75 per game I had been getting in Wilkes-Barre. I played for the Argonauts and, briefly, for the Ottawa Rough Riders. But eventually I got cut by both teams. I think it was a combination of things, the main one of which was that they had quotas for the number of American players they could have on their rosters. I was good enough that they had wanted me to play for them but not quite good enough to make the cut when they had to get the number of American players on their rosters under the limit. Between the American football season with the Vets and the Canadian season with first Toronto and then Ottawa, I was able to cobble a living together for a few years and keep my hopes of better things alive. And I had one more chance to make a big time NFL team.

Not long after I finally left Erie for good and was temporarily living in Detroit, I got a letter from the Chicago Football Cardinals. They were short on defensive backs and were willing to offer me a tryout. After my initial experience with the Lions, I had a lot fewer illusions than I had had the first time. But in many ways this was a godsend. I looked at it as a chance to start over. I had a lot more semi pro experience under my belt, and who knew—maybe I'd catch on this time?

I gave it a good run. The Cardinals' training facility in Lake

Forest, Illinois was intimidating in the same way the Lions' camp had been. There were some great football players there in those years. I was going to be playing defense against Ollie Matson and opposite Night Train Lane. [22] (The year had to be 1954 because that was the year Lane left the Los Angeles Rams and came to the Cardinals.) They had—like the Lions—some of the top college players, too. Ollie Matson and Night Train Lane went on to become Hall of Famers. These guys were good. It was exciting just to have the chance to play with them. And I did pretty well, I thought. I played with a lot more confidence than I had with the Lions. I got hurt after my first exhibition game, though, and I never really came back from it.

The exhibition game I started in was at Wrigley Field against the Los Angeles Rams. I made my tackles and didn't get hurt, and after the game I was cautiously optimistic. I thought I couldn't have looked too bad to them, and if they really needed help in the defensive backfield, then maybe I'd get my chance. But a practice scrimmage the next day changed everything.

It was the Cardinals' defense against the Cardinals' offense. I was playing left cornerback. The play started to the right and I went with the flow, but it was a reverse. I tried to change direction as quickly as I could. I didn't even see the offensive end, who was waiting for me and cut me down with a block below the knee. (It's called a "chop block" and you get penalized if you do it now, but everybody did it then.) When I got hit, my cleats held the ground and kept my foot and leg from turning while the rest of me turned with the force of the block. My knee couldn't take the strain, and I blew it pretty badly. It ended up being the occasion of another lesson about the way things worked in the NFL in those years.

I was just marginally a member of the Cardinals, but as I learned later, they couldn't let me go if I was injured. The team owners had ways of getting around it, though, and that's what they did with me. When I was about seventy-five percent of the way back from my injury and able to run and do calisthenics with the team, one of the coaches came to me and said, "Jim, we have an exhibition game coming up and we need to know if you'll be able to play. We need to see what you can do. Do you feel good enough to return a few punts?"

When you haven't made the team yet, when you know you're on the bubble, you want to do everything you can to please the coaches. I said, sure, I would give it a try. I still remember it. The punt was low and got to me ahead of the coverage. I saw a seam and ran it all the way back for a touchdown. I thought that would really impress them. Maybe that was what I needed to do to get them to keep me on the roster? The next day one of the assistant coaches came and told me to go get my playbook and report to the head coach.

I was angry when I got to the head coach's office. "I'm hurt," I said. "You can't fire me." "You aren't hurt," he said. "We have film of you running that punt back." I was speechless and embarrassed about how easily I had been tricked. "I'm sorry, Jim," the coach said, "there's just no place on the team for you right now. I hope you can catch on somewhere else." And that was that. It hurt, but after my experience with the Detroit Lions, it wasn't a total surprise. Pro football was a business. If I hadn't learned that by now, it was my fault.

When all is said and done, it was with the Erie Vets that I came into my own as a football player and almost made it big. For a three or four year stretch there, no matter who I played with in Canada or that I tried to make it with the Chicago Cardinals, Erie was my home base and, at the beginning, the Vets were my family. It's where I got the most playing time. It's where I got the most exposure in the press. And the Vets played some good teams. We had some real talent on that team.

When I first got to Erie, the president of the Vets told me where to find a room for myself at the Pope Hotel. It was the only black hotel in Erie, and it was owned by Ernie Wright, who was quite an operator—and quite a character. He owned the Pope Hotel; he was the biggest numbers man in Erie, with connections in Cleveland; and he owned a baseball team in the Negro Leagues. According to a recent history of the Negro Leagues [1], his team was called the Buckeyes, and they played in the same league with the Birmingham Black Barons; the Indianapolis Clowns; the Kansas City Monarchs where Jackie Robinson played till 1945; the Chicago American Giants; and the Memphis Red Sox. A modern history of the Negro Leagues says the following about Ernie Wright:

> Wilburn Hayes and Ernie Wright controlled the Cleveland Buckeyes in the 1940's. Hayes operated a shoeshine business in Cleveland and worked as a local sports promoter before becoming the General Manager of the Buckeyes. Wright lived in Erie, Pennsylvania, but worked the numbers game in Erie and Cleveland and also owned the Pope Hotel and the Buckeyes. Both men had numerous contacts in the community they could call on for support. Hayes knew the sports community and Wright had a constant cash flow as well as a hotel where the visiting teams could stay. (From The Negro Leagues, 1869-1960, by Leslie A, Heaphly, p. 97)

\

I didn't know anything about any of that stuff at the time. I was just out of the army and trying to catch on with a football team, pro or semi-pro. It didn't matter which at this point. But in Erie I was coming in contact, for the first time, with the fringes of the world of big time sports, gambling, and celebrity in both

---

[1]   See Appendix A: the History of the Negro Leagues

the black community and later the white. I didn't know it yet, but it was a world I was going to get to know very well and that I was going to spend much of the rest of my life working in or near.

At the time, however, football was what I was in Erie for, and I had a nice little run if I do say so myself. The Erie Vets were spending some money and making an effort to get better. Besides me they had Shag Thomas and Jimmy Clark, who had played for Ohio State. Thomas was a tackle, Jimmy Clark was a halfback, and I was a defensive specialist at cornerback and sometimes halfback. I played halfback on offense sometimes, too.

We won a lot of games in my first year. My speed helped me a lot as a defensive back. I had some great afternoons, and I started getting used to seeing my name in the sports pages. Here are some examples I cut out and saved (All from the *Erie Times*):

> The game's most sparkling play was reserved for the final minutes. Jimmy Long tossed a beautiful 50-yard pass to Frank Leibel, who made a great catch on the 10, and sprinted into paydirt. A Pepper to Zuravieff pass with a lateral to Clark good for 18 yards scored the first six-pointer in the third quarter. Jimmy Long raced 22 yards around left end for the other score. The alert defensive work of the Vet pass defenders paid off time and time again and stopped all but one Giant thrust. Six times Dean Dill had passes intercepted, with Jimmy Long grabbing three of them.

I was especially proud of those three interceptions against the New York Football Giants. I think at the time I would have been in the record book for it, but because the game was an exhibition game, none of the stats was permanently recorded.

The point I want to make, though, is that we were playing good ball and there were some very good players in these leagues. The Vets played a game against a team whose quarterback was some guy named John Unitas! [23] Nobody knew who he was going to become at that time—that was when he was playing sandlot ball--but I'm sure you see what I mean: these weren't bush league games. I was happy to be a part of this team, and it kept my hopes alive for eventually making it to the NFL. I also had some big successes in those years as an amateur boxer, too, one year winning the Golden Gloves heavyweight championship in the open category. It was off the field—out of the ring—where I started having problems.

LEARNING THE HARD WAY

When I started trying to play professional football and began living on my own in first Wilkes-Barre and then Erie, there were a lot of things I hadn't seen coming and wasn't prepared for. I wasn't in a foster home any more, and I wasn't in the service. Although the situation was pretty fluid in the foster home, there were still rules. People would eventually come around to check on you. If either you or your foster family weren't doing what they were supposed to, the county could blow the whistle. Obviously there were plenty of rules in the service, and people making sure you followed them. My situation was different now. When I was on the practice field, I knew what I was supposed to do. I knew what role I was supposed to play. But when practice was over for the day, I was a legal adult now, and I was on my own. I had to start making a lot of decisions about small stuff, like how I would spend my free time, and bigger stuff, like what kind of life I was going to lead. Like I suppose a lot of young people my age, I didn't always make the best decisions. But it was hard. Although I had grown up in Detroit, I had been a little kid and didn't know much about the world of the bright lights downtown. I hadn't seen the nightlife in big cities like Los Angeles, New York, and Chicago yet, either. The result was that even though it was just Erie, Pennsylvania, I was seeing things I had never seen before. The "adult" world in Erie was a real eye opener for me.

It seems like off the field, everything that was "happening" in my life during those years got started at the Pope Hotel. I remember it was at the corner of Holland Avenue and East 12th Street. It's where the black players from the visiting team and all the big name black entertainers who came through Erie stayed, and it was something of a hub for the local black community. I didn't even try to stay away from the action. There was good entertainment and a nice bar. The numbers people and black gamblers used to gather there, and people used to come for the bands and the dancing on the weekends. A lot of blacks came just to hang out and maybe meet people. Because I was living there, that was the crowd I started getting to know and mix in with. It was a real education in a lot of ways, and it was exciting but sometimes a little scary. I was flying without a net now, and I didn't have enough experience to appreciate the danger.

One of the most attractive and potentially dangerous things about the world I was suddenly living in was the sudden exposure to drinking and smoking, bad talking, trash talking, and high living! I had never seen anything like it. In Uncles Chris' and Allen's home in Detroit they had alcohol about twice a year, usually on Christmas and New Year's, and they were particular about the kind of language they used, especially around the children. Being in the various branches of the service had been an introduction to both drinking and some pretty rowdy language at times. But it was nothing like what I got used to hearing and seeing at the Pope Hotel. The guys working the numbers in Erie came in regularly and would start drinking and whooping it up almost the minute they came through the door. Pimps from Cleveland would bring girls up to work in the red light district in Erie, which was not far away. When they came in at the end of the week to collect their money, they would often take the girls to the Pope for an evening out. It goes without saying that where there was sex and gambling, there were plenty of drugs.

In that section of Erie, the "houses" where the girls worked were all on one block. Everybody knew where they were and pretended they didn't. The particular group of houses I was most familiar with was for whites only, and apparently some pretty important people in Erie could occasionally been seen visiting them. I know this because there was a vacant lot across the street from one of the busiest houses, and sometimes when I had free time I liked to get up a game of touch football with the neighborhood kids in their early teens. All of a sudden one day the police came by and told us that this lot was private and they had better not catch us playing football there again. The reason, I learned, was that anyone in the vacant lot had a clear view of the front and side entrance to the whorehouses, and the Big Shot clients didn't want anyone seeing who was going in and out.

In and around the Pope Hotel I got to know all kinds of people. I got to know some of the prostitutes. I got to know some of the numbers guys. And I got to know some real characters. I remember there was one old guy whose elevator I don't think went all the way to the top. This was in 1953, and he used to walk by the hotel every day and say to anyone who would listen, "Well... Eisenhower is the president." He used to draw the word out: ""Ei—sen—how--er." Then there were just the colorful hangers around. I had three friends with the nicknames "Geech," "Fizz," and "Chipmunk," who introduced me to marijuana, which everybody there called reefer. I never was a drinker. I didn't especially like alcohol, and I was well aware of what it could do to people. But from the time I first tried reefer I got along famously with it. I used it for years and can't say that it ever had an adverse effect on me. All in all, it wouldn't be stretching the truth much to say the Pope Hotel was really where I went to school to the wilder side of life.

I met Martha, my first wife, at the Pope Hotel. It started the way most of these things do. I was in the bar one night having a drink and looking the ladies up and down. The bar at the Pope was a great place not only for all the reasons I've just mentioned but also because a lot of young black women came there pretty much doing the same thing, and they were dressed up and especially beautiful on the weekends. While I was sitting there, three young ladies came in together, and one of them caught my eye.

She was petite and full of life, and I thought she was a knock out. When her friends were away from the bar for a minute and she was alone, I went up and introduced myself and offered to buy her a drink. That was how it all began.

Her name was Martha Butler, and I liked her right away. I don't know that I swept her off her feet that first evening, but we got on well enough that we began seeing one another, every now and then at first and then more steadily.

Not long after Martha and I had begun seeing one another, I was down in the kitchen in the basement of the hotel. That's where the people who were staying at the hotel could get their meals, and it was a great place to eat. I would have gone there regularly even if I hadn't been living there. The kitchen was run by three very nice older black women, and one night when I was there by myself, one of them started asking me about my relationship with Martha.

She began by saying something like, "Hey, Jim. You're a good-looking guy. You're young and you're a big football star, have you met anybody yet? Do you have a girlfriend?" I didn't quite know what to say for a minute, and so she decided to put her cards on the table and asked, "What do you know about Martha Butler?"

"She's pretty," I said. "We get along." That sounds like kind of a nothing thing to say, but at this point I didn't really know where this was going or how much I wanted to talk about.

"Jim", she said, "You seem like a very nice young man. Martha Butler could turn out to be a real problem for you," and she and her friends proceeded to tell me why. According to the ladies in the kitchen Martha had a history that included a previous marriage and two children by a man named Henry. But that wasn't all. While she was married to Henry, Martha found out that he was fooling around with another woman. The story was that she confronted him about it and went after him with a knife, cutting him in the face and giving him scars that he would carry to his grave. In the opinion of the ladies in the kitchen, she was nobody to fool around with.

There was more. They told me that Martha was now living with her aunt and uncle. Her uncle owned the Kentucky Barbecue, at that time the biggest black restaurant in Erie. (It was on the corner of the street where all the houses of prostitution were. After a good dinner, you would come out of the restaurant, turn right, and there you were.) She had another uncle—Uncle Bum—who was so light skinned some people thought he was Greek and who was the biggest bail bondsman for blacks in Erie. Their point was that even though her mother was an alcoholic the family lived well and thought pretty highly of themselves in the black community. They had social pretensions. "Martha's mother is not going to like you," they said, "because you're so dark skinned."

I knew about the color thing already. Just this year (2010) a book came out quoting Speaker of the House Harry Reid, a white senator from Nevada, as saying that it was a help to President Obama that he was light skinned. [24] When the media got hold of that, there was all sorts of criticism and controversy. How embarrassing, they said. How could he say such a thing? How insensitive! In my opinion, the senator was right on the money. Black people of my generation at least, know that it's true by the time they're two years old. In the world I live in, marrying a light-skinned black person is marrying up. Marrying dark is going in the other direction. It's brutal, but all black people have to live with it and encounter it everywhere. You start learning it as early as the playground. In junior high in Detroit, we talked about the most popular girls as, "light, bright, and damn near white." I've heard that there's a saying when black sororities are deciding who to invite to become members: "Too black, step back. If you're brown, stick around." I've even known of black churches where the congregation was predominantly light-skinned. They didn't absolutely throw dark-skinned blacks out, but they made it pretty uncomfortable for them. I remember my being dark-skinned started bothering me most when I was in junior high and high school and interested in dating the good looking girls. At first I was having a hard time getting them to pay any attention to me. I saw some of them dating dark-skinned guys and asked a friend what those guys had that I didn't. "They're athletes," he said. "It makes a difference." Eventually, it worked the same way for me. I don't think I went out for sports entirely to get dates, but after I became a football star, things got better. I remember I was sweet on a girl named Gwendolyn Edison and began to walk her home from school, met her mother, the whole nine yards. One day when I had walked her home, we were sitting on her front porch when her father came home and stared hard at me as he went on into the house. Next thing I knew we could hear him saying to her mother, "Who is that black nigger on the porch?" I heard her say, "That's James Long, the football player." The next thing I knew Gwendolyn's father was out on the porch introducing himself and shaking my hand. Nothing ever really happened between Gwendolyn and me, but I never forgot that lesson, and so I took what the ladies in the kitchen at the Pope Hotel were saying to me seriously. But I was too far gone to take their advice. But when you're young and strong and having some success, and feeling pretty good about yourself in general, who listens to good, well-meant advice that they don't really want to hear? Martha and I continued seeing one another. The attraction grew on both sides, and for all I know it may have been made even hotter because there was some opposition to it. Whatever the reason, we just got closer and closer together.

I was doing a lot of travelling then. In this period, when I was mainly based in Erie, I was always going back and forth between places where I lived temporarily because when football was over my income stopped, and I needed work in the off-season to make ends meet. As a rule I had been going back to Detroit where I had some connections and could usually find part time work, but now that Martha and I were heating up, I tried to find work in Erie instead.

One of my first off-season jobs in Erie was at a foundry, but it didn't last long. A friend of mine told me he could get me in there. I agreed and he picked me up and took me to work with him the next day. He dropped me at the office to do the paperwork and went on to his job, so when I was ready to go to work, I went by myself. I had never been there before, and when I opened to door of the room where the furnaces were I was nearly blown away. There was smoke everywhere. They were pouring steel and there were great showers of sparks that I was afraid were going to burn me. The noise was disorienting, too. I got to my workstation at about 7:30 a.m. and at 8:00 there was a twenty-minute break. The minute it started I walked straight to my locker, got my things, and headed out the door. My friend saw me going and shouted, "Where you goin', Jim?" I yelled back as loud as I could, "Anywhere but here." "You don't want to work here?" he asked. I said "No," and I was out the door.

The next job worked out better. I caught on at a Ford dealership in Erie. I detailed new cars, meaning I washed them when they came new off the delivery trucks and got them ready to be shown on the floor. I also drove people home when they came and left their cars off for servicing. It wasn't a hard job and it paid the bills when I wasn't playing football. I kept it for about two years and left it for what I thought was a better job on an assembly line at a General Electric plant, which I eventually lost when a wave of layoffs hit and I didn't have much seniority. I also had some Italian friends who got me off-season jobs in construction, which I liked because they kept me in shape.

While all this was going on, Martha's and my relationship was heating up. All it needed was something to push it over the edge, and that something came in the form of a decision of mine to return to Detroit till the season started. Maybe absence really does make the heart grow fonder because that's all it took. When we were apart, we decided to get married—and in secret.

At that time Martha worked days at a store in Erie. One day—a weekday—she left the house with everyone thinking she was going to work as usual. But she went to the bus station instead and got on a bus to Toledo, Ohio. I took a bus from Detroit and met her there, and a Justice of the Peace married us. Then, she got back on the bus and managed to get back to Erie at about the same time she normally got home from work. Nobody in her family was the wiser.

The way her family finally learned about us is a great story. Martha said she came home one day and her family, who still did not like the idea of Martha and me even being serious about one another, were talking about me and calling me a "black son of a bitch." Martha told me she couldn't take it anymore, and so she said to her mother, "Guess what? That black son of a bitch is your son-in-law!" She didn't tell me what they said after that but the cat was definitely out of the bag, and for a very brief time I was extremely happy. Getting married without her parents knowing was exciting and seemed romantic. It looked like I was going to have a home of my own and my own family. However, after that initial period of happiness nothing went right for Martha and me. My marriage fell apart and ended with tragedy, violence, and bad feeling. It got so bad that here were times when I thought everything in my life was collapsing. Before it was over, I had spent time in a mental institution. I eventually made it through to the other side, but it was as hard a time as I can remember having in my life, and the worst of it was that it began and ended at home. The way it happened was this. As a result of the pressure from Martha and her family, I finally moved back to Erie permanently. But there was still the season itself, and it had its own pressures. When I was away in Canada, Martha's so-called friends would start filling her head with the idea that I was probably fooling around every chance I got up there. They would tell her that I probably had my pick of those Canadian white girls. And then there would be the times when I would call home and Martha wasn't there, and that would get me thinking, too. Much of the relationship that had been so warm and exciting a short while ago was poisoned by suspicion and distrust.

I thought that if we had a child, it might help smooth things out in the family, and it might make the bond between Martha and me stronger. But that's not what happened. Martha learned she was pregnant when I was playing up in Canada. It was one of those times when her friends were filling her head with all sorts of ideas about what I was probably doing, so she got on a bus to join me. When she had a miscarriage and lost the baby she said it was because of the bus ride and blamed me.

That was tough, and of course especially hard on Martha, but we got through it, patched things up between ourselves, and started over, and it wasn't long before Martha was pregnant again. It was toward the end of a season. I had an injury that was going to keep me from playing till next year, and so I came home to be with her when she had the baby. Everything seemed fine with this pregnancy. I was going to be there this time. What could go wrong?

As long as I live, I will remember the night the baby came. When it was time, we went to the hospital. I paced around out in the waiting room like fathers did in those days. Time passed—I have no idea how much—and just as I was starting to think that I ought to be hearing something soon, I saw a doctor coming my way, and then I heard a piercing scream. I had never heard a sound like that in my life, and I looked to the doctor, who said nothing but motioned me to follow him.

The person screaming was Martha. It was the sound she made when they first brought our daughter to her. It was every parent's nightmare. She checked everything the way a mother does: the arms the legs, the fingers and toes. The baby wasn't right. In most respects she was a beautiful little girl, but one arm was noticeably shorter than the other and she was missing fingers on both hands.

The effect on me was powerful and not in my control. When I saw that our baby wasn't right, I was shaken so badly that I ran out of the hospital and went straight to a friend's and hid there. I wasn't really hidden, though. My friend called Martha's family and told them where I was. He said, "Diz is going to be OK. He just needs to figure out how to live with this." And that was exactly right. I was a physical person. I was making it in the world because of my physical ability. I was terrified for my little daughter. She wasn't right physically. What was she going to do? What was I going to do now?

I did figure out how to live with it. I knew I should have been with Martha the whole time, and I felt terribly guilty about having run away. And so I came back and we worked things out as best we could. Donna—that's what we named her—was a beautiful little girl, and I learned to accept the things that weren't perfect. But because there was so much poison in the family, the baby didn't bring us together; she pulled us further apart. People in Martha's family and some of her friends began to raise questions about whose fault it was that Donna was born the way she was. Things like that. We went back to a state that was as normal as possible under the circumstances. But beneath the surface things were getting ready to blow.

When the new season rolled around, I went back to Canada to play ball, and the trouble started all over again. I would call home to talk to Martha and find out about Donna, but Martha wouldn't be home. This happened more and more regularly. Martha's sister would tell me only that Martha was out with her mother, but I knew it was more than that. Martha's mother was an alcoholic. They were going to bars. I thought I ought to find out what was going on, so as I sometimes did, I caught a bus after our game in Toronto (we played on Thursdays) and was back in Erie on Friday night. When I got to the house, Martha's sister told me where they were and I went to the bar to get Martha. She wouldn't come at first, and when I grabbed her arm, she quick as a flash stabbed the back of my hand with something small and sharp (I'm not sure what it was). The suddenness and the violence startled me. I couldn't think of anything to do, so I turned around and walked out.

Things just went from bad to worse after that. When the season was over and I was working back in Erie, I found out— or thought I found out—that Martha was cheating on me. After worrying about it for quite a while but saying nothing, I confronted her and asked her to get in the car and go for a ride with me so we could talk about it. She refused. It just made her angry to talk about it. From then on, though, it hung in the air between us.

About a week later we were at a picnic and got into a big argument when we got home. I think Martha was tired of being on the defensive, so she went on the attack. She accused me of flirting with one of the ladies there, and she wouldn't let up about it. Eventually I decided the best thing I could do was get out of the house before I said things I would regret and maybe also to give Martha some time to cool off. I didn't make it, though. While I was walking to our car, Martha ran into the kitchen, got a knife, and came after me with it. Just as I got to the car, I heard the front door open and saw Martha coming after me, and when I saw the knife I panicked. Seeing it brought back all the stories about how she cut her first husband, and I was frightened. There was a child's baseball bat in the car, and I grabbed it and hit her in the face before she could cut me. I hit her hard, and she went straight down, dropped like a stone.

After that, I wasn't thinking too clearly. When I saw that she couldn't get at me, at least for the moment, I got it the car and drove off. That evening a warrant was issued for my arrest. When I learned about it, I immediately turned myself in and was charged with aggravated assault. Then began one of the most difficult and frightening episodes in my life.

When I was arraigned, I went before Judge Roberts, Martha and her family wanted him to put me away –send me to prison. Instead he sent me to a mental hospital in Warren, Pennsylvania, for psychiatric observation. I spent thirty days there, and it was a nightmare.

I had a room of my own, but I spent a lot of time in the common room with the other inmates. What I realized immediately was that many of them were genuinely insane, and in the short time I was there I saw and heard things I could never have imagined if I hadn't actually seen and heard them. There were people in padded cells, and even though I had my own room, you could hear them screaming at all hours of the day and night. I saw the attendants put people who had fits into tubs of ice, I think to shock them into calming down. I saw with my own eyes an attendant beat a violent male patient so badly that the man eventually died. I sat in my room at night trying not to think too much about the things I was seeing and finding it hard not to wonder what it was about me that had caused Judge Roberts to send me here. I have never felt more alone than I did during those thirty days. What was going to happen to me? I wondered. What was I doing in a place like this?

While I was at Warren only two people came to see me. One was a girl named Eleanor, who I had been friendly with in Erie, and the other, to my surprise, was Martha's Uncle Bum, who turned out to be my one friend in that family. It wasn't much contact with people, but it helped me get through those nights when all I could think about was how completely alone in the world I was and how few people seemed to care about me. To keep myself busy during the day, I volunteered to work in the kitchen. I had meetings twice a week, sometimes with psychiatrists and sometimes with social workers. The work in the kitchen was the most normal thing I did, and it helped me keep my sanity. I think that's how I made it through.

After the thirty days of observation were over I had to appear before a board made up of institution staff, social workers, and psychiatrists. They were the people who would make a decision about what was next for me. That's when I found out why the staff sent me there. There had apparently been real concern that I was suicidal. Of all the things I had thought of while I was there, suicide had never entered my mind, but the fact that they thought I was at risk told me a lot about how I must have looked to them. I must have been in worse shape than I thought.

At the meeting with the board they asked me a lot of questions like "Do you think someone in their right mind would commit suicide?" "Have you ever thought about suicide?" Things like that. I think I surprised them when I brought up Frank Sinatra. The story was that he had attempted suicide when he and Ava Gardner broke up. I said, "We don't view Frank Sinatra as suicidal, do we?" I said, "Sometimes things happen in people's lives that are just too heavy for them to bear and for maybe for a little while they don't want to live. If they really get depressed they might temporarily consider suicide—but they get over it and they don't do it. They're not suicidal. They just had some bad moments."

Nobody said anything for a minute.

"Hey," I said, "If I really wanted to commit suicide, I could have done it here."

"How?" a couple of them asked at the same time.

I told them it would have been easy. I worked in the kitchen. I could have grabbed a kitchen knife and cut my wrists. Or when the delivery trucks came to the kitchen and the back door was open for a minute, I could have run out, jumped in front of a car or truck, any number of things. I said, "You people are the ones who think I'm suicidal, not me. I don't want to commit suicide. I want to go home."

Not long after that I left the room and they talked about my case for a while. The long and the short of it was that they decided that I wasn't suicidal and remanded me back to Judge Roberts' court, which had sent me there in the first place. They kept me in the Erie County jail for two days, and then I had my day in court.

I remember it well. When I walked into the courtroom the first thing I saw was Judge Roberts. The second was the prosecutor, and sitting in a row behind him were Martha, her mother, her sister, and Uncle Bum. There was nobody for me except the public defender. The prosecutor wanted me to do hard time, and finally Judge Roberts asked Martha what she thought ought to be done with me. She said she thought I should be sent to prison, and so did everyone in her family but Uncle Bum.

When Judge Roberts had heard the arguments on both sides, he went into his chambers to make his decision, and I was taken to a holding cell. In about four or five hours we were all called back into the courtroom to hear his decision. It's a moment I'll never forget. He said that he was not going to recommend that I be sent to prison. He said what I had done could be considered self-defense, especially because Martha was known to have a history of using a knife. He went on to say that a factor in his decision was the fact that I had been a well-known sports figure in Erie with no previous record there of violence or bad behavior. He therefore saw no reason to sentence me to hard time. What he did, however, was order me to leave Erie. The only circumstances under which I would be allowed to return would be to visit my daughter, Donna, and the court would determine the date and time of those visits.

The story didn't end there, of course. Martha and I didn't even get divorced for a while. On one trip back to see Donna— who was just taking her first steps—a former girlfriend of Martha's took me aside and said, "What happened to the baby,

Diz, it wasn't your fault." She went on to tell me that while I was in Canada and Martha was pregnant with Donna, she had tried a sort of homemade abortion that didn't work. That's what they thought was probably the cause of Donna's birth defects. Nobody can know for sure, but it made me feel a lot less guilty.

And then Martha was at it again. After we separated, she took up with a guy named Johnny. When she discovered he was cheating on her, she stabbed him and killed him and this time was sent to prison herself. When she went to prison, I went through with divorce proceedings and finally ended the marriage. The divorce was finalized in 1959, but I wasn't off the hook entirely yet. Martha got out of prison around Christmas a few years later. I was living in Cleveland by then, but I heard she was getting out, and because I thought it would be the best for Donna, I actually drove to Erie and asked Martha if she would marry me again and come and live with Donna and me in Cleveland. Martha said no. She said she was angry that I had divorced her while she was in prison and she was going to marry someone else, which she did. That finally was the end of my relationship with her.

Donna is another story. When I think about her, it breaks my heart. Donna was a straight "A" student and a delight as a little girl. She went to a small college in Pennsylvania, but from the late teen years on she became convinced that her deformities were making the boys reject her. She just couldn't overcome her fears about the effects of her difference from other kids. So much potential and yet she just kept going downhill and no one could do anything to stop her. It seemed like the odds against her were just too great, and few things in my life have been as painful, as hard to watch play out. In fact, I don't think I was the same person after the time I spent in Erie.

THE REST OF MY WIVES

You would have thought I might have learned my lesson about jumping into marriage after the experience with Martha Butler, but I didn't. In the next fourteen years I got married and divorced five more times, and the time between my first wife, Martha, and my last wife, Delores—was one of the most important periods in my life.

As I can see now, I was pulled strongly in two quite different directions. On the one hand, it was obviously very important to me to try to create a home, family, and relatively conventional life. Exactly what I didn't have when I was growing up. On the other hand, from the time I began to be attracted to the kind of life that swirled around the Pope Hotel in Erie, the life of glamour, high rollers, money, and crime, I began to be pulled in that direction, too. What I believe I eventually learned was that I could have either the one or the other but not both. And I'm not so sure about the marriage thing in any case. Maybe I just wasn't cut out for it. It took me a long time to realize it, though. After I was divorced from Martha I married (and divorced) Loretta, Joan, Mary, Eleanor, and Delores. They were very different people, but the end result was always the same.

I met my second wife, Loretta, in Cleveland. When I left Erie and my marriage to Martha behind, that was when I went to the Chicago Cardinals' football camp for that one last try to make it in the NFL. When that attempt failed I didn't want to go back to Detroit. I had heard that my old friends from Wilkes-

Barre, Suitcase Simpson and Al Smith, were with the Indians now, and so I got in touch with them. They suggested I come to Cleveland and stay with them until I could find something. I lived with them and shared the rent till I got a job working at Bellefaire [25], a facility for problem kids located in University Heights, a suburb of Cleveland.

Bellefaire was originally founded as a Jewish orphanage in 1868. Since then it has become one of the nation's leading providers of child welfare and behavioral healthcare for children, youth, and their families. Because of my athletic history, I got a pretty good job there running a sports program for the kids. Some of the children came just for the day, but there was a small campus and some were housed there. I lived on campus and got room and board, which saved me a lot of money.

Working at Bellefaire, which I did for three years, was just what the doctor ordered after my terrible experiences in Erie. I didn't have the pressure of trying to make a professional team or the worry about getting hurt. I was in a well-to-do suburb of Cleveland at a highly respected institution. They paid for me to take a couple of courses, in psychology and child psychology at Case Western Reserve University. I felt like that meant they saw promise and had faith in me, and it gave me a real boost. The work came naturally, and for a change the paychecks started coming regularly. Besides being in charge of athletic programs, I was responsible for a group of boys. I saw to it that they got to their classes and appointments, and I wrote regular reports on their activities. I think the time I spent at places like the Moore School and Boys Vocational helped me a lot in my work at Bellefaire. I understood where troubled kids were coming from. I had been there myself, and I think they sensed that. It seemed a "win, win" situation: If I was doing some good for them, they were also helping me. The peace and stability of my daily routine were just what I needed and maybe more than I needed. At one point Jackie Presser's [26] son was under my care. I remember he had a lot of moxie. One time he said to me, "Hey, Diz. If you ever decide you don't like this place and need work, my father can get you a job." I said something like, "That's nice" and forgot about it. I didn't know more about Jackie Presser at the time than that he was William Presser's son.

The point is, that things were going pretty well for me then. Not long after I settled in I met Loretta. She was a counselor for the girls, her job was similar to mine, and she lived on campus, too. We discovered that we got along, and we started seeing a lot of one another. After a workday we began going to my apartment or hers for a drink and to talk about the day and unwind. One thing led to another and before long we became lovers, but we were, I thought, being careful. So when Loretta came and told me she was pregnant, I was genuinely surprised. I asked her what she thought we should do, and I was not really unhappy when she said she thought we should get married. Maybe that was just what I needed—not an apartment but a home and the beginning of a family. So I told her I agreed and when we talked with Dr. Mayer, our supervisor, he told us there would be no problem from Bellefaire's point of view. We didn't waste much time after that. We got a license, went down to City Hall, and before you knew it we were husband and wife. However, about two months later, another woman friend and co-worker stopped by my apartment for a drink. After maybe the second round she asked did I mind if she asked me a question. I said, "Go ahead," and she asked me why I had decided to marry Loretta.

I told her about the pregnancy, and she started laughing. When I asked what was so funny, she said, "You are. You're a fool, Jim. She's not pregnant."

I was angry and told her she didn't know what she was talking about. She just laughed again and said, "Hey. It's up to you. You think what you want. I'm not going to say another word."

When she left I was upset and couldn't stop thinking about it. Loretta was away so I couldn't settle it at the moment. But it was on my mind all night, and the next day, when we had a minute alone, I asked her if she'd like to take a walk. When we were by ourselves, I asked her if it was true that she wasn't pregnant.

"Who have you been talking to?" she asked.

"Just answer me. I've made a doctor's appointment." I said. "It's tomorrow. We can find out right then if you're pregnant or not."

"Why are you doing this, Jim?" The tears were starting to come now.

"A little bird told me that you aren't pregnant. I want to know the truth."

The crying started then, and I knew I had my answer.

"Why did you do this to me?" I asked.

"Because I love you, and I thought, with all the other girls here, it was my only chance."

The marriage was over as far as I was concerned, and Loretta knew it.

In a day or so we went to talk about our situation with Dr. Mayer. He was a decent man, and certainly sympathetic, but the long and the short of it was that if we were getting divorced, one of us was going to have to leave Bellefaire. Being married would have been alright he said. But many of the kids in the programs there came from broken homes, and he felt he just couldn't have the staff appearing to repeat the same drama the kids had already experienced at home. There wasn't an easy way to decide which one of us would be the one to leave, but since Loretta had worked there longer than I had, Dr. Mayer felt she had seniority. I could understand that; it seemed fair under the circumstances, and so I was the one to go.

When I left Bellefaire, I got an apartment in Cleveland and got another job at a school for boys in Hudson, Ohio. The setup there was something like it had been at Boys' Vocational. The kids lived in cottages and there were usually a man and woman who lived in and were in charge of each cottage. They were fine with me commuting from Cleveland, though, and at the time I thought it was a pretty good job. Maybe I could even have made something out of it, but I'll never know because it was a long commute every day from downtown Cleveland, especially in the winter. And this was the period when I was getting more and more attracted to the people and the night life downtown. Even while I was still working as a counselor, I was heading for the city at night. Eventually I quit my job in Hudson and got a somewhat similar job at the Detention Center in Cleveland. I also coached a little football at East Technical High School. But it was because of the new crowd I was starting to run with that I met my next wife, Joan.

The first time I saw her was at a fashion show. John H. Johnson [27], publisher of *Negro Digest* and *Ebony* and *Jet* magazines, was highly successful by this time and used to tour a black fashion show through the black communities in the bigger cities. Joan was a model for *Ebony* and some of the other top black magazines. When Mr. Johnson's fashion show came to Cleveland, I went to it. When I saw her up on the runway strutting her stuff, I couldn't take my eyes off her. I wanted to meet her, and through some friends I was able to do so. We hit it off right away and from there things just snowballed. We started seeing each other regularly, and in three months' time we were married. It took about the same number of months before the whole thing fell apart.

I can see now why parents so often tell young people who want to get married that they ought to take their time, get to know one another as completely as they can. Joan and I got caught up in the glamour of a whirlwind courtship, but when the parties were over and we started living together day to day, we learned pretty quickly that we weren't made for each other. Joan was disciplined, strict, and what I thought was compulsive. The way I was living then, the hours I was used to keeping, the routines I had gotten used to grate on her, just as hers grated on me. The straw that broke the camel's back was one night when I came in and threw my jacket on a table in the hall.

"Pick up your jacket," she said, "and hang it in the closet where it belongs."

"Look," I said, "this is my home, too."

"No it isn't. It's my apartment."

Technically she was right. It was her apartment. But when you're trying to be a couple and you've gotten to this point, there's not a lot more to say, and I think we both knew it. Of course it wasn't something as simple as hanging up a coat or not. That was just the tip of a much bigger iceberg.

"If that's the way you think about it," I said. "If you think this is your apartment, then as far as I'm concerned, you can have it. Just give me a couple of hours to pack up, and it's all yours."

In a little more than six hours I was gone, and I have to admit I was discouraged. I'd already had two marriages turn out very differently than I had planned, and now it had happened again. Maybe I could have been a counselor in one boys' school or another for the rest of my life, but honestly it wasn't what I wanted. However, I was upset and not at all sure what I did want then, and so I decided a change of scene might be a good thing. I went back to Ypsilanti, because I hadn't as yet been in Cleveland that long and I still thought of the Detroit and Ypsilanti area as home. I still knew people there, and I think maybe I just wanted to touch base.

Now that I look back on it, I think I was more unsettled by the marriage not working than I had thought at the time. Maybe I wanted to get a little distance from the glamorous but risky and violent world I could feel myself getting pulled into? I don't know. These are things I think about now. At the time, it just seemed a good idea to get away for a while, so that's what I did. That's when I met my fourth wife, Mary.

I met her at work. Because of my experience at Bellefaire and the detention home in Cleveland, I didn't have much trouble landing a job in a mental hospital outside of Ypsilanti working with delinquent boys. They also had a home for troubled girls, and that's where Mary King was working.

I didn't just jump into marriage this time. Mary and I got to know one another slowly, at first mainly at work. The fact that we had both had previous marriages and we both had children made each of us cautious. Martha got custody of Donna, but Mary's children--two girls and a boy--were living with her. (Her former husband, the children's father, had been killed in a car accident on the way to meet another woman at a motel—another reason why Mary was inclined to be cautious about rushing into anything.) So we took our time. We saw one another, increasingly steadily, for about a year before I asked her to marry me. She said yes, and this time things genuinely seemed to be different.

Mary had a small home in Inkster, Michigan, about twenty miles from where we both worked. She had put down roots in the community, was a member of a church, and we had a lovely church wedding. It was a summer wedding. We went to Cleveland for our honeymoon. We stayed in a fancy suite at the Sheraton. Friends took us out to a nice restaurant for dinner. When we got up on the last morning and had coffee in the hotel before driving back to Michigan to start our life together, it looked like this was going to be the one that worked. But it wasn't.

The biggest problem was Mary's children by her first husband. I got along fine with the little boy, but the girls never accepted me as their father. The boy didn't remember too much about his father, but the girls were older, and they did. In their hearts they never accepted me into the family. The tension they caused put a serious strain on our marriage, and so did the fact that I was dark skinned. But an even bigger problem was my involvement in a very high profile incident involving the Cleveland Browns' star running back, Jim Brown [28].

If you're anywhere near close to my age and you know anything about Cleveland football, you know how big Jim Brown was in the early 1960's. When he was touched by possible scandal, it was front-page news, and he was more than just touched. Allegedly, on a June night in 1966 at about three in the morning, an eighteen-year-old girl named Brenda Ayres knocked on the door of Jim Brown's room at a Howard Johnson Motor Lodge on East 107th and Euclid Avenue in Cleveland. What happened next quickly became a much written about matter of dispute, but the long and the short of it was that Ayres accused Jim Brown—married man, superstar, and celebrity—of striking her and of being the father of her fifteen-month-old daughter.

The trial was a media circus that drew national attention. It had everything: rich powerful superstar apparently victimizing helpless young girl. Black man catting around town taking advantage where he could. You name it, they wrote it. Jim Brown's private life suddenly became public knowledge. For a while it was a media feeding frenzy. Ultimately, though, Brown was acquitted on the assault charge. But there was still the question of whether he was the father of Brenda Ayres' child. That was where I came in.

I had gotten to know Jim Brown in the late fifties and early sixties, partly because we would often end up at the same black clubs and bars in downtown Cleveland and partly because I used to play basketball at the YMCA. Jim and his buddies like John Wooten and Bobby Mitchell [29] used to hang out there and I got to be one of the regulars in their pick-up games. I hit it off with Jim Brown right away, and it was exciting to be included in those basketball games with the Browns' big stars. We would talk a lot after the games, and I think that's how he knew I had a connection to Brenda Ayres.

The connection was East Tech. When I was a security guard at East Tech, I often was assigned to be a monitor in study hall. That's when I first met Brenda. She was good looking and aggressive. She started flirting with me in study hall, and it got to the point where I didn't want to lose my job and told her that nothing was going to go on between us while she was at school. However, she also started seeing Jim Brown and got kicked out of school, and what can I say? I wasn't married at the time and after she was no longer going to that school I took up with her, too. Jim Brown knew about this, and so when Brenda Ayres accused him of being the father of her child, his lawyer called me one night. I was in Michigan and married to Mary at the time, but I agreed to come back to Cleveland and testify that I had also had sex with Brenda Ayres during the time she was going with Jim Brown.

Jim's lawyer paid all my expenses, and my impression is

that my testimony was a major reason why the jury found in Jim Brown's favor. But the publicity that followed the trial and my role in the acquittal were the straw that broke the camel's back in my relationship with Mary. The trouble with her older girls worsened after that, and eventually it started affecting our relationship in ways that eventually ended it. As the weather got stormier and stormier at home, I started spending more time away, some of it in Cleveland. We were finally divorced in 1968.

The divorce was especially painful because while the marriage looked like it was going to work, we had made some fairly big decisions. Mary sold her house in Inkster, and we assumed the mortgage on a nicer home in Detroit. While Mary continued to work as a girls' counselor, I called a guy I had played football with, and he got me a pretty good job working at Chrysler in the Import-Export Division. At about that time, we came to the decision that our marriage wasn't going to work. I think I probably could have found a place for myself at Chrysler, but, down in the dumps again, I decided staying around would just keep reminding me of everything that had gone wrong between Mary and me. So I went on back to Cleveland, where I have lived since.

The year I got divorced from Mary—1968--was also the year that Carl Stokes [30] was elected Mayor of Cleveland. Mary and I were separated and I was back in Cleveland well before the divorce became final, and in that time I had met Carl Stokes, begun doing some security work for him, and also began to get involved in his mayoral campaign. Over the next few years, Carl Stokes helped get me a job as an Inspector for the City, and I got more and more involved the numbers rackets and the life of the streets. But it was when I was working on Carl's campaign that I met my next wife, Eleanor.

The first time I saw her was at a political meeting. Her father was Mexican and she had a black mother, and you could see both sides of the family in her face. She was a little thing but full of energy, and, as I was later to discover, extremely strong willed. She was smart and had some education, and she was as cute as she could be. I remember we were talking about how to get the vote out for Carl, and she was full of ideas, and I wanted to know more about her.

On that evening she was obviously with a man. At the next meeting she was by herself, and I went up and started talking with her. We had plenty to talk about because we were both involved in Carl's campaign, and I remember we talked a lot about what we thought needed to be done to get him elected. We hit it off, and exchanged phone numbers. I called her a couple of days later, and she agreed to go out to lunch.

We talked about ourselves at lunch. I learned that she had been married young and had an eight and a fifteen-year-old son. She was divorced now, and the eight-year-old boy, David, was living with her. I told her about myself, not everything but, you know, the way you do. She said she had heard about "Diz" but she hadn't known my real name.

We started going out after that. Took it slow. On our third date I asked her about the guy I had seen her with. How serious were they? She said he was more serious than she was, and so I asked, well how about her and me? She turned it right around on me and asked me how I felt. I told her I'd like to be seeing her regularly, that I was serious about her, and she said she'd have to tell the other guy. From that point on we were a couple, and after we'd been seeing one another regularly for about two or three months, we decided to get married.

We were married at a very nice ceremony at a friend's house. Eleanor had been living in the Projects, but after we were married we moved into an apartment in the Lake Park Towers, on Superior Road that was big enough that her son, David, could stay with us. Carl Stokes was the mayor by that time; I had a decently paying job as a city inspector. It looked for all the world like we were good to go. However, in about a year's time things started going downhill. Partly it was the same thing as with my wife, Joan, the fashion model. Eleanor and I made much better friends than we did husband and wife. Partly it was a trust thing. Eleanor and I both worked for the city. She was a nurse with the Sheriff's Department, and she worked at the Sheriff's Office downtown. Being a city worker myself, I was downtown a lot and after a certain point I started getting suspicious. People I knew who also knew Eleanor started acting funny around me, being careful—like, if they wanted to they could tell me things. It was just a vibe, but I started getting it a lot. I tried talking with her about it, and she came right back at me with rumors she said she'd heard about things that I had been doing that I shouldn't have been. We were both strong-willed and stubborn, and neither one of us was willing to give in or let it go.

When things had been at this point for a while, it wasn't a big step to take to decide that that our marriage wasn't working. We didn't get a divorce right away, though. Instead, we separated and tried living in the same apartment building but in separate apartments—I was paying for one for her and David and one for myself. Our deal was—or so I thought—that as long as were just separated but not divorced, we could each see other people. But as long as we were living in the same apartment building (and as long as I was paying for her apartment) we would agree not to bring people we might be seeing home with us. That is, I wouldn't be so rude as to be having sex with someone in the same building where she lived and *vice versa*.

While we were living like this it happened that I went out one night, and as I was driving away from the apartment building, a little girl ran out from between two parked cars right in front of me, and I hit her. We called the police, she was taken to the hospital, and although she wasn't hurt badly I was really shaken by the incident. She ran out so quickly that there was no way I could stop the car in time, and I wasn't charged with anything, but I was very upset. I needed to talk with a friend about what had just happened, someone who would listen, so I went back to the building where I was living and straight to Eleanor's apartment.

The minute Eleanor came to the door I knew something was up, but I didn't know what. I wasn't thinking especially clearly, but even in my upset state, it didn't take long to realize that for some reason Eleanor wanted me out of the apartment. I needed to talk to her, though. I started telling her about what I'd just been through, how upset I was, but it seemed like she wasn't paying that much attention, and I was really surprised. It wasn't like her. Finally, I said I had to go to the bathroom, and before I came back to the living room I bent over the sink and splashed my face with cold water to try to clear my head. That's when I saw the little boxer shorts.

There they were lying on top of the clothes hamper, and even in the state I was in something about them didn't make sense. The little shorts were small enough to have been her son, David's, but he wore briefs. When I came back to the living room I asked Eleanor what was with the boxer shorts in the bathroom. For just the tiniest fraction of a second, she looked at the closet in the hall, and that was all I needed. I walked straight to it and slid the door wide open. At first I didn't see a thing out of the ordinary—just clothes on hangers. But that was because I was looking at about eye level for me and for someone roughly normal size. I was about to shut the door and go look other places, but something made me look down, and there—as God is my witness—was a midget, naked as the day he was born and scared out of his mind.

Then it seemed like everything happened at once. Eleanor started screaming at me: "Get out. You get the hell out of my apartment." The midget let out a yell, too, and when I turned to look at Eleanor, he took off running down the hall to the door, his little thing flapping as he ran and his little naked butt bouncing up and down. Eleanor ran to a phone to call the police, and while she did that I ran after the midget. As I came out of Eleanor's apartment into the hall I saw him standing by the elevator punching the buttons as hard as he could, not a stitch on him. I was on him in a second. I grabbed him, lifted him off his tiny feet. While he was trying to run with his feet not touching the ground, he kept yelling, "Put me down. Put me down." I carried him back, threw him into the apartment, and told him to get his god dammed clothes on and get the hell out of there, which he did as fast as he possibly could.

I was in a state of near shock, but I wasn't really angry with the midget. He wouldn't have been in that apartment if Eleanor hadn't invited him. I was furious with her for breaking our agreement, which I had been very careful to keep—and for God's sake, with a midget. And then all of a sudden she came running at me, screaming from wherever she'd been till then. She had something in her hand that she was trying to hit me with, and I just lost it. I laid a pretty good one on her and she went down—out like a light. The police were there before long. In a few minutes it was a zoo, and I was in court the next morning.

Not surprisingly, that was the end of my marriage to Eleanor, and in the divorce proceedings that followed the midget episode gave me a little leverage that I didn't expect. Eleanor wanted a divorce badly. Working through my lawyer, I agreed to give her one, make the whole thing easy, if she would be willing to drop the charges against me for hitting her. I think she was so traumatized by my catching her with the midget and then hitting her that she would have agreed to anything to prevent problems getting out of the marriage. I'll never forget the day it all went down, though.

On the day when all the papers were to be signed, we were in a conference room, big polished wooden table, her lawyers on one side and mine on the other. We worked our way slowly through all the legal mumbo jumbo and finally got to the point where both parties agreed and signed on the dotted line—or they didn't. My lawyer assured me he had it all worked out. Everything was going to be fine. But when it came time for Eleanor to say she agreed and sign the papers, she paused and then said, "Well, I just don't know." I went crazy when she said that. *We had an agreement.* What the hell was going on now? I had been behaving because my lawyer had assured me that there would be no problems. It would all be over. Now it wasn't going to be?

I short-circuited. I wasn't thinking at all. I started to jump across the table to get my hands on Eleanor and make her sign. Fortunately my lawyer hung onto me, and Eleanor's lawyers snatched her out of harm's way. And my outburst didn't ruin everything, as I was sure it was going to. After a lot of huffing and puffing, Eleanor did sign the papers, and I think she did because after seeing me coming across the table after her she thought it would be worse to have to stay married to me than to just get it over with. Whatever the reason, I was out of the marriage.

I remember exactly how I first saw my last wife, Delores. I

was waiting my turn in a barbershop on 105th Street, when she came walking past the window. I found out later that she lived in the neighborhood. At the time I didn't care where she lived. All I could think about was how good-looking she was. I got up and went outside to get a better look, but by that time she was half way down the block.

"Who is *that*?" I asked the barber.

"That's Delores Howard."

"Is she married?"

"Yes," he said. "To a damn fool!"

Now I was interested. I learned that she had come from a small town in Ohio and maybe had married young just to get away. She had five children but was separated from her husband when I first saw her and divorced by the time I started dating her.

The way I heard it people were a little bit afraid of her former husband. It wasn't that he was a big, tough guy. He was a little guy. But he was known to carry a gun and was supposed to be a bit unpredictable. Made people nervous. I remember that after I started seeing Delores I met him—in the barbershop. He was in one chair and I was in another. The barber introduced us. He said he had heard about me, and I said I had heard about him, and we talked a little more, and without talking about it directly it was more or less settled that there wasn't going to be any trouble.

I actually met Delores for the first time at Lancers Steak House [31], which was a really nice place in those days. Some of the most important black lawyers and businessmen in Cleveland used to eat there regularly. What I mean is that there were some pretty, successful, well-to-do people that used to go there, and even so, Delores stood out from the crowd. She was petite, very pretty, and dressed beautifully. I liked her and was attracted to her the minute I met her. We found it easy to talk to one another, and before too long we started seeing one another regularly.

We didn't do anything crazy. We dated for nearly a year. She took me home to meet her children. Her oldest daughter, Michelle, and I hit it off right away, and we still stay in touch. And all of the other kids but one liked me—the one being a different daughter who was partial to a different man her mother had been seeing before me. But things looked promising, and when we decided to get married, we had the ceremony at Amasa Stone Chapel on the campus of Case Western Reserve University. That came about because I had always liked the way it looked I thought it was a beautiful old church, and one day I just walked in and asked someone if I could get married there—and we could. I designed her wedding ring—a beautiful combination of diamonds and sapphires. We said our vows. The ceremony was beautiful. I thought we were off to a great start. I was making pretty good money then, Delores had a job at National City Bank, and we got a nice apartment in a hotel across the street from the Chesterfield downtown on East 12th. I really thought this marriage was going to work. It didn't, finally, because of the kind of work I did, the kind of life I had begun to lead, and Delores' suspicions.

Delores had a hard first marriage that I think directly affected the way she thought about ours. She had a tough time accepting the calls I would get late at night. Most were a result of my increasing involvement in the numbers, sometimes the calls were from women, too. I guess I had a bit of a reputation by that time, and what made it worse was that she had friends that were always encouraging her suspicions, fanning the flames. I tried to make her see that she didn't have anything to worry about, but my lifestyle was just too different from hers, and in the end too hard for her to accept. (For most of one of the years we were still married, I took the job as a bodyguard for Harold Robbins. The money was great, but I was not only away most of the time, but living in Sin City and at most of Harold's notorious parties that some people called "orgies.")

Things just went from bad to worse. We were divorced in 1973, and I never married again after that. It's probably a good thing, too, because the rest of the 1970's were both violent and dangerous, and by that time my life and lifestyle had changed considerably. As I look back from this distance, I want to say that when all is said and done, while I didn't stop seeing women, it's probably a good thing I stopped getting married. And if I ever had any doubts about it, the following little episode certainly convinced me.

Just a few years ago, I was out shopping—in the supermarket—when a well-dressed woman my age pushed past me with her cart and said, "Hello, Diz." I didn't recognize her and said something like "Hey, baby" or "Hey, sweetie." The kinds of things you say. She stopped her cart, and looked me straight in the eye and said, "You don't have any idea who I am, do you?" I didn't, so I just shrugged my shoulders and put my hands up, palms out, like "You got me."

"You were married to me," she said. "I'm Loretta."

Maybe I just wasn't cut out for it.

A WALK ON THE WILD SIDE

The year is 1958. It is 2:30 AM Monday morning at the Chatterbox in Cleveland. The band and the customers are gone. The stage is dark. The weekend crowds have been big, though—both blacks and whites. It's been standing room only. Billie Holliday [32] did two shows on Saturday—one from 9:00 to 11:00 and another from 12:30 to 2:30. Same on Sunday. Now that it's Monday, things will start heating up again in a few hours—the famous "Blue Monday" that was the custom here and at the Rose Room at the Majestic [33], but Billie Holliday's performance is over. The hard life she's led has taken its toll, and so have the drugs. At the moment, however, she is calm and wide-awake. An attendant, a woman who always travels with her, gets her things together. When she is ready to go, a young, good-looking emcee comes to get her to take her out for a breakfast of orange duck and champagne. She takes a liking to him and after breakfast, they go back to her room at the Majestic Hotel and she tells him stories about her life. The young emcee is me.

You know that song that goes, "How ya gonna keep 'em down on the farm, after they've seen Paree"? That's how I was with the worlds of the old Majestic Hotel, The Chatterbox, and the black nightlife in Cleveland. Even in the earliest days working at Bellefaire, even after I was married to my various wives, once I'd gotten a taste of it, I couldn't stay away.

When I came to Cleveland in 1958, blacks weren't allowed to

stay at any of the better downtown hotels, but the Majestic was ours. Located at 55th and Central on the East Side of Cleveland, it was the center—the heart--of the black entertainment and celebrity community. The great black jazz musicians in those years all played there. The great black singers and groups performed there. Black athletes just starting to be accepted into American professional sports hung out there when they were in Cleveland. The big numbers people hung out there. Organized crime people hung out there. The pimps and drug pushers hung out there. High-class call girls hung out there. Everything that follows money and celebrity could be found there, and the music was amazing.

I didn't have to look for the Majestic. Everybody in the black community knew about it. Everybody who could tried to be there when they could. While I worked at Bellefaire I had weekends to myself, and I would go down on Saturdays and Sundays and often after work during the week. If I had access to a car it was a twenty-minute drive. If I had to take the bus, it took a little longer.

I was just the right age to be drawn in by the glamour and excitement. I was old enough to appreciate what I was seeing and young enough to be confident that I could be a part of it. With all the confidence of youth, I felt it was a world that had a place for me in it. I didn't just sit around hoping that something good would happen, either. I made it happen.

They had a regular amateur night at the Majestic where anyone who wanted could take the mike. I was feeling pretty good one night, and I took a chance, got up on the stage and did a stand-up comedy routine that people loved. I went back a few more times, got the same kind of reception, and started to get a reputation as both a stand up comic and an emcee. Before long the Majestic offered me a few night jobs emceeing their shows, and I also got work at a couple of the other top places in black Cleveland—The Chatterbox at 55th and Woodland (owned by John "Chin" Ballard, one of the biggest numbers men in Cleveland) and The House of Blues, which was right next door. It was an extraordinary opportunity for someone like me, and of course that's how the Billie Holliday thing happened.

That time I took her out for breakfast, we went in my car. There was a Chinese restaurant she liked over on 79th and Cedar that was open all night. I took her there Saturday and had reserved a table for us for after the Sunday shows. I was more comfortable around her this second night, and I could tell there was something up. There had been a little episode before she went on stage on Sunday, and she wanted to talk about it.

Her singing, her presence, was still dynamite, but she was near the end of her career and as it turned out the end of her life. She was a heavy heroin user, and because of it she could no longer work in New York. She would still occasionally come to Cleveland fairly clean and play the Majestic on a Friday, Saturday, and Sunday. When she performed, she wore long white gloves to hide the needle marks in her arms. She would be in pretty good shape on Friday, but the need for drugs would start to grow, and she got shakier and shakier till payday—Sunday—when her drug connection would come in from Buffalo and bring her what she needed to build herself back up. That's what the episode was about.

As she was getting ready for her second Sunday show, I went to check on her and found the guy who brought her drugs in her dressing room. I was young and felt responsible for the way the show went. Also, I could see plainly what the stuff was doing to her. So I told him to get out. He looked at me and then at Billie, and then said he wasn't going anywhere unless Billie told him to leave. It was kind of a tough spot for me. I was either going to win this standoff or lose face big time. I didn't look at the guy at all. I looked at Billie and said, " I don't know how much stuff you've had already, and I don't care, but I'm your friend—I'm saying this to you as a friend—I don't want you using any more tonight."

She didn't say anything for a minute, but I was in too far to back down. "Tell him to get out," I said. "If there's money involved, tell him to see your manager." A few seconds passed when nobody said anything, and then Billie told the guy to leave. I could tell she was still thinking about it, and when we were at the restaurant. She told me she liked the way I had handled things (with the drug guy), and I told her I knew how hard it must have been to turn the drugs down, and that I was grateful to her for backing me. After that we were friends for the rest of the evening.

She was still wide awake when we finished our breakfast, and so I drove her back to the Majestic, went up to her room with her, and just let her talk till she was able to come down from the evening. She talked about what it was like growing up in the south. She said her color was always against her, by which she meant that she was light skinned—what blacks call "high yellow"— and that she took a lot of grief from blacker blacks because of it. She talked a little bit about some of the men in her life, especially one of them. She said I reminded her of him. He was just an ordinary guy when she met him, but she liked him and gave him a taste of the good life, bought him expensive clothes, a car. She said he didn't use drugs and did everything he could think of to help her break her habit. She didn't say what ever happened with them.

I was still young but not a kid anymore. I was in my thirties and I knew how special a moment like this was. How could I turn my back on it and go back to working at Bellfaire or such places or being a coach, a nine to five guy. The answer was, I couldn't. It was like I was being pulled along by a current that was taking me away from Bellefaire, and Hudson, and a more ordinary kind of life. It didn't happen all at once, and that experience with Billie Holliday was exceptional—things like that didn't happen every day. But the current just kept getting stronger, pulling me along. Although it's not the whole story, it's probably accurate to say the same current pulled me away from some of my later marriages, too. It was certainly true of my marriages to Delores, and maybe Eleanor. My lifestyle was definitely a part of what eventually went wrong with both those relationships. But I let the current take me, because it was taking me where I wanted to go. I took to the world of the Majestic Hotel and the black clubs like a fish takes to water.

Before long I was getting regular work as an emcee. On my nights, I would cradle the standing microphone confidently, run through a little patter of my own, and then say something like, "But you've listened to me for long enough. Now it's time to get to what you came for. Let me present *Miss Dinah Washington!*" The more I did it, the more comfortable I got. In a short time I was opening some of the biggest acts.

I developed my own routines. I would come out and say something like, "Good evening, ladies and gentlemen. I'm really glad to see you here tonight, especially all the ladies." (I would give them a look when I said that about the ladies, and the laughing would start about then). I would look around the audience, pick somebody out and say, "You. Yeah, you there. You came to see some big names and you probably want to know who I am and what I'm doing up here—don't you?" They would be laughing by then or sometimes flustered. Then I would say, "I'm just a country boy—but I come from good people. Yes, that's right. My parents were in iron and steel." I would pause a minute and then say, "My mother ironed and my father stole."

I had a whole bunch of corny jokes like that, and if people were in the mood or getting there, they usually worked pretty well. Sometimes I had a friend planted in the audience. I would come out, introduce myself, and maybe start to sing "Stardust" or something like that. Then he would shout out, "Hey, we're paying money to hear *good* singers." I would pretend to get my back up and say something like, "Don't you tell me how to do my job" and crack on him, and then we would camp it up and the people would realize it was staged and have fun watching us go at it for a minute or so.

I don't know where they came from, but I had all the right instincts on stage. I knew where the lines were that I shouldn't cross. I knew what I could joke about and what I couldn't, and I had a pretty good sense of when enough was enough and it was time for the headliners to come on. The applause was always long and loud, and of course it was for Dinah Washington or Nancy Wilson, or whoever, but I was up there on the stage, too. Up there in the lights I felt more like I was in a place I belonged that at any of the places I had been so far except maybe for a few good moments in the paratroopers.

Every black entertainer who was anybody played the Majestic, the Chatterbox, or the House of Blues when they came through Cleveland, and I heard and before I was done I introduced most of them: comics like Flip Wilson and Redd Foxx, the great Motown groups—Diana Ross and the Supremes, the great jazz musicians and blues singers, Duke Ellington, Ray Charles, and Dizzy Gillespie [34]. I loved Dizzy Gillespie's music so much that my friends started calling me Diz and the nickname stuck from that time on.

That job as an emcee at the Majestic and the Chatterbox was

the beginning of almost everything else that happened to me in those years. It was my ticket to the world of black power, money, celebrity, and crime in Cleveland. After they got used to seeing me on the stage, the entertainers, the celebrities, and the numbers crowd accepted me. Because of that, I started taking myself more seriously and believing I belonged there. Powerful and important people at the Majestic recognized me. They knew my name and I knew theirs. I got to see how they operated, hear how they talked, see how they dressed, learn what made them tick, how things really worked. Above all, I got comfortable being around them and operating in their world.

The change in the direction of my life took place over a period of quite a few years. As I said, when I first came to Cleveland in 1958 and was working full-time at Bellefaire I was getting downtown as often as I could, but on the surface of it my life was still pretty conventional. The same was true when I worked briefly at the school in Hudson. Things began to change when I started working for Carl Stokes and for the City of Cleveland. In those years I had a lot more time to myself. I divided it pretty equally between my day jobs and my night jobs, and my night jobs began to include greater involvement in the black numbers rackets. I kept getting in deeper and deeper, and eighteen years later, by the time I was shot and nearly killed in 1976, I had committed entirely to the world of the streets and the clubs, the world of fast living, glamour, money, celebrity, and crime. It would be the world I would live in to one degree or another for much of the rest of my life.

In hindsight, the steps that led me there were predictable. The journey began, I think, when I lost my job at Bellefaire. For a time after that I was fairly discouraged. I was in my mid-thirties and had to face the fact that professional sports was not really an option any more. I had been good enough to come close but never got the break I would have needed. I have often wondered whether if I had gone to a name college and gotten the notice that the college stars—the All Americans—get it would have made a difference. But that's water under the bridge. The reality was I was too old now, and I had to find something to do that would pay the bills. And I was setting my sights higher.

I was still emceeing, which was fine when I was at Bellefaire and on a regular salary, but it wasn't a full-time job. All I got for doing it was $50 a night, and I usually worked weekends only. Occasionally I got work out of town because the Majestic had one of the top black agents in the region. Sometimes he would call me up and say, "Hey, Diz. I'm sending a singer and exotic dancer to such and such a club in Erie. I need an emcee. Can you do it?" I usually could do it, but it was still $50 a night and I had to pay my own travel expenses. As glamorous and exciting as I found it, it wasn't a way to make a living, and it was especially frustrating because while I was doing it, I was surrounded by people who had a lot of money and spent it freely. I was getting more and more comfortable in their world, but I was still an outsider, and I couldn't live like they could. I wanted to be an insider. I wanted to live like they did. That was when I decided to talk seriously with the people who ran the numbers game in Cleveland.

I knew who to talk to, and I felt like I didn't have to beat around the bush. When I asked them if there was anything I could do for them that would help me make some real money, they knew exactly what I was asking. I was big and strong, and obviously eager. But they had questions. Yes, maybe I could help them, but only if I was willing to do some things that were going to be hard, only if I was OK with the fact that the job they had in mind was sometimes going to involve violence.

Of course I knew what they meant. There were basically three kinds of numbers people. There were the bookies, the big shots, who ran the local games. There were the pick-up men, the guys who worked the neighborhoods, took the bets, and made the collections and payoffs. Then there was the muscle. These were the people who stepped in when somebody wouldn't pay up when they owed or who were otherwise causing trouble. That's the job they were offering me. They said there was a guy who wasn't paying what he owed. They said he was big and mean and that their regular collectors were afraid of him. Did I think I could handle it for them? It was a good question and one I wondered myself. I knew I was strong and athletic. I knew I could box and fight. Could I use violence to collect money? I didn't know but I decided I was willing to try.

The way the numbers [35] worked in the black neighborhoods then was exactly the way the state run lottery works now. People would pick three numbers and bet them. Then the next day the winning numbers would be known. Although sometimes there were drawings, usually the winning numbers were the final three numbers in each day's Dow Jones averages, available in the morning and afternoon papers.

If a person hit, they could make some money. The odds were 500 to 1. If a person bet $1.00 and had the winning numbers, he or she would collect $500 and so on down the line; $10 would get you $5,000, etc. Pick-up men would come into the neighborhoods each day (working from a different house or yard each time) where they would take the bets and collect the money, which they would then carry to the bookies. When the winning number came out, the pick-up men also made the payoffs. The profits came, of course, from the money that was left over each day after the payoffs had been made, and the profits were considerable.

The numbers were enormously popular in the black

175

neighborhoods. There were a lot of theories and superstitions about how to pick a winning number. Most people used the old dream books, which were part of an elaborate system of numerology and had long lists of all the common things people might dream about. In these books each dream subject had a three-digit number. For example, if you dreamed about an actor or actress, that was number 498; a baby was 183, a hatbox 413, and so on.

Literally anyone could play. Some people would bet pennies, hoping to turn them into five dollars each! Others bet considerably more, and some people were what we would now probably call addicts. They had to bet every day, and if they didn't have the money, they would try to get credit—run a tab—which was usually up to the bookie. It was fairly common for bookies to give people credit. Sometimes it was because they just needed to get to the next pay-day. Sometimes it was because they regularly dropped a lot of money into the system and you didn't want to kill the goose that laid the golden egg by telling them they couldn't play. Usually they paid eventually. But sometimes they were compulsive gamblers, who ran up debts they couldn't or wouldn't pay. That was where the muscle part of it came in.

I found out that I could do it, but sometimes it was rough. I handled the guy that they asked me to—the one the pick-up men were afraid of. When the word got around that I took care of that business and some other hard cases, I started to get a reputation that made my job slightly easier—but only slightly.

When I had to go talk to someone who owed, I would always start out low key. I would say something like, "I don't want trouble. There are two ways we can handle this. We can handle it like gentlemen, or we can handle it in a way that you won't like and I won't like, either." I would usually know right away whether things were going to have to get rough or not. Most times there was a little give somewhere. I might ask, "How come you didn't pay up?" Usually they would shake their heads and look away. Sometimes they had hard luck stories. I saw a lot of grown men cry. Each case was different, though, and I had some leeway. If I thought it would work, I might say something like, "Look. You gotta give me something. You owe $40, how about $20 now and the rest later? I'll give you $20 worth of credit for a week, but that means you have to pay it all back the next time I come around."

They would say all sorts of stuff. They would say they had been laid off, hadn't worked for weeks. They would say they had no money, just food stamps. They would say they just had enough to pay for food for their kids. It was painful at first, but after a while I didn't even hear them. If they said all they had was food stamps, then I said that was what I wanted. If they said they could either pay what they owed or feed their family, I said pay up—or else. If nothing else worked, I would give them a beating that they wouldn't forget.

It wasn't long before the numbers was a major source of income for me, and, since it wasn't nine to five work, I was able to do other things besides, even move around a bit. For example, in the next several years while continuing to do some muscle work for the numbers people, I also took the job at the detention home and later the job at East Tech. But after a certain point, I always knew where my bread was really being buttered. I worked for some of the biggest numbers men in Cleveland, Don King [36], Big Joe Allen, Little Brother Drake--I knew Virgil Ogiltree. I knew them all. I was living higher on the hog than I had ever been. I was playing pickup basket basketball with Jim Brown and John Wooten at the YMCA. And it was during those years—and through Jim Brown--that I met Harold Robbins and took some time off to work for him as a bodyguard for his family, a job that took me to Hollywood and bigger money and higher living that I had yet seen.

CELEBRITY BODYGUARD

I met Harold Robbins [37] at a good time for me. I was ready to be what he needed. I had come back to Cleveland after the Jim Brown-Brenda Ayres trial (1966) and after things began to go wrong between Mary King and me. When Carl Stokes was elected mayor in 1967, I got an inspector' job with the city but I had also served as a bodyguard for him during his campaign and for his children and family after that. The children went to University School, and I took them to school and picked them up. I also took Mayor Stokes' wife places she wanted to go, and in general I did small jobs for him. To do the kind of security work I was doing, I had to get legal permission to carry a gun, so I entered a program in the Law-Medicine Center School of Law Enforcement Training and Research at Case Western Reserve University. I actually got a degree for the "satisfactory completion of the Private Police Training Course" and still have my diploma. While I was doing this, I also had occasional numbers work as well. I was doing all right, but I wasn't a kid anymore. If I could, I wanted to live better than I was living then.

I remember that during the Christmas holidays in 1969 or 1970, after the divorce from Mary, a friend of mine who I knew from the streets and the Majestic Hotel was also a writer. He had the manuscript of a novel—the working title was something like *Blood Black & White*. As you may remember, in 1966, while Jim Brown was making *The Dirty Dozen*, Art Modell insisted that he leave the set and come to the Browns' training camp that fall. That's when Jim retired from football and went to Hollywood. He had been there ever since, he kept in touch with his Cleveland connections, and he was interested in my friend's draft novel. He wanted him to come to Hollywood to talk about turning it into a movie, and since Jim and I had become good friends, especially after the Brenda Ayres thing, he invited me to go along.

I jumped at the chance. *The Dirty Dozen* had been a huge success at the box office, and Jim Brown was riding pretty high in Hollywood. It was fun to see him again and hang out with him and his friends, and of course just be in Hollywood. Off his recent success with *The Dozen,* he moved in some pretty fast circles, went to a lot of parties, and I hadn't been there long before he invited me to come with him to one of Harold Robbins' famous affairs.

I remember the address because eventually I got to know it very well: it was 905 North Beverly Drive. When I handed the car to the valet to park and followed Jim Brown through the front door, I stepped into a world the likes of which I had never seen before, even at the Majestic. Walking around with drinks in their hands were the people I was used to seeing on the big screen or on TV. I met Vince Edwards that night. Shook his hand. I met Willie Shoemaker, the most famous jockey of his time, Barbara Eden, Lawrence Harvey, and Lana Turner— towards the end of her career but still a beautiful woman and a "star" if there ever was one.

When Jim introduced me to Harold Robbins, he built me up pretty big. Made a thing about my being in the muscle end of the numbers in Cleveland. After that we moved around and mixed with the crowd, and I soon realized that Harold Robbins was watching me. Several times I would look up and meet his eye. My friend the writer told me that Harold had been asking him about me, too. It was flattering but mysterious. I couldn't figure out why he would be interested in me. I didn't get any bad vibes about it, so I didn't worry. I was just curious.

I was having such a good time at the party that I lost track of Jim and my writer friend, who both left before I did. It didn't bother me in particular; I knew how to get back to where I was staying. But when the crowd thinned out, Harold came over and asked me if I could give him a minute. What he wanted to know was whether I would I be interested in working for him. That's why he had been watching me. I agreed to come to his office on Sunset Boulevard the next day around 11:00 so we could talk more about it.

Harold Robbins needed a bodyguard. He was seriously behind deadline on a current book, and his publisher, Simon & Schuster, was pressing him. He realized that he couldn't stay in Beverly Hills and get the book done on time and decided that he had to go away so he could finish it. He was a very wealthy man by that time and in the limelight. There were problems with kidnappings in Hollywood as elsewhere, and he wanted to know his family was safe while he was away.

I'm guessing, of course, but as I put it together, Jim Brown must have impressed him with the fact that I could do the job physically, and I suspect as he watched me at his party what he saw was that I wasn't just a tough street black who wouldn't know how to act in his world. Because of my emceeing experience, I was at point in my life where I was impressed but not dazzled by celebrities. I had gotten to know Dinah Washington. I had sat up all night with Billie Holiday. I was surprised to suddenly be in the same room with Ben Casey, but fundamentally I was comfortable around people like that. For that matter, my work at the Majestic had also made me comfortable around people with money and power. I knew how to be discreet, and if I say so myself, I dressed well. I never looked like a street tough.

My suspicions were correct. When I met Harold the next day, I realized immediately that I was in his office at all because he was convinced that I could handle the muscle part of things if necessary and that I could fit into the world his wife and family were living in—the world of Rodeo Drive, palm trees and stretch limos, privilege, and seriously big money. At his office, we got right down to business. He told me about his deadline with Simon & Schuster and about his family, which consisted of his wife, Grace, and a young daughter, Adriana. My job would be protecting them.

We talked a little bit about some of the work I had done in Cleveland and how I saw the job he was offering me. I tried to make clear that I was interested but not committed to the idea, and when he asked me what kind of money I would want I said $60,000. That was a lot of money in those days. It was certainly more than I was making at the time. But I had decided ahead of time that if I was going to consider doing this, I should come in high and act from the beginning as if I was top of the line and expected to be paid as such. Also, I was married--to Delores--and I knew this body-guarding job, if I got it, would mean a lot of time away from home and might put a strain on our marriage. If I was going to take the risk, I wanted it to be worth it. Harold didn't bat an eye at the figure I gave him. We talked a bit more, and then he offered me a contract for a year.

I didn't jump at it at first because I had done quite a bit of thinking before I came to the office. I wanted to find out about a few things. I told him I needed to know where I would stay and what my duties would be. I had known people who had done some body guarding, and I knew enough to know that if you didn't get these kinds of details straight at the beginning you could end up doing dishes, washing windows, and chauffeuring people around. It was clear, however, that what concerned him was protecting his family and nothing else, and so I agreed to come out to the house, meet his wife and daughter, and work out final details then. We met at his home at 5:00 the next day. I met his family, took a look at the layout, and by the end of the evening I had accepted his offer.

My job was to be on the property at all times except when Grace and Adriana had to go someplace to which I would accompany them. I had a cabana by the pool where I could sleep and a bedroom in the house if I chose. I liked the cabana because it was very quiet there at night, and I could hear if anyone tried to get onto the grounds from the back. It was so quiet at night that once I learned the normal sounds of the house, I could tell right away if anything didn't sound right. Inside the house, of course, I was on the spot—much closer to where I would need to be if I was needed. The way it eventually worked was that I slept sometimes in one place, sometimes in the other, varying my routine so that no one who might be scouting out the house could be certain where I was on a given day.

Grace frequently went out and I always went with her. Harold had several expensive cars, and I had my choice of a Rolls Royce or a Lincoln. Given the cars I would be driving and the places we would be going, I needed to dress appropriately because, obviously, when I went to Hollywood parties, restaurants, and public functions with Grace, I needed to look like I belonged. That meant Armani suits, Italian shoes, Rollex watches—the whole nine yards. Harold's business manager took care of the money for everything. I just told him what I wanted, and Harold took it off his taxes as a professional expense. In that short year, I got a taste for fancy clothes and the good life that stayed with me for a long time. When I first started work, Harold's manager said to me, "You have hitched your wagon to a star."

I started work the day after meeting Harold's family. Harold left for Cannes, France, three days later. While he was still in Hollywood, I drove him to work and then went back to the house to begin getting to know Grace, Adriana, and the household staff. For the most part I didn't need to know a lot about the gardeners and people who took care of the pool, people like that—I just had to know who belonged and who didn't. Grace's personal maid was a different story. She had been a maid to the actress Merle Oberon and was quite a character. She told me stories about Merle Oberon, and as we got to know one another better, she asked me about my job—what was my understanding of what I was supposed to do. When I told her, she made a point of saying, "Stick to your contract because I can tell you right now what's going to happen. Grace is going to try to get you to do extra things. You're going to have to watch out for her."

She was right, and I knew it already. I hadn't been there a week before I realized that if I was going to have any problems, they were going to be with Grace. She was Harold's second wife and had been his secretary. She came from a poor Italian family, and because she wasn't born to Hollywood, high living, status, and being seen at the right places meant a lot to her, and so did feeling like she could look down on other people. We had our first run-in almost immediately after Harold left for France.

Grace liked lunches out at expensive places, and of course I drove. After a week or two she asked me if I would mind wearing a chauffeur's uniform. Other women she knew had chauffeurs, and she wanted to be seen around with one, too. I knew I had to draw some lines right then, and I said, "No." I said it nicely but so she would know I meant it. "I'm not a chauffeur," I said, "I'm a bodyguard. I have to go wherever you go and be there if you need me. I have to see everything but not stand out, not attract attention. I can't do my work if

I'm wearing a chauffeur's uniform. Mr. Robbins left you and Adriana in my care, and I have to do it as I see fit." And that was that. I know Grace didn't like it, but she backed off. After that, there was a kind of uneasy truce between us.

For a while after that, we got into a routine that worked for all of us. I took Grace everywhere she went, and if it was a party of more than three, I was authorized to, and did, hire some extra help. The way to be a good bodyguard is to think ahead about what the dangers might be, what you'd need to do "if." If you are good at thinking ahead, anticipating possible problems, then usually nothing happens, and that's exactly what you want. If Grace was going to a nice restaurant, I would need to dress in a way that allowed me to blend—to not stand out. Without drawing undue attention to myself, I had to position myself properly—so I could see where trouble might come from if it came, where was the nearest exit, and so on. If Grace went to a ball or a large party of any kind, I needed to be able to keep her in sight at all times but not be obvious and get in her way.

How did I know how to do this stuff? Certainly the body guarding I had recently done for Carl Stokes and his family was a big help. A lot of on-the-job learning went on there. I didn't think about it at the time, but as I look back I can see that I learned some things as a boy in Detroit. When I was old enough—ten or eleven—my Uncle Hosea, who was the butler for the Fisher family---would sometimes let me come up when the family had big parties and do some minor serving. When the dinner was over and the men had retired to the library for drinks, I was sometimes allowed to bring them things and take empty glasses away, that kind of thing. I also got to talk to the other servants, some of whom were bodyguards, who told me things about what they did when they were working and why they did them. Maybe I remembered some of it.

Whatever the case, between what I had learned and the instincts I discovered I had, I did, if I may say so, a pretty good job. Specifically, I mean that nothing bad happened to anyone in the family on my watch. Every once in a while we would be at a restaurant or a big party, and I would see that someone was bothering Grace or getting on her nerves. Harold Robbins was a wealthy, powerful man in Hollywood in those days, and I think sometimes people were trying to get to Harold through Grace. When I would see something like this happening, my job was to make it stop without causing a disturbance or making a scene. I would usually walk over slowly, touch the troublemaker on the shoulder and ask if I could have a word, stressing that it was important. They always came, and when we got to a place where we had a little privacy I would say something like, "I'm security for Mrs. Robbins. She doesn't want you bothering her anymore, and I'll be grateful if you'll just move on and let her alone." They always did.

Body guarding Adriana was a lot more fun. She was a cute little thing, full of life and fun, and we got along famously from the start. Within weeks she was calling me "Uncle Diz." When I was at home and keeping an eye on her, I got to meet all sorts of famous people. Vincent Minnelli lived catty corner from the Robbins' and had a fancy tree house on his property that he built for his young daughters, Liza and Lorna. Adriana used to play with them and I would go along. Pat Boone lived across the street, and sometimes when I would take Adriana to the movies, little Debbie Boone would come along. I met Pat several times and liked him. I thought he was nice and down to earth. I met Merv Griffin several times when we were both out walking our dogs. He lived on the same street and we had what they call a nodding acquaintance. When we passed, I would say, "Hello, Mr. Griffin", and he would say, "How's it going, Diz?" It wasn't long before I started taking meetings like that for granted.

Before long we also got into regular routines in the Robbins' house, and things went pretty well until Grace's father and mother came to stay with us. Grace's mother was a load. I tried to get along with her, but she was critical about everything I did. She got on me about the grocery bills. She didn't like the things I would buy or wanted to have for dinner. She even got angry when I tried calling her "mother." She was having none of it.

I think the real problem was that neither Grace nor her mother was ever comfortable with the authority Harold had given me when he left for Cannes. With the mother, I think it was more that she wanted to be in charge, and I kept getting in her way. (I talked with Harold's manager about it, and he said he wasn't surprised I was having this kind of trouble. He'd fully expected it.) With Grace I think it was something more. I remember once I had done a big favor for one of their friends and the friend threw a party at which he made a point of thanking me publicly. In fact, before I left that night, the man I had done the favor for, a big name Hollywood director, took me aside and said, "I'll never forget you, Jim." I think all the attention I got really got to Grace because later in the evening I overheard someone asking her who I was. What they said was, "Who's that black guy?" Grace said, "He's nobody. He's just our chauffeur."

Grace had to be able to look down on people.

The situation in the house between me and Grace and Grace's mother never went nuclear but I think Harold must have gotten wind of it, because he came back a few months earlier than he had planned and made a big production of taking Grace and Adriana back with him to France. Harold was always good to me and good with me, and he paid me in full even though there were a couple of months to go on my contract.

I saw a lot, and experienced a lot, and learned a lot in that not quite a year I spent in Hollywood. It was a pretty wild time sexually speaking. Everyone was still in the mindset of the late sixties, free love, make love, not war, anything goes. As I soon learned, some of the parties Harold had been throwing were beyond "X" rated, and everyone seemed to be experimenting. The writer I came out from Cleveland with came very close to having an affair with Debbie Reynolds, who was just coming off a divorce from her second husband. I know this because Harold told me, and Harold knew about it because some people asked him to speak to the writer and try to set him straight. (The thinking was that my writer friend would listen to Harold because he stood to gain so much from Harold's friendship.) What I'm told Harold said to him was something like this: "If you want a white woman, there are dozens of them around here who will oblige. Just leave *her* alone. The scandal could really kill her."

I had offers all the time. They were almost always from older, very wealthy white women—some married, some not married--who got it into their head that they wanted to know what sex would be like with a black man. I think they believed that since I was working for Harold Robbins I could be counted on to be discreet. But I was pretty careful about things like that. I had my own work to do, and I didn't want to put my job at risk by crossing lines that I wasn't supposed to cross.

There was one "opportunity" that is worth remembering, though. She wasn't a headliner, but if I told you her name you'd know it immediately. She had been around Hollywood for quite a while by the time I met her, and she had some credits in impressive films. Just the fact that she'd stayed around as long as she had was pretty impressive. When I knew her she was mainly getting "mature" parts and was the founder of a fairly successful cosmetics company. I could tell that she was interested in me, and one night she came to the house and found her way out to where I was staying in the cabana. She asked me to take off everything but my shorts because she wanted to show me one of her special lotions. She started massaging me with it, head to toe, and the rest, as they say, is history.

The other episode from that year that involved a movie star didn't involve sex at all but it was certainly memorable. Lana Turner was at Harold's one night and for whatever reason (I don't know what it was) became lightheaded and woozy and clearly needed some help. Harold asked me if I would drive her home and make sure she got in safely. We took her car, a Lincoln Town Car. She got into the backseat and I played the role of chauffeur. However, while we were driving she started fumbling with the door in the back and nearly fell out. I was terrified that something would happen to her while I was supposed to be looking out for her, so I stopped the car and persuaded to come up and sit in the front seat with me.

When we got to her house, it turned out that it was her maid's night off. Miss Turner fumbled with her keys but was so out of it that she couldn't get the door open. I helped and we got inside where she fell onto the couch and went out like a light. I didn't want her to wake up in the night and do harm to herself because she didn't know where she was, and I didn't want the maid to come in next morning and find that I had left here there like that. So I picked her up and carried her into the bedroom. I got her down to her slip, put her in bed and tucked the covers up. (She never woke up the whole time.) Then I went to the living room and called Harold, and he got me the number of Miss Turner's maid. I called her and told her what had happened and what I had done, and then I left the house and locked the door behind me. The next day, Miss Turner called

Harold and told him she wanted to see me. When we met, she thanked me warmly and gave me $500. She said I should use it to buy myself a nice sweater or a pair of shoes.

Although I spent just a bit less than a year with Harold Robbins, I learned a lot about people, and got to be a part of a world I doubt I would otherwise have seen. If I occasionally had problems with Grace, I had none with Harold. As soon as I was on the staff, he always treated me as if I belonged there. He wasn't there a lot of the time, but when he was, I would sometimes come to talk with him when he was with someone, and he would look up and say, "Diz, I'd like you to meet Ernest Borgnine, or Edward G. Robinson, or Billy Wilder." (I met them all that way.) They were always as nice as they could be, never treated me like a servant who was cutting in on their time.

The world Harold Robbins lived in wasn't just a world full of celebrities. It was a world of big money—white, big money. What I mean is, I had begun to know of blacks who had a lot of money—for blacks. Ernie Wright who owned the Majestic Hotel, was worth hundreds of thousands of dollars—but not millions. And athletes—even the superstars like Jim Brown—didn't make anywhere near what the players make today. In Harold's world there were multimillionaires. I remember one time I had to ask Harold about something, and when I found him he was on the phone really being hard with somebody. I got there at the part where he said, "This is the end of this. I don't want to talk with you about this anymore." Then he saw that I was there. He hung up the phone and said, by way of explanation, "This is a guy who wants to invest a million dollars in my new movie. He thinks he's going to make a killing if he does. But he doesn't have a lot more than a million. He can't afford to lose it, and this movie could bomb. I don't want that on my conscience." I nodded like I knew what he meant, and I did understand about someone playing with money he couldn't afford to lose. But the stakes were higher than anything I had known about before. Here was where I learned what the phrase "big money" really meant.

We parted on good terms. I know that because Harold gave me a good recommendation to Reuben Sturman later on. I had done what I was hired to do for Harold, and he had always been straight with me. When we were saying last goodbyes as they were about to leave for France, Adriana looked at everyone and asked, "Can Uncle Diz come, too."

COLOR, RACE, AND WORKING FOR WHITE MEN

Race is a subject I haven't talked about much, and now is perhaps a good time. In a lot of ways, working for Harold Robbins as a bodyguard changed my life. To be successful in that particular job, I had to learn how to act around a lot of powerful white men—and women--with money. To do that, I had to see the facts of life about race and racial discrimination clearly. I not only had to learn how to act; I had to learn what the lines were that I couldn't cross.

To my mind, racial discrimination and the question of equality with whites are separate issues. In my opinion, discrimination involves behaviors or laws—things you can point to like separate drinking fountains and bathrooms. The idea of equality, to my way of thinking, is more an attitude—a way of looking at people. I never spent a lot of time in my life thinking all these things through, but at a certain point I felt like I could see how things were. I saw that they were never going to change, and so I learned to accept and deal with them.

There wasn't any talk about equality for blacks when I was growing up in the 1920's and 30's and blacks certainly understood that there was discrimination. Even women didn't get a vote in America till 1920. The forms racial discrimination took were obvious, up front. Blacks couldn't serve in the military when I was born. In lots of states they couldn't use the same washrooms, swimming pools, or drinking fountains. Obviously a lot has happened since then, and people talk about progress and more equality for blacks all the time now. There are television shows about it, and all sorts of debate, and I think a lot of the things they say now are a bunch of hooey. I know that some big things have happened, like the end of separate drinking fountains and swimming pools, and riding on the bus, but over all I don't see the changes as being all that great. In my experience, the facts a black person needed to know when I was growing up and still needs to know are pretty simple.

There's a joke question black people that I know like to ask: "Where is the one place a black man can be equal to a white man?" The answer is, "On the highway." What they mean is that if you've got the money—and some blacks do—you can drive anything a white man can drive. You can be equal on the highway. Money can't always buy you a house—still—in the neighborhood you want, but you can own and drive anything you can pay for. Other than that, forget it. Lots of black—and white—people will try to tell you otherwise, but I don't think they know what they're talking about. Either that or it's just a big scam.

It sometimes makes me angry to listen to Johnny come lately black people talking about all the progress that's been made, about how far we've come. You hear this a lot from younger black politicians and ministers. Maybe they actually believe it, but I don't see how. I've lived a long time. I've got eyes, and I know what I've seen.

When I'm angry about it, I like to imagine what it would be like to talk from a stage in an auditorium to a big audience of black people. I would be on one side of the stage, and an idealistic young politician and a naïve young minister would be on the other. They would say what they felt they were supposed to say and what they thought people wanted to hear, and then I would tell it like it is. For example they might say the Bill of

Rights guarantees that all men are created equal, and I would point out that blacks weren't even considered men when the Bill of Rights was written. I'm not convinced we are yet. They might say, well, we are all equal under law, and I would say, "Please." "That may be the theory, but look at what's happening in practice. Look at who's crowding the jails in this country. Look at who gets long sentences and who gets light ones." They might say that in this country we've all got freedom of speech. I would say maybe in private, but if you're black you've got to be careful in public. Has everyone forgotten what happened to Tommy smith and Juan Carlos after they raised their Black Power fists on the podium at the 1968 Summer Olympics? It's not rocket science. You just have to watch what's really happening.

Unlike many blacks, especially the ones who grew up in the south, I can't point to any specific example of painful racial discrimination in my childhood. The earliest home I had was with my grandmother and my uncles Chris and Allen, and in their house nobody talked about race or racial issues at all, at least not that I knew of. This was, of course, in the late 1920s and early 1930s—not the 1960s—and so I suppose there could have been a lot of reasons why nobody talked about it then, but the fact was they didn't.

I didn't encounter anything serious in grammar school or in my neighborhood as a child, either. My kindergarten teacher, Mrs. Goetz, was one of the first white people I remember ever seeing, but she was always kind to me, and that was an entirely good experience. So were the kids in my neighborhood, which as I've said, was integrated for a while. We were kids, and the schoolyard was the schoolyard. Even as kids we knew the words. But it wasn't the way it became later. On a given day— when I was six or seven, say--my Italian neighbor might call me a "nigger" and maybe I would call him a "Wop", and in the end we would both laugh about it. Even if we got into a fight, we made up quickly and didn't take it personally. At the time and at our ages it was like calling each other "stupid" or a "dummy." You knew it was supposed to be an insult, but it didn't mean anything more than that.

The first experiences I had with words or attitudes that had clear overtones of race were after the poor blacks started moving up from the south to work in the mills and car companies in Detroit. They brought a lot of suspicion and attitude with them. When my white neighbor Mrs. Sowinski would tell me to pick up something maybe I had just thrown on her lawn, I would hop to it because I knew she would tell my grandmother if I didn't. When she would say the same thing to one of the new kids from the south, they might tell her she wasn't their mother and to mind her own business—or worse. But by the time things started to get really bad in the neighborhood, and the new freeways started being built and cutting us off from surrounding neighborhoods, and the white families started moving out, it wasn't long before I went into the service.

At the time I was in it, the military was, God knows, not perfect. But it wasn't a bad place to be if you were a young black man. Okay, it wasn't integrated yet. Blacks didn't serve with whites, and knew I was never going to be a five star general. But I had no such expectations, and the way we all—black and white--got treated in the service reminds me of a story people used to tell about Vince Lombardi, the famous coach of the football championship Green Bay Packers. Black players liked playing for Lombardi because they said that he treated all the players—black and white—the same: badly! They appreciated the fact that, while he was a tough taskmaster, he treated all the players alike. At my level, that's the way it was in the three branches of the military where I served briefly. And it was better than that. If I could box or run faster than anyone else, then they were fine with letting me try. If I misbehaved, they whacked me around pretty good—just like they did anyone else. (I really don't count that episode with the German prisoner who called me racial names. I think there was something else going on there.)

After I left the service, I tried semi-professional and professional football. As with the military, it wasn't perfect, but it was somewhere where blacks were starting to get a foothold. There weren't a lot of back professional football players yet, but there were some, and the number was growing. It was growing slowly, but it was definitely growing. Although they didn't invite me home to meet their sisters, I was accepted by the white athletes I played with as an athlete and even had friends among them. And when I finally had to face the fact that a career in professional football wasn't going to happen, it wasn't long before I came to Cleveland, where I lived primarily in an all-black world—the world of the black numbers, and the Majestic Hotel. I wasn't competing in a white world, and therefore I didn't encounter racial discrimination. People—at least the ones I hung around with--weren't as self-conscious about racial issues in those days, either. It never really occurred to me to come to Cleveland and try to make it in the white world, and I never gave much thought to why it never occurred to me.

When I did cross over into the world of white men, and white money, and white power was when I began body guarding, first for Harold Robbins and then for Reuben Sturman. The kind of money they were offering and the lifestyle that went with the job was the stuff that poor blacks only dream about—or maybe not because it's so far out of an ordinary black person's reach. It was being offered to me, and I was ready to accept it and make it work not because I had learned to deal with racial discrimination (which I felt like I had not seen much of)) but because I had learned some crucial things about white men, equality, and power.

In the years before I had the opportunity to work for Harold Robbins and Reuben Sturman, I had had two experiences that taught me a lesson I've never forgotten. The experiences were being locked up in St. Elizabeth's Hospital and in the insane asylum in Warren, Pa, both after episodes in which my behavior was violent and over the line.

That I had a violent streak and a temper was obvious to me after that. There have been periods in my life when I have tried to figure out why? Where did all the anger come from? I wasn't beaten up as a child more than lots of kids I knew, and a lot of the time when I was disciplined it was my fault—I had it coming. You might even say it was my choice—like cutting school and going to the movies—things that I could have avoided if I had wanted to. Was it because I felt I always had to take care of things myself? Was I angry at my parents for not being there? Was it something else? To this day I have no idea. Sometimes I thought it was an unintended result of my military training, especially in the Marines. They were very big on making you proud and aggressive. "You're a Marine. You can handle anything—go get it. Attack and conquer. You don't have to take any shit from anybody, you're a Marine!" I don't know. I could never come up with an answer about where the violence came from, and at this stage of my life I don't care. But I cared then, because I had two powerful examples of what could happen if I let it out and threatened the people who ran things, the people with power.

I learned they had the power to put me in places like St. Elizabeth's Hospital and the insane asylum, and they could keep me there as long as they pleased. I had power in my arms. I had power in my legs and could run like the wind. I had power in my fists. But I didn't have any power that was remotely like the power "they" had, and by "they I mean the white establishment, the white people who made the laws and who applied and enforced the laws, and who ran things. It was a whole world of people: the police, the courts, the social workers, and the court appointed psychologists. I knew now that if they had me in their power, they could decide to lock me up and throw away the key. If I tried to take them on, they would win. If I stepped too far out of line, they could do pretty much whatever they wanted with me, and the lesson was clear: I had to learn not to cross the lines that were really important. That meant I had to learn where the lines were. I had to learn how to win powerful white people's respect and trust without threatening them, and by the time I went to work for Harold Robbins, I had learned.

I remember as a child when I would be visiting my Uncle Hosea at the Fisher mansion, there would sometimes be big parties for the top brass at Ford—or in the whole auto industry. When I was old enough, I would sometimes be allowed to help clean up, carry things back and forth from the kitchen and so on. And I remembered overhearing the powerful white men talk about the union movement. There was talk that the sizeable black population that worked for them were going to be a part of it. They didn't like the idea of unions black or white, but the idea that blacks might have a vote in these unions and become a factor in negotiations threatened them directly. The fact that it was black people they were talking about somehow made it worse. Even a kid could see it.

I also began to see that some things were not white-black things but that others were. Violence that went out of control was not a white vs black thing. Anyone in the army—black, white, or brown--who threatened a superior officer physically or who hit a prisoner would have been punished. But I also learned—just by watching—that when blacks and white's worked together, the whites obviously had a sense that blacks had their "place" and they ought to know it and stay in it. Any black person who grew up in those years, if they're honest, would say that's true. And by the time I had the opportunities I did with Harold and Reuben, I knew what I needed to do.

I was physically much bigger, stronger, and tougher than Harold Robbins or Reuben Sturman. If I'd wanted to, I could have mopped up the floor with either of them. But I made sure it was a possibility that never even entered their minds. I was a different person than I had been as a kid in the army. They were the boss; I was the employee. They told me what to do; I did it. I never became an Uncle Tom. I knew how and when—and how far—I could assert myself, like I did with Grace. I didn't let people push me around, but I knew how to do it without threatening anybody, without pushing the wrong buttons. I looked like they wanted me to look. I drove what they wanted me to drive. I went where they wanted me to go. I even took risks for them. And I got a lot in return. It wasn't just the style of life I was able to lead in those years, although that was extremely important to me. It was also that, because I knew what lines I couldn't cross, they trusted me with their families and sometimes with their secrets.

Harold Robbins sometimes talked with me about private things in a way he never would have considered if I had had been running around in a dashiki with an attitude and an afro. (If I had been doing things like that, he never would have hired me in the first place.) Reuben told me things that he knew could have put him in prison if I had told anyone about them. But he knew I wouldn't tell anyone. And all these things happened because I understood the rules of relationships between a black man like me and powerful white men like Harold and Reuben.

A very small example: During the time when I was doing some work for Frank Sinatra, I always carefully addressed him as "Mr. Sinatra." One day we were riding up in an elevator together. He was standing at the front of the elevator looking at the door, and I was standing behind and to his left so that I couldn't see his face and he couldn't see mine. I started to say something to him and began by saying, "Mr. Sinatra," and without looking around he said, "Frank. You can call me Frank." It came as a complete surprise, and I was actually moved. I quickly corrected myself, and said, "Frank." But I never called him that in front of other people because I knew better. It was the same with Harold and Reuben. We were sometimes fairly close in private but I was never over-familiar in public.

The other thing I knew better than to do around powerful white men was in any way to suggest that I was interested in white women. The subject of black men and white women has always been a powder keg, and everybody knows it—certainly blacks know it if they have a brain in their heads. There were times both with Harold and with Reuben when I had my chances. As I said, there were times when I worked for Harold Robbins that opportunities with white women came my way and I took them. But when I did, I was as discreet as it was possible to be. And I never openly expressed—to anyone—an interest in white women. With Reuben especially, and some of his people, there were times when someone would say, "Hey, Diz, you looking for a little action tonight? When you get off work, want me to send a couple of girls to your room?" Stuff like that. I made a decision early on about how I would handle it if it came up. I always made a joke about it. I might say something like, "As long as they're black, send 'em on up. I don't' want any white women." That's what I always said—or something like it—and I never broke that pattern, not even when it seemed like opportunity was knocking hard.

When I took Lana Turner home when she was semi-conscious at best, she was still a beautiful woman. If I had tried something it might have worked. The state she was in she might not have remembered if she did, it might have been all right with her—or she might not have wanted the hassle and publicity that would have gone with making an issue of it. Honestly, I never considered it. There was too much at stake for me. Harold was comfortable suggesting that I take her home by myself because he felt he could trust me with her, and he could. That kind of trust and the lifestyle I was living because of it were a lot more valuable to me than anything you might now call "Black Pride."

I know that now there are a lot of different ways to look at what I'm saying and what I did. All I can say it that it made sense to me at the time, and it still does. If I had tried to swim against the current, if I had tried to assert my rights—or whatever you would want to call it--nothing would have happened except that I would have lost everything I had. And what I had was extremely important to me. It was the lifestyle, of course, but the friendships meant a lot as well. Harold Robbins trusted me with his wife and his little girl. I loved Adrianna. I loved it when she would call me "Uncle Diz." When I was leaving Harold Robbins' employ and Adrianna asked if Uncle Diz was coming it broke my heart. My relationship with Reuben's young wife, Naomi Delgado also meant a lot to me. She was young, beautiful, independent minded, and full of fun, and she became a friend. And think about what I've just said. I was friends with a beautiful, young, white girl, who was the wife of my boss. He expected me to look out for her—and his daughter Erica. He trusted me with her, and he did so because I never gave him any reason not to—or to suspect there could be a reason not to. I didn't see anything wrong with that then and I don't know. I also don't think the world has changed a bit for black men since then. But that's neither here nor there. It worked for me.

I'm not saying that after working for Harold Robbins I was a totally changed man, or that I was somehow housebroken. When I left Harold and came back to Cleveland, I got back into the old life of the streets and the old ways pretty quickly until the opportunity with Reuben Sturman came along. But from the time I worked for Harold Robbins, I knew what I had to do if I was going to work for or be around white people, especially white people with money and power.

Diz & Nancy Wilson on stage at the old Majestic Hotel

Teenage Friends, Eddie Horton & Diz

Diz at the mike at the Majestic

Team Picture of the Lake Erie Vets, Diz #72. Circa 1950

Diz with Friends Jim Brown (3rd from left)
& Paul Hornung (5th from left)

Ollie Matson, Diz, Night Train Lane & Marion Motley

Diz & his first wife Martha Butler

Diz & Loretta, wife # 6

Third Wife, Joan, a model for Ebony Magazine

Diz & Reuben Sturman at Sturman's home in Shaker Heights

Old Blue Eyes & Diz

Diz and Mary King on their wedding day

REGENCY ARTISTS, LTD.

Sarah Vaughan

PERSONAL MANAGEMENT & RECORDS
RAMS HALL CORP.
13063 VENTURA BLVD.
STUDIO CITY, CA. 91604
213/ 788-8683

Publicity photo of Sarah Vaughn, one of the greats
Diz introduced at the Majestic

The authors William Siebenschuh & Diz
at Diz's apartment at the Abinbgton

Diz at the Abington late in his life

BACK ON THE STREET

When I got back to Cleveland after the year I spent with Harold Robbins it was easy to pick up where I had left off. Through my previous connection with Carl Strokes, I got a job in security with the City of Cleveland. At the time somebody was stealing gasoline and equipment from city lots. I had a city car at my disposal, and it was my job to make regular inspections and try to find out who was doing it. I also continued to be available to work for Carl Stokes personally when he needed me.

I liked Carl Stokes from the first time I met him. He was the best, the most trusted and successful black politician I've known in Cleveland, and I knew a lot of them. He was a handsome man, with a smile that could light up a room. He was a strong man, too. He knew how make decisions and he knew the black community in Cleveland from the high end to the low. He could move comfortably in the world of money and power, but he also knew the streets. I first met him when he was, I think, a state whiskey inspector. He used to play pool at a place across the street from Lancer's Restaurant. He treated the people there and in the neighborhoods with respect. He had a great sense of humor, and the longer I worked for him, the closer we got.

At the same time that I was getting to know Carl Stokes and doing more and more things for him, I got back into the numbers in a big way, too. In fact, at the time everything was working for me but my private life, which for a while got a bit out of control.

I knew the numbers operation backward and forward by now. Sometimes I was there for the drawings that always took place in somebody's back yard or basement. We had the numbered balls in a bag, shook them up good and then drew the three winners, always with a bunch of people standing around to watch. What the people never knew was that sometimes, if the bosses were afraid that certain combinations might break the bank, they would rig the drawing. We would put the balls we wanted chosen in the icebox all morning. When the drawing took place, the guy with his hand in the bag would make it look like he was being careful to choose three balls at random. What he was really doing was hunting for the cold ones.

Sometimes I carried the money either back to the bookies or from the bookies to the winners. I also got back into the muscle part of it in a big way. I had a reputation by then, and now I didn't just deal with the ones who thought they were tough guys. If Don King or Big Joe Allen or any of the other big bosses thought somebody was skimming from them or coming up short, they would send me out to have a talk with them. If they couldn't pay what they owed, I would give them what we called on the street a "big ass whuppin."

I did some muscle work for Carl during this period, too. One job I remember in particular was the one with Jimmy Smith. Jimmy Smith was about as good on the jazz organ as it gets [38]. We knew he was good then, and I've learned that in 2005 he was awarded the Jazz Masters Award from the National Endowment for the Arts. It's the highest honor a jazz musician can get.

I don't remember how Carl met Jimmy, but I know Carl was excited when he got a commitment from him to play for the lunch crowd at noon at the Mall right across from City Hall.

The Mayor got a lot of publicity out of it, built it up big. When Jimmy Smith didn't show, Carl was *not* happy. He had very publicly given his word, and he hadn't produced what he promised. Politicians can't afford to have that happen too many times, and so he called me and another guy who did the same kind of work I did into his office. "Don't you think," he said, "that Jimmy Smith just showed me a lot of disrespect? Don't you think he should be reminded of that?" We felt like it was clear what he wanted us to do.

The other guy's name was Ronnie Bey, and he had a reputation as an enforcer just like I did. It wasn't hard to find out where Jimmy Smith was staying. We got there a little before noon. When we asked for the room number, the clerk wouldn't tell us at first. He said he wasn't supposed to give out the room. Very quietly I said, "We are going to ask you one more time." You could see he didn't know what to do, but he hesitated too long for his own good, and I knocked him down hard. Then he told us.

When we knocked on Jimmy Smith's door he had a girl in bed with him and told us to go away. We talked through the door and got him to open it, and when he did we were in. The girl was terrified. We told her to get her clothes on and get out, and we didn't have to tell her twice.

Jimmy Smith wasn't used to being rousted like this, and he was angry at first. "What do you guys want?" he asked, I think trying to sound tough. "Where were you supposed to be at noon yesterday?" I said. "I couldn't make it," he said, like that ought to be enough for us. That's when Ronnie hit him, and then I unloaded on him, too.

We gave him a beating and then went to the Lancer's Steak House on Carnegie for a bite to eat. Jimmy Smith must have called somebody big because before we were finished with our meal, in came Gerald McFaul, who was a deputy sheriff then. He got in our faces right away. "What the hell did you guys think you were doing to Jimmy Smith?" he said. We said, "Why don't you go ask Carl Stokes what's happening?" That made him think for a minute. Then he made a big production of showing us that he was wearing a gun. We said "We got guns, too. Why don't you go talk to the mayor about this?" Then we just stared at one another for a long minute, and then he left. It was over, and he knew it. We didn't hear anything more about it.

I remember another job I did for Carl. There was a Black Nationalist group that was shaking down a guy who went to Carl to complain about it. Carl wanted it stopped and he again asked Ronnie Bey and me if we would handle it. We got the details, and we knew the guys who were causing the trouble, so we called a meeting. It was a little tense at first, but we made it clear that the mayor wanted this stopped. We told them, "Nobody wants trouble. We respect you, but you have to respect us on this one." And they did.

In those years, I sometimes worked for people besides Carl Stokes and the numbers people. People on the street knew about me now and what I could do. For example, I remember I was in bed one night and got a very late call from a man who was in a gambling joint. He had just won a lot of money—over $1,000—and the people he won it from were not amused. He was afraid to walk out to his car in the parking lot with his winnings, and so he had his girlfriend call me and ask if I would come over and get him to his car safely. It was a few minutes work for which he said he would pay me $200, and I got out of bed and went. When I got back home, Delores, my new wife, hit the roof. She was angry and suspicious about my getting a call from a girl in the middle of the night—and then getting out of bed and going out! I told her what I was doing and showed her the money when I got home. It didn't calm her down much, and then I got angry and said, "Where do you think I get the money to pay for your big car, and our apartment, and all your jewelry? It's not from working for the city!" She wasn't happy, but she didn't have anything to come back with.

Another thing I was doing in these years was getting involved with the trade in cocaine, but in a very special way. One day I was approached by a man named Charley Warren, who wanted to know if I would be interested in getting into the drug business. He said he had been watching me doing a lot of small jobs for the people in the numbers. He liked what he'd seen and was sure I was ready to do bigger things and make a lot more money than I was making. He said that if he didn't believe he could trust me he wouldn't be talking with me. "You know how to keep your mouth shut," he said.

I was interested, but I wanted to be up front with him. I told him that I didn't know anything about the drug game. I knew that a few of my friends used cocaine, but that was about all. He said that was exactly why he was talking with me. People knew I wasn't involved with the drug trade. I didn't deal and never had, and the police knew I was clean. That was why I would be able to help him.

What he wanted me to do was keep his drugs for him when they arrived in Cleveland. He didn't have a lot of clients, only four or five. But they were big clients, black doctors and lawyers who were willing to pay top dollar for a source they knew they could count on and trust. Charley, I was to learn, got extremely high-quality cocaine from his sources in Florida and at times Peru. He had an almost perfect set up. He had a small group of regular, highly reputable clients who could pay top dollar, and who no one was likely to suspect. He had a premium source. His problem was that although the police and the DEA had not been able to catch him and make anything stick yet, they knew he was a cocaine dealer and they were watching him like a hawk. That's where he saw me fitting in.

Having decided that he could trust me, what was important to him was that as far as drugs were concerned I stayed clean as a whistle. He knew that the police could get a warrant to break into his apartment or search him or his car any time they wanted. They didn't associate me with cocaine at all. I could not only keep it safely but if need be I could transport it without much fear of search or arrest. Maybe the law enforcement people knew that I worked for the numbers people occasionally, but I had always kept my city job. I was respectably employed and had never hung out with big users. Though I had been arrested once or twice in my life, I had never been convicted of anything. I was about as clean as he could get.

What he wanted me to do at first was simple and not too risky. He brought a kilo a month into Cleveland, and all he wanted me to do was keep it for him in my apartment. When he wanted to pick all or some of it up, he would come by the apartment building and get what he needed. Easy as pie, he said. I said why didn't we try it and see how it went.

The first time we tried was about two weeks later. He came to see me at my apartment. In a briefcase he brought along one kilo—street value at the time of about $60,000. For the rest of the month, he would drop by when he needed to pick some up. I got $1,000 just for keeping it in my apartment, and when he dropped it off he gave me some cocaine for myself. He said it was for my personal use "so you don't have to be tempted to steal from the 'key' that you're keeping for me." The final thing he told me was that if any of my friends asked me where I got the cocaine he was giving me for my own use, I was never to tell them. He said just to say that I got it from a friend of a friend, and let it go at that.

Charley got a new shipment every month, and after working with for a couple of months, he decided he could trust me, and he let me a bit further into the way he handled his operation. After three deliveries, he raised my salary to $2000 a month and increased the personal "source" he gave me each time. I could use it or sell it, but I could never tell people where it came from—and I never did. I worked for Charley for a long time. I worked for him after I got shot and even after I began to work for Reuben Sturman.

Charley and I became good friends. We had a lot in common. We liked nice things and classy women. We both knew how to dress; looking good mattered to us, and we liked to drink and eat only the best. He helped me make a ton of money, and I learned a lot from him. For example, I learned a lot about the particulars of the drug business. I learned how to test cocaine to see if it was good, and if so, how good. I learned what color you had to look for when you mixed it with the right kind of chemicals in a vial. I learned about putting a little bit first on your finger and then on your tongue to see if you got the "freeze"—the numbness you were supposed to get. I learned how to measure it properly for distribution—in $50, $100, and $200 sized bags.

I also learned to appreciate how careful Charley was. He was never going to get caught carrying the stuff around. When one of his clients called with an order, he would drop by my apartment and pick it up. Then he would meet the client at a prearranged place, make the deal in a matter of seconds, and be on his way. It was in his possession for as short a time as he could make it. The only times I ever saw him carrying coke around was when he was hitting the clubs and bars looking for women. Women loved the stuff. Honest to god, I think in those days you might go up to a good-looking woman and offer her $200 for a little pleasure, and she might turn you down. Offer her a little coke, and she was on your arm in a New York minute. I saw it work for Charley dozens of times. He would go into a place where they knew who he was and buy a round of drinks. The women would be all over him with, "Hey, Charley. You got anything?" If he did, he might palm them a $50 bag and say, "Hey, baby. Here you go. You can split this" and they were his for the evening.

Charley was as successful as he was because he was discreet. His client's knew they could trust him; and he didn't cut his coke too much. Nobody I knew who dealt cocaine dealt it pure. The best dealer's, like Charley, cut it once, maybe twice at the most. In doing so they doubled and tripled their profits, but they didn't seriously dilute the quality like the more fly-by-night dealers did. He was a class act in every sense. He knew how to live, and he didn't save his money. He spent it like there was no tomorrow. He had a beautiful condo, and, because he was one of those people who go grey early (and Charley went white), with that white hair of his and the killer clothes, he always stood out from the crowd. We had a beautiful partnership and a friendship that was to last for close to twenty years. He's gone now, but I still have a picture of him on a table beside my bed.

Since I've just said so much about my keeping cocaine for Charley, I maybe should say something here about my own involvement with drugs, such as it was. Charley's idea about me—that I didn't use or sell—was correct. But it's not like I never tried things. From the time I was a kid in Detroit, wherever I had lived there had always been drugs ready to hand. I never did heroin, and I only did coke socially and not that much. I would do it if that's what everyone else was doing, but I was careful with it for my own reasons. Too much coke, and it started to affect the way you could perform sexually. To be blunt about it, if you took more than a couple of light hits, you could wind up not being able to get it up, and in those days, good sex meant a lot more to me than good drugs.

Although I did use cocaine socially, the only drug I ever used at all regularly was marijuana, which we always called "reefer". I was never addicted, and I think that stuff about, you take one hit and you become an addict is a bunch of crap. The people who I've seen become addicts haven't done so because the drug was strong but because they were weak. I'll say this, though. Every once in a while people would offer me heroin. I would turn them down, and they would say, "Hey, come on. You don't have to shoot it—put it in your veins. You can just 'skin pop' it—just put it right under the skin." I never did it, though, because I knew you could hit a vein by mistake, and why even take a chance?

I never cared much for alcohol, either, except, again, socially. What I liked—and still do—was reefer. I remember when I was in junior high and still in Detroit, I was sneaking a glass of wine with some buddies, and an older kid gave me some advice. "Don't drink that stuff", he said, "It'll kill you. You're an athlete, you don't want to wreck your body." Then he handed me a joint. "Here, he said," try some of this." I did, and have done so many times since and never had any ill effects from it. If I am addicted to anything, though, it's probably food. I love to eat well. I always have, and I know what it means to do so.

Where I lived and worked, drugs were just part of the territory. Everybody worked out their own way of using or not using them. A lot more was going on that just drugs, though. These years I've just been talking about—the last years of the 1960's and into the 1970's in Cleveland--were wild times on the streets. Crime families were moving in from out of the city, rival gangs were getting closer and closer to open warfare. Down in the neighborhoods and the clubs you could feel the temperature rising. And it was like it was catching. I did some of the craziest things I ever did in those years, and maybe the craziest was what happened with me, a girl I was living with named Dorothy (who came after Eleanor but before Delores), and Herman Stevens, a colorful character and a big time cocaine dealer in Cleveland whose nickname was "Scatter."

Herman Stevens' nickname was "Scatter" because he had a reputation for being scatterbrained. He didn't like to be called Scatter, and not many people were willing to do so to his face on the streets, but the name stuck like glue. In his day, he was something of a celebrity in the Cleveland black community. He drove a big, flashy Cadillac and at one point bought an expensive Austin Healy, the car James Bond drove. He was always dressed to the nines and liked to be seen with beautiful women. He owned a barbecue place on West 105th where black celebrities always came when they were in town because Scatter was their cocaine connection. Sammy Davis Jr., Count Basie, Sugar Ray Robinson, they all came to Scatter's.

He loved the high life. He was the guy you would always see at the Kentucky Derby if you knew where to look. He was the life of the sections where black people with money were allowed to sit. He would walk around, meeting and greeting everyone, looking like a million bucks. He would also be at ringside at the biggest fights, working the crowd, flashy clothes and jewelry, seeing and being seen. At both places he handled a lot of big time betting. I got to know him because sometimes when he went to the Derby or the fights he had quite a bit of money with him and I carried it for him to keep it safe. When I had my trouble with him was when he started moving in on Dorothy.

Before she knew me, Dorothy had been with Scatter and had had a child by him. But she was my woman now, and we had been together for a while. Dorothy worked at The Corner Tavern, Don King's nightclub at 79th and Cedar. I went to pick her up after work one night but she wasn't there. They told me that Scatter had come by and picked her up in a big white Cadillac, and I didn't like the sound of that at all. The more I thought about it, the more upset I got, and so I decided to go looking for them.

I went to a couple of other clubs for blacks downtown, one on Prospect and one on another place on Cedar but no luck. The more I drove around, the angrier I got. Things had fallen apart with Eleanor not long ago. She had been cheating on me--and now this. I didn't like being played with—by anyone. I decided I was going to find Scatter and Dorothy if it took all night, so I went to his barbecue place, figuring if he wasn't there maybe they would know where he was.

I don't know exactly what I looked like when I walked in the door, but Elsie, the woman who managed the place for Scatter, took one look at me and put her hands out in front of her. She said, "You have to calm down, Diz," and she walked me over to a table and tried talking with me. I know she could see it didn't do much good, but she made me promise not to do anything drastic till the anger had passed. Maybe it helped a little but not much. I was really getting myself into a state.

Wherever they had gone, I soon realized that I wasn't going to find them by driving around. I couldn't find her, and I felt like I had to do *something*, so I went back to my apartment, which was on 93rd Street just off of Hough Avenue, and started throwing out some of the expensive clothes I had bought Dorothy. I remember I took one shoe each from a bunch of pairs of shoes I had bought her and took them all and some sweaters and threw them down the garbage chute. Then I had the idea if I hid somewhere outside the entrance to the apartment building, I could catch them both when Scatter brought her home.

When I got downstairs and went outside, I saw right away that there weren't many places a man my size could hide. What I ended up doing is one of the craziest things I ever did in my life: I climbed a tree. All I can tell you is that it seemed like a good idea at the time.

I did it because I wanted to be able to have a clear view the front of the apartment, the place where Scatter would drive up to let Dorothy off. Except for a good sized tree just across the street, there was nowhere I could hide and get the view I wanted. I decided that was what I was going to have to do, looked around to see if anyone was watching, and up I went. To get the sight line I wanted, I had to hunker down on a fairly big branch, hold onto another above it for balance, and stay that way till Scatter and Dorothy drove up. I ended up being in this uncomfortable squat for between a half an hour and an hour. I sometimes asked myself what I thought I was doing. But I was too far into it to give it up then.

While I was up there two white guys came walking by under the tree. One of them happened to look up and notice me, and said to his friend, "By God, there's a nigger in that tree." All I could think was that this would be when Scatter pulled up and these guys would give me away. "Get the fuck away from here before I kick your ass," I hissed pretty loudly. They looked at me for a few seconds and then took off.

Not too long after that Scatter pulled up, and sure enough there was Dorothy with him in the white Cadillac. He got out and walked over to her side and opened the door for her and they started kissing good night. I had them dead to rights, and I jumped down out of the tree. But my legs had gone completely asleep from being hunkered down all that time, and I fell onto the tree lawn in a heap, making a huge racket when I landed.

They both jumped a foot in the air when I hit the ground. Dorothy's eyes were as big as saucers and she yelled, "Diz, *What* are you doing?" From the ground where I was sitting, furious that I couldn't get on my feet, I shouted "Bitch, when I can get back on my legs I'll show you what I'm doing." When she heard that, Dorothy was gone. She ran for the apartment building as fast as she could go, and Scatter, who realized right away what was happening, jumped back in the car and took off with me still not able to stand but yelling that I was going to kick his ass, too. When the circulation came back to my legs, I ran after Dorothy, but by the time I got to our apartment I could see right away that she had grabbed a few personal things and was gone—out the back entrance.

The next morning I heard through the grapevine that Dorothy was holed up in Shaker Heights in the home of a friend named Dolly Mapp. Dolly Mapp was someone you needed to take seriously [39]. She had always run with a fast crowd and was something of a legend in the Cleveland area in the 1950s and 1960s. She was a knockout when she was younger and had been married to big name fighters like Larry Bivins and Archie Moore. She was also involved in a landmark legal case involving the use of evidence obtained in an illegal search that went all the way to the Supreme Court—the Warren Court. (The Supreme Court found in her favor and against the State of Ohio [40].) She was still connected and tough and not someone you mess with.

When I got to her house and asked about Dorothy, she said, "Dorothy doesn't want to talk with you right now. You can't come in here lookin' for any trouble, Diz," and I didn't try. But now this was now becoming a thing with me. I felt like I had to get Dorothy back and get her to talk with me. It was a matter of self-respect. She was going to talk with me or else. I wasn't going to cross Dolly. But when I found out later that day that Dorothy had left her house and gone to work, I decided that was where I could catch up with her. I drove back down Cedar to the Corner Tavern, but when I parked and got out of the car, I saw a bunch of mean looking black men, some of the toughest black gangsters in Cleveland, standing between me and the door of the Tavern.

"Where you goin', Diz?" they asked.

"In to see Dorothy."

"No, you're not," they said and they all took a step towards me. I stopped and squared up on them and said, "That's my woman, and I'm goin' in there.

"No, you're not," was the answer.

I said, "OK, went back and got in my car and drove away— to a pawn shop I knew about, where I pawned one of my rings and bought a shotgun and some shells with the money. I was so angry that they would butt in like this, try and stop me, that I was almost literally seeing red. If they tried to stop me, they were going to get blown away.

When I got back to the Corner Tavern, I didn't get out of the car with the shotgun in my hand. I thought I would see if they had changed their minds. They were still there standing on the corner, though, and when I started towards the tavern they said, "Where the hell you think you're goin'?" I said I was going inside to see my woman, and they said no I wasn't and lined up again between me and the door. At that point I turned around, walked back to the car and took out the shotgun.

When the toughs on the corner saw the shotgun, they started singing a different tune. One of them yelled, "Look out. He's gonna kill us all!" and they took off running in all directions.

When I saw that, I headed straight for the door and Dorothy, but I never got there.

What stopped me was Aggie Greene. Aggie Greene was a private cop who was well known in the neighborhood. He was big and tough. He carried two pistols, and he wouldn't let any harm come to a woman when he was around. That's why he came over when he found out what was going on.

By that time, everything seemed like it had had slowed down, and a crowd was gathering. Then Aggie said, "What are you doing, Diz?" I held up the shotgun and said, "I'm going to kill anyone who tries to keep me from seeing my woman."

Aggie Greene looked at me for a long minute. Then he said, "I don't want to see you get in trouble, Diz. You go back to your car, put the gun away and stay there, and I'll bring Dorothy out to you."

We just stood there and glared at one another, and then I did what he asked. He wasn't challenging me personally or calling me out like the guys on the corner, and I trusted him to keep his word. I think maybe at that point I was looking for a way out without anything bad happening, and he gave it to me. I sat in my car like he asked. He went into the Corner Tavern and in a little while he came out with Dorothy. She was really scared, but I was over my anger. I think what had gotten it up so high was being told no, being challenged by the guys in the street. Dorothy and I talked for a while and then we made up and went home. When we finally broke up, it wasn't because of any of this. That's just how crazy it was. Honest to God, it was like the old West on the streets of Cleveland in those years, and as the decade of the 1970's went on, it just got worse.

BOMB CITY: THE MOB WARS OF THE 1970'S

Without question, the most dramatic thing that happened to me in the last years of the 1970s was getting shot and nearly killed. To understand the why of it, though, you need to know not only what was going on in my life in those years but also what was going on in the city of Cleveland. The following article in the *Cleveland Plain Dealer*, linked my shooting to the general climate of racketeering and mob activity. After a headline that read, *Long Denies Dealing with Racketeers*, the report was that:

> James E. (Diz) Long, a city street department investigator who was shot April 2, denied yesterday that numbers slips and financial records found in his apartment are his.

> Long, 47, said in an interview at Huron Road Hospital that he was not connected with the numbers racket in Cleveland and has no direct dealings with anyone who is. . .(*The Cleveland Plain Dealer*, Apr. 26, 1976)

I suppose technically the reason I was shot was related to my involvement in the black numbers rackets. But I could understand why the police might have thought it was connected with something bigger.

The decade of the 1970's was one of the most violent periods in Cleveland's modern history [41] The *Cleveland Press* was calling Cleveland "Bomb City." In 1976, the year I was shot, there were 36 bombings. In the previous year, 1975, Alex "Shondor" Birns [42], a legendary and feared enforcer in the numbers rackets, was blown up in the parking lot behind Christy's Lounge on West 25th. According to newspaper and magazine accounts, "Parts of the car landed on St. Malachi Catholic Church 1,000 feet away." In 1977, the year following my shooting, Danny Greene [43], who ran his own mob and defied Shondor Burns, was also blown to smithereens in a parking lot. The papers said the blast "blew off his left arm, throwing it 1,000 feet away, the gold ring with five green stones still firmly on a finger."

A special issue of *Cleveland Magazine* in 2007 put it this way:

> Before there was Tony Soprano, there was Alex "Shondor" Birns and Danny Greene. Clevelanders in the '70s didn't need color TV — they had something better: a Technicolor drama chock full of colorful characters in their own front yard. . . "Last year, in fact, more bombs were placed and set off in Cleveland than in any other major city," Edward P. Whelan noted in 1977.

I wasn't an insider with either Shondor Birns or Danny Greene, but I knew them, and I knew the people around them. I occasionally rode with Shondor Birns. I remember that whenever we were going somewhere where we would have to leave the car, I always used to tell him never to park in a parking lot—where it was hard to see if anyone was messing with your car. "Park on the street," I said. "It's out in the open; people can see if anything funny is going on." As it turned out, he should have listened to me.

I knew Danny Greene because I would occasionally go to the old Stirling Hotel where he and his guys used to hang out. I was friends with one of his main enforcers, Eugene "the Animal" Ciasullo," who was badly injured by a bomb during those years and hospitalized for months. My own situation was that because of what I did and the reputation I had, I was a part of that world, but never at the highest levels—where the bombs were going off. I did things for lots of different people, and you need to understand what my part in it was to understand how the fact that I got shot fits in.

It begins with the numbers, which just kept getting bigger and more lucrative during these years, with the kind of results you'd expect. When people began to realize how much money was there to be made, everybody wanted to get into the act. There were lots of competing bookies, some offering better odds than others. This had always been a problem but it became especially so in these years. Also, because the volume of betting was so high, there were times when the bookies—the bosses—feared that they had taken more bets than they could pay off if too many people hit. When that situation occurred, they started what we called "laying off" the excess to people from the mob in Youngstown and Pittsburgh, who had deeper pockets. In return, the Youngstown and Pittsburgh people took a nice cut of the profits. With so many people trying to get their cut, it was a very unstable situation. In the black community, the solution to the problems being created by this out-of-control competition ended up being Shondor Birns.

Shondor Birns, a Jew whose family had come from that part of Hungary that has since become Czechoslovakia, isn't someone you'd automatically think would be the answer for the black numbers rackets. But what was needed was someone who could keep the peace, someone who could guarantee that the playing field was level, that everyone was giving the same odds. Shondor was able to do that.

There have been lots of books and articles written about Shondor Birns in the years since he was killed. But the reason he was so effective is easy to state in a few words: People who crossed him didn't live long. That's why he was able to keep the peace. He was also something of a public figure. He could regularly be seen around town at his favorite bars and restaurants. The papers said he was charming and people—politicians, the news media, people who were fascinated by the mob--were drawn to him. I would ride with him sometimes, both for company and for extra protection. Sometimes if he was taking a lot of money somewhere, I would carry it. I remember he used to have a favorite spot in the old Theatrical Grill where he would always stand and drink and if people wanted him they could find him there. I remember he used to go around a lot with a cigar in his mouth, but he never lit up. He was a character. He played the role to the hilt, and there were always plenty of people turned on by the idea of hobnobbing with someone that dangerous.

In the years just before and just after Shondor was killed, a number of factors kept increasing the tension in the city. Having been brought into the Cleveland numbers action more regularly, the mobs in Youngstown and Pittsburgh were always looking for a bigger piece of the action. A year after Shondor died, the godfather of the Cleveland Mafia died following heart surgery [44] and, as you would expect, there was competition for the top spot. Danny Greene was still around; and all those things increased the possibility of violence.

Because of my reputation as an enforcer and I think especially because I had proved to everyone that I could be discreet, I did a lot of different things for a lot of different people in those years. I continued to work as an enforcer for the big numbers bosses, but I also did some work for the Cleveland Browns. For example, there was the time Art Model was worried because he'd heard that Brian Sipe, the quarterback of the old Cardiac Kids, was messing around with a blonde he shouldn't have been. Model wanted to prevent scandal but he also wanted to get the facts straight, so through the Brown's chief of security he hired me to get some proof. We got the seat numbers for the tickets Sipe was giving to friends before a game and I checked them all out and when I found the blonde I got a picture for Model. He, of course, took it from there. It wasn't my job to know how he handled it.

I remember another job I did for the Browns. They had heard that a star player was smoking marijuana, and they wanted to know who his source was and how he was getting it. I found out what was going on from contacts I had on the street and was able to tell them where the player was getting his stash, how it went down, and from whom. I did a number of things like this, the kind of things a private detective might have done. I think people came to me because by now I had a lot of contacts, and again because they knew I could be trusted.

I was a member of the Teamsters Union for twenty years, and I sometimes did things for them that were like the things I did for the Browns: getting information, confirming suspicions, and so on. The point I want to make is that in these years I wasn't working for any one person. I was what I called "on the street." People knew who I was and that I was available.

As I said earlier, the shooter nearly got me. I was in the hospital for a month. After I came out of the operating room I was taken to the recovery room and then to a private room. I had friends who paid for the room and a private guard. They told me they didn't want whoever shot me to come back and try to finish the job.

I was in no condition to read anything at the time, but people saved the articles for me, and when I got around to them they were interesting. The stories in the *Call & Post* were more colorful than the ones in the *Plain Dealer*. For example the *Call*

& Post's reporter wrote things like,

> Long underwent surgery the day after he was shot, and though he is listed in serious condition his status is now fair, a hospital spokesman said.
>
> A building resident said "the shot had not dimmed (Long's) senses," explaining that he was told Long walked down the stairs instead of waiting for the elevator. "Hell, he could have bled to death waiting on these slow (expletive deleted) elevators," the resident added. (*Call & Post*)

The *Plain Dealer* focused more on information. For example they gave a lot of play to the fact that numbers paraphernalia were found in my apartment by the investigating officers. They quoted me as protesting that the numbers stuff didn't belong to me. I said I had confiscated it in my investigations for the city. I was closing in on the bad guys, I said, and maybe that's why I was shot.

It made a good story and I stuck to it. There was nothing anyone could prove against me and nothing they could do.

I was in the hospital for a month because they had to repair what the bullet had done to the whole left side of my face. When I was finally able to come home, the people I worked for sent me to Las Vegas for several weeks, all expenses paid. They even gave me some money to gamble with. I spent a lot of time in the casinos and by the pool just resting and getting my strength back. It also allowed for some time for things to cool off back home and gave me time to think.

By the time I came back to Cleveland, I thought I knew why I had been shot. The numbers people I worked for had raised the payoff ratio from 5 to 1 to 6 to 1. You weren't supposed to do that on your own, and I was pretty sure that killing me was supposed to have been a warning. What bothered me when I came back was that I didn't know whether this thing was over yet—whether they were still going to go after me. I wasn't going to be able to sleep easy till I had this settled, so I asked my friends to try to find out who it was that shot me, and eventually they did.

I knew him and I quickly found out what his routines were. He liked to bowl on Fridays, and I found out where he went. Then one Friday I found his car in the parking lot near the bowling alley and waited by it till he came out.

It was perfect. I saw him before he saw me, and he was alone. He came straight to the car, and when he saw me he tried to play it cool: "Hey, Diz. Haven't seen you for a while, how are you," and so on. I told him about just getting back from Vegas and that I didn't have any idea who shot me, and then I said why didn't we go for a ride. What could he say? If he acted nervous and tried to beg off, it would have been a dead giveaway. There was nothing he could do but get into the car

We drove down to the lake, to a black yacht club near Gordon Park. It was a warm night and we got out, walked over to the big rocks on the break wall, and sat down. Nobody said anything for a minute or two. Then,

"You did a cowardly thing," I said. "I know it was you."

"No. No." He said. But his eyes gave him away.

"Don't lie to me," I said. "Don't insult my intelligence. I know it was you."

He gave up. You could see it in his body language. He was afraid I was going to hurt or kill him, and he dropped down to his knees and started begging me not to hurt him. But it was over by then. I had what I wanted. He knew I knew who it was, and I was sure I wasn't going to have any more trouble from him.

I went home and slept soundly that night, and I never saw hide or hair of him again. Now that it was finally over, I could go back, I thought, to my old way of life.

It wasn't that hard to get back into the old routines. The fact was that while I had certainly been involved in the numbers rackets, I was never part of the wars going on between Shondor, Danny, the various crime families, and the government. I was a small fish surrounded by all sorts of bigger fish, and so I was able to swim away pretty easily. Because of the connections I had made over the years, I had no trouble getting my job back with the city of Cleveland. I still had my arrangement with Charley Warren, and I started keeping his cocaine for him again and getting a nice chunk of money every month for doing it. I got back into the numbers, too, but with a twist.

While I had been gone, a guy I knew named James Tate, a bookie who ran a numbers operation, had died. When I got back on the street, his wife, Lorraine, approached me and asked me to take over the operation. I agreed, but not until I was sure my back was covered. I had been around long enough and seen enough to know that if I took this on, there would be times when I would need some protection. So before I shook hands on it, I paid a visit to the people in Little Italy. The operation I was going to take over wasn't a big one, but I promised to make regular contributions if they would agree to back me, which they did. It was a good thing, too.

I hadn't been running my operation for more than a week when I had a visit from a tough guy from the black community—a competitor. He came to tell me that if I knew what was good for me and wanted to stay in business, I would have to pay him and his people off or there would be problems. I said all right and suggested that we meet in a day or so at the Majestic Hotel to work out the details.

I got us a room and set it up to look exactly like a business meeting. When we got down to business, I asked him how much he wanted. He said we'd start at a bill ($100) a week. I pretended to think about it and then said, "You know, I think I'll give you exactly what you deserve." Then I pulled out a pistol and cracked him hard on the side of the head. He was stunned and fell to the floor. While he was lying there, I put my foot on his chest and pointed the gun directly at his eyes. "Who the fuck do you think you are?" I said. "You get the fuck out of here and don't let me see you again. Ever." He was out of that room like a shot. Obviously he and his people did some checking and found out who was behind me, and I didn't have any more trouble from them.

After that, the word got around. From then on if I even heard rumors that I had a possible problem, all I had to do was take a walk up the hill to Little Italy and tell the people there that I thought I had heard there had been some kind of misunderstanding in the neighborhoods about my operation. They would say, "OK, Diz, we'll take care of it." And that would be the last I would hear of the matter. And so, things were going along pretty smoothly for me in the old grooves, and then something happened that changed everything: I met Reuben Sturman.

REUBEN STURMAN

I met Reuben Sturman [45] for the first time at the downtown YMCA, where I had begun to go regularly again. Reuben lived in Shaker Heights and was a regular at the "Y" as well, and one day in the locker room, we got to talking. He was especially interested when I told him that I had been a bodyguard for Harold Robbins. Larry Flynt [46] had just been shot (on March 6, 1978) and Reuben had obviously begun to worry about the same thing happening to him. He asked me about details—what exactly I had done for Harold Robbins, how it had worked. But he didn't go any further with it at the time. I remember I had the impression that he didn't take me seriously, maybe didn't even believe me.

A couple of weeks passed, and then I ran into Reuben again at the "Y," this time in the sauna. We started talking and he told me that he had met a friend of mine in California—Harold Robbins. (I found out later that he had been to California to take care of some problems out there in the factories that made the sex toys and paraphernalia that he sold in his stores.) He told me Harold had good things to say about me as a bodyguard. He said I was loyal and practically became part of the family. Harold told him he "couldn't find a better man," and that was enough for Reuben. He offered me the job and suggested I come to his office the next day to work out the details.

When we talked at his office, a lot of the things he said he would expect me to do were the kinds of things I had done for Harold Robbins. There were some differences, though, and some of them I had to think hard about. He told me I would have to travel with him, but I expected that. What concerned me more was that Reuben made no bones about the fact that my duties would include carrying money to the big crime families in New York and Boston. That was new for me, and I was concerned that I might be getting in over my head. But Reuben was a good salesman; the money was good, and in the end I decided to take the job. My connection with Reuben that started then would last for the next fourteen years and make some real changes in my life.

The job was in fact quite a bit different from the work I had done for Harold Robbins because from the start it involved more than just being a bodyguard for Reuben himself and his immediate family. Reuben was a different breed of cat from Harold Robbins. Although he had started small, selling comic books out of his car in the 1950s, Reuben had an empire by the time I got to know him. He had chains of stores that sold adult products and provided peep booths all over Cleveland, in major cities, and on both coasts, and he was involved to one degree or another in similar operations in a number of countries in Europe. He was at the top of his game when I went to work for him, and although some of my duties did involve going places with him for protection or as muscle, I also became a bodyguard for the operation itself.

At the time Reuben was based in Cleveland. He had a big house in Shaker Heights, at the corner of Attleboro and South Woodland. After I was working for him regularly, I had a key to the big house, and I had my own apartment. I went with Reuben when he traveled, but even if he wasn't traveling and didn't need me with him I was on call 24 hours a day. Sometimes if he thought a clerk or managers in one of his stores was skimming money, he would ask me to investigate. But mostly what I provided was protection for the stores.

All of Reuben's Cleveland store managers had my phone number. I might be at home in my apartment at night, maybe even asleep, but when there was trouble I was the one they would call. I remember there were a lot of stores out on Brook Park Road. They were open all night, and so there was always the possibility of trouble that there is in any all-night operation where the clientele isn't exactly high society. Trouble was almost bound to happen occasionally, and no matter what time it was, when the phone rang I would get dressed, put on my shoulder holster, get in my car, and drive on out.

Surprisingly often the people causing the trouble were still there by the time I arrived. Usually it was drunks, or maybe punks looking for trouble. They were never hard to spot, but I would always go to the clerk and ask him who the leader was or seemed to be. When he told me, that's the one I went after.

Because of my experience as muscle in the numbers rackets for all those years, I had a lot of practice in situations like this, and I knew what worked. I would get out my pistol and whack the leader on the side of the head before he knew what was happening. That always got everyone's attention, especially if there was a little blood. I always carried my big pistol on these jobs, the .44 magnum. When people saw it, it was sometimes enough to calm things down by itself. I would look right at the troublemakers and ask them what the hell was going on. What did they think they were doing? By the time they had seen me knock their friend down and noticed the gun, most times nobody had anything to say. So I would tell them to get the fuck out and that if I ever heard about them coming back I would kill them. Usually that would solve the problem, at least for a while. Sometimes, however, things got more serious.

One day Reuben called me in to tell me about a problem he was having at one of his adult products stores in Carson City, California. The people causing the trouble weren't just punks or night owls and drunks. It was a couple of small time gangsters who had no idea that this was one of Reuben's stores. They thought they were big time and were trying to shake the clerk down for protection. Apparently they had already gotten rough and were making some pretty serious threats if the clerk wouldn't pay up. Reuben was already paying fairly big money to the crime families in Boston and New York so that he could operate freely in those states. He couldn't afford to have punks trying to freelance like these guys in California, so he told me he wanted me to fly out there and take care of it. I was on a plane later that night.

When I got to Carson City and found the store, the clerk told me when the toughs had said they were coming for their money. That's when I knew these guys weren't pros. If they had been, they never would have told the clerk exactly when they were coming. Since they had, it was easy for me to be there to greet them. I had my .44 magnum, and I was ready. On the day they were supposed to show, I was sitting in a chair at the back of the store waiting for them. When they came in the door I knew they were the ones because the clerk got really nervous. "There" he whispered, "Those are the guys that want the money."

At about that minute they noticed me, and one of them thought he was tough and asked me what I was doing there.

I said, "Oh, nothing" and started to get up from the chair.

By the time I was on my feet, the pistol was out, and the two of them couldn't take their eyes off it. I said, "Let's go into the back room," and I walked them in ahead of me.

No more tough guy from them now. They were scared. The clerk came in, and I asked him to shut the door. Then I asked him, "Which one is the one that hit you?" He pointed, and I told the guy he pointed at to step toward me. When he was close enough I pistol whipped him and then told him to go stand by the desk facing the wall. Then I asked the clerk, "Which *hand* did he hit you with?" He pointed again--the right hand—and I told the guy, who was still facing the wall, to reach back and put his right hand on the desk. When he did, I smashed it up pretty badly with the big gun.

By this time there was blood all over the place, and these guys were so terrified they were shivering. I had their full attention now, and I said, "You are way out of your league, and I hope you know it." I took their wallets and made a point of letting them see that I was writing down their addresses from their driver's licenses. "Now I know where you live," I said. "If I hear about anything happening to this store or the people who work here, if there is even a pane of glass broken and I find out about it, I'm going to come back. Next time I won't be waiting in plain sight in this store. You won't see me coming, and you won't even know what hit you."

After that, I threw them out, and they took off running. I was on a plane back to Cleveland the next day fairly certain that we wouldn't hear anything more from them. They were just small time hoods who had no idea what they were getting themselves into.

I did some other kinds of work for Reuben that involved violence or the threat of it. By the time I knew him he had a team of well-paid, high-powered lawyers, but there were always situations he would get into where it wasn't a lawyer that he needed. It was a lot simpler just to send me. I remember once there was a guy in Detroit who opened up an adult store on his own and owed Reuben some money. Reuben said why didn't I go up to Detroit and straighten it out. The minute I walked into the store the guy took one look at me and said, "Diz, I know what you're here for. Believe me, I'm going to take care of this." We locked eyes and held for a second. Then I said, "I know you will" and left. I'm pretty good at sizing up people. When I got back I told Reuben it would be all right, and it was.

There were other times when I had to be more aggressive. Reuben wasn't a violent man himself, but when he needed it, I was his violence, and after I'd worked for him for a few years people understood that. In fact, Reuben and I sometimes made a pretty good team. For example, there was an incident with a couple of guys from Chicago. The way I heard it was that when Reuben had gone to Chicago to collect some money from them he hit on one of their daughters. The father was angry and threatened Reuben. When Reuben heard about the threats, he called a meeting with them in Cleveland, and when they arrived, I was at the meeting. They were upset the minute they saw me. "What's he doing here?" they asked.

Reuben said, "Diz is here because you threatened me."

They started looking around and tried to deny it, but Reuben wasn't buying it. Then I took over.

"Let me explain something," I said. "You guys live in Chicago and probably don't take me seriously, but I want you to know something. I want you to know that if anything should happen to Reuben, even if it's an accident, even if he chokes on a chicken bone, anything at all—I'll come to Chicago. I know people there, and I'll have plenty of help if I need it. I'll find you, and I'll kill you and your daughters and your mothers, and everyone in your family."

You could have heard a pin drop.

They were seriously spooked and upset at this point, full of apology: "He doesn't have to talk that way to us. It's just a big misunderstanding."

Reuben just looked at them as if to say it was out of his control. "Hey, that's just Diz," he said.

Then I said, "I know you boys will do the right thing. If I thought you weren't going to take this warning seriously, I'd kill you right now, right here in this room," and I let them see the gun and shoulder holster. They apologized all the way out the door.

Reuben and I did that kind of thing a number of times. He heard later, through the grapevine, that the Chicago guys went home and told people that "that black sonofabitch Reuben's got working for him is crazy." We didn't do anything to discourage people from thinking that. In fact we sometimes played the kind of game that you read that President Nixon and his Secretary of State, Henry Kissinger, used to do. Nixon would foam at the mouth and talk about bombing so and so back to the Stone Age, and then Kissinger would take the listeners aside than tell them that he hoped they wouldn't make trouble because he didn't know if he could control that guy. Reuben and I often worked something close to that. I was fearless in those days; I wasn't afraid of anyone or anything. When I was shot, it was a very close call. I looked death in the eye and survived, and for the next few years I was up for anything. I felt as strong and sure of myself as I ever have in my life.

I remember another incident, this one in Boston. Reuben had a deal with the local crime family there, and he thought it was solid. But all of a sudden they were talking like they wanted a bigger cut. Reuben couldn't afford to have that kind of thing happen. If the people he dealt with started thinking he could be pushed around that easily, there was never going to be an end to it. So he agreed to fly to Boston for a meeting, but he sent me on ahead of him.

I met him at Logan airport and took him to the hotel, where

I had booked adjoining rooms for us. Reuben called the guys and gave them the room number, and then we made a plan. The walls between the two rooms were thin enough that I could hear what was going on in Reuben's room pretty clearly, so we agreed on a code word. If I heard Reuben say, "OK, OK, I'll take care of it," that would be the signal for me to come in and do my thing. I of course heard when the two guys came in, and it wasn't long before Reuben gave the signal.

It was perfect. They didn't know what was going on when I walked in and sat down.

"I thought this was a private meeting," they said, clearly uneasy.

Reuben just played it straight. He didn't bat an eye. He said, "This is Diz Long. He takes care of security for my company. You can speak freely in front of him."

They didn't say a word, so Reuben went on.

"Diz," he said calmly, "these guys have brought me a problem."

"How?" I said. "What kind of problem?"

It was just Reuben and me now.

"We are having a disagreement about finances," Reuben said.

At that point I turned in my chair, looked squarely at the two of them, and said, "I take care of problems for Reuben Sturman. If he has a problem, then it's my problem, too. I'm not from Boston, but I have a lot of friends here, and so maybe what we need to do is settle things right now."

They backed down.

"There's been a misunderstanding," they said.

They made a bunch of small talk, kept saying there was no problem, and eased their way out the door. Reuben and I flew back to Cleveland, and the next day Reuben told me that he'd gotten a call from Boston, and in the end his protection payment was a lot less than those guys had been asking. He was laughing. The people who called were the bosses, not the lower level types who had come to his room for the meeting. He told me the bosses said, "We heard about that big black guy. We thought it was going to be a private meeting. You didn't have to do something like that." Reuben just smiled. He was pretty shrewd. He was paying the families in Boston a lot of money as it was. He gambled that they wouldn't want to risk rocking that boat with some kind of violence that would end up being public and might bring the heat down on them. And he was right.

Another thing I did fairly regularly was carry money for him, usually payoff money to the people in Boston, New York, or sometimes L.A. By the time I started working for him, Reuben was a marked man who the government and both local and federal law enforcement agencies had been trying to nail, unsuccessfully, for years. Although he had been the subject of numerous attempted arrests for obscenity and pornography, he was probably most vulnerable to the IRS, to the tax laws. He and his team of lawyers spent a great deal of time covering his financial tracks on paper, and when he needed to make big payments, especially protection payments, he paid in cash and had people carry it for him. I was one of those people.

The law enforcement people used profiling techniques in those days, too, and if I had tried carrying large sums of money looking like some kind of street black, they would have been on me like a coat of paint. But I didn't look like that. I was always dressed in expensive, conservative suits. I usually carried a flashy briefcase that had no money in it. They could search it all they wanted. I carried the money in midsized bills taped or glued lightly up and down both legs and sometimes around my body as well. When I got to New York or Boston, I would come off the airplane, go into a restroom, shut myself into a stall, unstick all the bills, put them all in the briefcase, spruce myself back up and then make my delivery. Even though I was black, I never set off any alarm bells and was never stopped. The only time I was ever stopped was once when I was carrying quite a bit of money of my own for an investment I wanted to get in on. I have no idea what tipped them off on that one, but it was the only time.

What I've just described was pretty much my routine in the early years with Reuben. It changed when he got married again, which happened all of a sudden. Reuben was based in Cleveland and lived in Shaker Heights when I first started to work for him. But he did a lot of traveling and had a lot of business in California, and one day I remember he was all excited. He told me he had met a beautiful woman in L.A., and he looked at me and said, "Diz, we are going to take a trip to California." It was the start of a whole new chapter in Reuben's life and therefore in mine.

Reuben had a first wife and grown children, but when I met him he was divorced and in mid-life. He had more money than he knew what to do with, he liked young girls, and it turned out that he wanted a trophy wife. Naomi Del Gado was a drop dead gorgeous coed at UCLA with hopes for an acting or singing career and a desire to meet a rich man to help her on her way. That summer she and Reuben were like the Titanic and the iceberg: they were heading straight for a collision with one another.

The collision, when it came, was pretty impressive. Naomi blew Reuben away with her dazzling beauty, and Reuben's money talked. Did it ever. Naomi liked Reuben, and because she wanted the kind of life she could live as his wife she quit school to marry him. For a while after they were married, Reuben and Naomi had a condo, and I had a small apartment just off Sunset Boulevard about a block from the Playboy Club. But they didn't stay there long because Naomi wanted a mansion. In those early days, she got what she wanted, and I was part of the process.

Naomi knew exactly what she was looking for, and she didn't want to settle for anything less. I remember driving around with her and Reuben for weeks looking at beautiful home after beautiful home. For the longest time there was always something missing. This one didn't have the kind of pool she wanted. It would be hard to add the kind of gym and sauna that she wanted to that one. Another one maybe didn't have the perfect view. She finally settled on a place that cost Reuben a small fortune, but he didn't even bat an eye. Reuben was enormously wealthy in those years, and for him to have money was to spend it.

As I've said, I had a taste of the world of big money when I was a body guard for Harold Robbins. But working for Reuben was being in another world altogether. I never saw anyone who was a free or as casual with huge sums of money. Besides the mansion in Shaker Heights, Reuben had a house in California, an apartment in New York. When he went to Europe he stayed in the best luxury hotels. Everything he did had to be just so. I remember on one of our first trips across the country, we were getting ready to check our bags, Reuben took a look at my luggage and said, "Hey, Diz, we can't travel with that junk." When we got to Los Angeles, he took me to Luis Vuitton and bought me a complete set of top-of-the-line luggage--including a briefcase--all of which cost in the neighborhood of twenty thousand dollars.

When we traveled between houses we didn't bring very

many clothes. If we needed anything we bought it there, and we usually left it behind—in New York or wherever we had been. When we came back, our clothes were always cleaned and pressed and waiting for us, and if we needed anything, Reuben bought it. One time in California when he thought I needed more clothes, Reuben took me to Rodeo Drive and got me three new suits in the $500 to $800 range, and a stack of dress shirts that were $200 apiece. Among the various houses I had three Rolls Royces at my disposal when I needed to take Reuben or Naomi anywhere.

He did the same kinds of things when we went to Europe. After the success of the porn film *Deep Throat* in 1972, the X-rated movie business had expanded far beyond the peep show, and Reuben was, of course, in the vanguard. He often went to the Cannes Film Festival, where he was a sort of X-rated celebrity. On our first trip to Cannes, we had a suite in a four-star hotel, where Reuben threw outrageously expensive parties for the Hollywood elite and the big money people in the film industry. Partly this was just to thumb his nose at the U.S. government, which was still trying unsuccessfully to prosecute him for violations of the obscenity laws. Partly it was to keep old contacts and make new ones in the Hollywood film industry, partly it was to try to bring investors on board, and partly it was just because Reuben was Reuben, and everything he did was on a huge scale. On another trip to the Film Festival a four star hotel wasn't good enough for him, so he rented a yacht where his whole party stayed and took meals. It came with a complete crew and an extra chef to make snacks for people at off hours.

On these trips, of course there were movie stars and celebrities everywhere you looked. And sometimes Reuben would look at me and say, "You can take the rest of the day off, Diz," and I would just hang around the hotel or the beach and watch people. One afternoon when I was people watching, I saw a crowd gathering on the beach. When I walked closer to get a look, I saw it was Pablo Picasso and his new wife. (I would later meet Picasso with Reuben and actually shake his hand.) That kind of thing happened all the time over there, and I appreciated the occasional time on my own that Reuben gave me. There were blacks there to be sure, but the only ones who weren't servants of some kind were some wealthy African blacks. In those years I was usually the only American black man in sight who wasn't a servant.

It was in those years that Reuben started giving me some special assignments that were a lot more than just muscle. Occasionally he would find himself in a situation where what he really needed was one of his top business people or one of his best lawyers, but the people involved were tough customers. I remember on one of our trips to Cannes, Reuben called me in for a meeting. He had recently sold a part of his huge porn empire to a guy in Nevada. The deal was that Reuben got $2 million up front and then a percentage of the business after that. The problem was that the deal had been made before Reuben left for Cannes and the guy was supposed to make the payments while Reuben was away, but it wasn't happening. What was different about this assignment for me was that Reuben wasn't just telling me to go lean on the guy. He was asking me to go back to the states and negotiate for him. I was a black man, and Reuben was trusting me to negotiate for him with a rich white man. He had a situation and he was telling *me* to handle it.

The first thing I did was talk the situation over with Reuben's accountant. I wanted to know the facts about the money and the understanding, and I wanted his advice. This guy I was going to see was apparently a genuinely tough customer, and some of his people had even threatened Reuben. Reuben didn't need the money right away, but he couldn't afford to have people welshing on him or disrespecting him, so the accountant suggested that I talk to the guy and offer him a deal. "He's got to pay something," he said. That made sense to me and so by the end of the day I was on a plane for the states.

When I met with the guy, I didn't come on as a thug. I was dressed to the nines. I was a partner representing Reuben and that's how he was expecting me. When we were done with small talk and got down to business, I reminded him that he had signed a contract. "We'll try to figure out a way to help you out if you need it, but you have to pay something." He didn't say anything for a minute and so I said, "You need to know that if you don't pay, you've got a problem." (This conversation, as polite as it was, was not chitchat over tea. It was serious business, and he needed to know it.)

This had not promised to be an easy negotiation and it wasn't. But the bottom line was that when it was over, he paid up. And it was more than that. Before we were finished I told him that it had gotten back to us that one of his people had made some threats against Reuben. I told him that I wanted that person to call Reuben and apologize, and he did. By the time I got back to Reuben, I had done everything he asked, and I was grateful to him for trusting me with the assignment. It proved that he could trust me with jobs or problems that required thinking and negotiation, and from then on he did.

I remember another assignment that was fairly dramatic. It was in the mid to late 1980s when the FBI and the IRS were closing in on Reuben and when some of his most loyal people were beginning to turn on him. There was a man named Chuck Higgins, one of Reuben's accountants, who was telling stories to the FBI about Reuben's connections with organized crime.

(He told the press that I was a hit man for mafia, which was not true. I wasn't a hit man, and I worked for Reuben, not the mafia.) Higgins sang like a canary. He told the FBI where they could find corporate documents damaging to Reuben, and besides that he was stealing from Reuben, putting money from one of Reuben's businesses into his own account. Reuben wanted this guy found and neutralized, and he wanted his money back; but before he could get him, Higgins disappeared. He owned two ranches and a string of thoroughbred horses and one day he just didn't come to work. His wife didn't know where he was. Nobody did for a while.

Finding him was some of the best detective work I ever did. He went deep into hiding, but I finally found out where he was from a contact I had at the bank where he kept his money. When he started using a bank account in his name, I had him. He was hiding out in Arizona, and he almost had a heart attack when he saw me waiting for him at his hotel. I took him upstairs and kept him in his hotel room. He kept pleading, "Diz, please don't kill me. Please." But I wasn't going to kill him. When I had him, I called Reuben, and he told me to sit tight, he would have two lawyers out there as fast as he could. We waited, the lawyers were there the next day, and they hammered out an agreement that got Reuben what he wanted including the guy signing over his ranch and string of horses to Reuben. This wasn't just muscle work. I had to use my head, and again Reuben trusted me to get the job done.

I wouldn't be giving you an accurate picture of my years with Reuben if I didn't talk about my friendship with Naomi Del Gado. Naomi and I hit it off right away, and as I think about it now, it wasn't surprising. She was a young girl—not finished with college--when Reuben swept her up into his world of wealth and celebrity. She was a California girl, and at first he brought her to Cleveland, and she didn't like it at all. There were so many ways in which she didn't fit in. She was young, healthy, beautiful, and California all the way—miniskirts and thigh high boots. She would walk down a Cleveland street and nearly cause traffic accidents. Cars would screech to a stop and guys would whistle. She once asked me, "What are they looking at?" and I said, "They're looking at you!" It wasn't the kind of attention she wanted—or needed. Reuben's family wasn't welcoming, either. (Reuben's mother said simply, "I don't like her. What does he want with her?") She had, that is, a hard time adjusting, and although Reuben showered her with attention when he was around, he wasn't always around. When he wasn't, it was my job to look out for her, and so we got thrown together a lot.

I remember exactly when I really started liking her and getting on with her. Reuben had some business to take care of, and we were all at one of his warehouses in Cleveland. Around noon or one somebody had sent out to a local deli for lunch. It wasn't awful, but it was just neighborhood food. Naomi was bored anyway, and when someone handed her a sandwich she opened the wrapper, took one look at it at said, "What the hell is this shit? I don't eat shit like this." Then she handed it to me and said, "*You* take it." It was such a surprise to hear her talk like that, it just cracked me up. I almost fell off my chair laughing, and then she started laughing, too. When I stopped laughing for a minute, I said, "Why are you giving that shit to me? I don't want that shit either." We were both laughing then. I gave Reuben a look and he nodded, and I took her to Jim's Steak House for lunch instead. We both talked the whole way there, first about what had just happened and then about her experiences in Cleveland so far. Jim's was a pretty nice place in those days. Naomi had nothing bad to say about it. We started talking a little bit about ourselves during the meal, about what it was like living in Reuben's world. By the time we had finished our lunch we were on our way to establishing a friendship that would last till the end of Reuben's days.

As I look back, it's easy to see why Naomi and I became close. In general, but especially when we were living in Cleveland, it was natural that Naomi and I would be friends. California was a world at least she knew, but in Cleveland she was alone. Reuben's family and grown children from his other marriage didn't like or approve of her, and it wasn't like they ever tried to conceal their feelings. We of course spent time together because I looked after her when Reuben wasn't around. We therefore were together a lot and quickly found that we shared a sense of humor. A lot of the time we felt like co-conspirators. When Reuben had people over and they were all talking business, Naomi and I used to get a kick out of talking over or around people. In a few years, especially after the baby came, Erica, we had shared enough experiences to be like old friends. By the end, she was almost like a sister. Nothing lasts forever, though. Those years when Reuben was flying high were good years for me. I sometimes thought I had it all. But eventually the government caught up with Reuben Sturman, and things started coming apart.

THE END OF THE RIDE

The end didn't come quickly for Reuben; he had an amazing run. However, slowly but surely the net began to close around him, and after a certain point it began to close faster and faster.

The government had tried unsuccessfully to get him on obscenity and pornography charges in 1964 and 1976. It was that period just after all the free love, "turn on and drop out" stuff of the late sixties, when the Reagan administration made a major and very public attempt to define pornography legally ("I know what it is when I see it." ". . .without any redeeming social value," etc.) They worked at it hard but in the early days they failed to nail Reuben every time they tried. They tried again in 1980, with the same results. In those years Reuben was identified by the Justice Department as the No. 1 distributor of hard core pornography. But they still couldn't get him.

In his way, I think Reuben was a genius. It's just that he was a genius at a certain kind of crime. A lot has already been written about the pursuit and eventual conviction. I will only talk briefly about the major events here, and concentrate instead on how I saw things from my point of view, most of the time behind the scenes.

I don't know all the things that were or had been going on in the Justice Department and the FBI during those years. But in my gut, I think I know when the beginning of the process that put Reuben in jail started. He used to throw huge parties every year at the Statler, a big downtown hotel in Cleveland. He invited friends, managers, celebrities, and big time porn dealers from around the country and around the world. In some ways it was like any big corporate party designed to celebrate the successes of the past year. In this case, however, the product was pornography of all kinds, and many of the biggest successes were examples of how Reuben and his people got away with things.

I never judged Reuben by what he did. He paid me very well and treated me like a friend. For most of my time with him I was fiercely loyal. But this night, I thought he made a mistake that was going to cost him. He had had a huge year financially. He had beaten the government's best lawyers again and again. Anybody on the streets knows that unless you can eliminate your enemies for good, you don't brag about it too much when you've won big because you don't want to give them incentive to come back at you. You have them down, you don't want to wake them up. Reuben didn't think about this that night. He was riding high and he bragged about everything he'd done, and he did it publicly. He gave the government the finger, almost laughed in their faces. I don't know if he intended it to come across that way or not, but that was the way I saw it. I knew it would get back to the FBI and the Justice Department. I knew it was going to cause him big trouble, and it did.

Again, I don't know details, but a whole host of legal agencies was after him after that, and eventually they caught up with him. In 1985 he was indicted by a grand jury in Chicago for conspiracy to defraud the government. In 1987 the Racketeer Influenced and Corrupt Organizations Act (RICO) was broadened to include obscenity violations. This made things hotter for Reuben because the government was having increasing success tying him to the big crime families in New York.

The net was beginning to close. As clever—even brilliant—as Reuben had always been about concealing the money trail, in 1989 he was convicted of tax evasion. After a prolonged period of appeal (and another indictment on obscenity charges that was declared a mistrial in 1991) in June of 1992 Reuben was remanded to a minimum-security prison in Boron, California, to serve a four-year term. In December of that year, he escaped and successfully hid in a rented apartment in Anaheim, California, living under the name of Abe Levine. That didn't last long, and when they caught him he was sent to a maximum-security prison in Lexington, Kentucky, where he died alone in the prison hospital on October 27, 1997.

Watching more or less from the sidelines was sometimes painful—and although it didn't really surprise me, it showed me a lot about human nature. The government had been trying to "turn" Reuben's top people, people with inside information, against him for years but they hadn't gotten anywhere. Reuben's people were extremely loyal to him, partly because he treated them well, and partly, I suppose, because it was clear how he was likely to treat people who tried to go against him. For a long time he was a rising tide that lifted everybody's boat. But by the mid-1980s Reuben appeared to be losing the battle, and when it looked more and more like he was going to go down, some of his top people began to turn on him while they could still cut a deal. Reuben had always been pretty cocky and never more so than when the government was trying to hit him with everything they had. He had a winner's confidence. But in these last years I saw him get desperate for the first time.

The most striking episode was the juror bribery thing. It's been written about quite a bit. The basics are that, as some of the newspapers reported it, Naomi Del Gado tried to seduce a juror, the idea being to get one of the jurors on our side (or get something to blackmail him with) and get a mistrial. I saw the whole thing go down from behind the scenes, and because Naomi and I had become such good friends, it was painful to watch it all play out the way it did.

It was, of course, Reuben who got the idea. He was watching the members of the jury carefully, and he saw that one of the younger men seemed attracted to Naomi, who always sat behind Reuben in the courtroom dressed to the nines. Reuben wasn't as confident that he could win his case as he had been in the past, and so he hatched this scheme to have Naomi actively try to attract this juror and if possible seduce him. The problem was that Naomi didn't want any part of it. That was the part that was painful for me. I was there, in the room, when Reuben started telling Naomi what he wanted her to do. I was watching her, and she was shocked. She just kept saying, "No. No. No." Reuben just kept telling her that she had to do it, that it was the only way out. That's when I began to realize how serious Reuben thought his situation was.

Reuben finally convinced Naomi that she had to do it, but it didn't work out the way Reuben wanted and in fact just made things worse. It started off well enough, though. I don't know how but somehow Reuben got a note to the juror from Naomi. The note said that she wanted to meet him, and he swallowed the bait. Of course it all had to be "hush hush." The way we did it was that I arranged to meet him in the parking lot at Winton Place on the Gold Coast along the lakeshore on Cleveland's west side. I had an apartment there, and they met in my apartment for a while and then had dinner at Pier W, a nice seafood restaurant that is part of Winton Place. After dinner I drove him back to his home in North Olmsted. Naomi went along, and occasionally, when I looked in the rearview mirror I saw them kissing in the back seat. Whenever I saw them, all I could think of was Naomi saying "No. No. No."

After we dropped the juror off, I drove Naomi back to Reuben's Attleboro Rd. home in Shaker Heights, and for a while, it looked like Reuben's plan might actually work. But the fact was that his luck had finally begun to run out. The government found out about it, and suddenly they were threatening to prosecute Naomi for jury tampering. However, by this time the FBI was looking for far bigger fish than Naomi Del Gado. Besides the attempted jury tampering, there were also rumors of a possible attempt to bribe the judge.

Sanford "Sandy" Atkins was one of Reuben's many lawyers, and he was at the time thinking of running for a judgeship. He happened to be friends with Judge White, who was the judge in Reuben's case. They went on skiing vacations at the same place and had become friends, and on the basis of inside information Atkins apparently thought he had, he told Reuben that he thought Judge White could be bought. He said that he thought for a bribe of half a million dollars, he [Reuben] could get the result he wanted out of this trial. Reuben was willing to try anything, and so he agreed. It was at this point that I began to realize how complicated Reuben's situation was and in how many ways the government was moving against him.

Reuben was willing to try the bribe, but first he had to get the money, which was not easy for him because he wasn't supposed to have that kind of money (according to the income tax information he was routinely sending the IRS) and because much of what he had was "on paper" and carefully hidden away in accounts all over the world. What very few people knew, even some fairly high up in Reuben's organization, was that he had a safe deposit box in Detroit where he always kept a considerable amount of emergency cash. I had a key, and Reuben told me everything I would need to know to use it. He said that nobody else knew about the deposit box, obviously not the government but also his own people. He knew that by telling me this, he was trusting me with both a considerable amount of his money and possibly his freedom. That's the way our relationship was. And so off I went, quietly, to Detroit, and came back with the cash in unsequenced $100 bills. We got the money to Sandy Atkins, and then things started to unravel big time.

As I look back, the way things really were at that time seems almost funny. We were being so secret. We were being so careful not to let anybody know what we were doing. But it turned out just about everyone immediately concerned knew everything. Everyone was spying on everyone. No sooner had we gotten the bribe money to Sandy Atkins than some of our sources told us that there was no point to trying. Judge White wasn't going to accept a bribe. I had another source (a guy who I used to know in Cleveland but who now worked in Washington, D.C.) who let me know that we had better not depend on Atkins because the government might be about to investigate him! And while we were trying to decide what to make of this information, the FBI called Naomi to their office downtown. They told her they knew all about the attempted jury tampering and about the bribe, and they made her an offer: if she would wear a wire and get something that would incriminate Sandy Atkins, they wouldn't prosecute her for the attempted jury tampering.

Naomi was beside herself. She had never been someone you would mistake for Mary Poppins, but jury tampering and wearing a wire for the FBI were not things that she had ever imagined doing. We went back to Shaker Heights and she talked it over with Reuben. He was, at times, an extremely cold, calculating man, and he looked at the situation in purely practical terms. He saw it as a way for her to beat the jury tampering rap, and he told her to do it. The way he put it was, "They want eagles, not sparrows." What he meant, of course, was that the government wasn't interested in small fish like Naomi. They wanted bigger fish like Atkins, people who, if they got something on them, could maybe be induced to give up whales like Reuben in order to save themselves. It went the same way as the wire thing. Naomi protested for a while, Reuben kept at it, and in the end, Naomi agreed.

It was crazy. Sandy Atkins' office in downtown Cleveland was right across the street from the offices of the FBI. On the day when it was supposed to go down, I was still body guarding Naomi, and we went to the FBI together. It was just like you see in the movies. They got a wire taped under her clothes and then coached her about what she was supposed to say. Basically what she was supposed to do was get some kind of proof that Atkins had the half million for the bribe. (My going along was for cover. Sandy would know that I was supposed to be body guarding Naomi and would probably have been suspicious if I hadn't been with her.) When we were ready—or as ready as we were going to be--we went downstairs and over to Atkins' office, which was right across the street.

I was with Naomi in Sandy Atkins' private office when she tried to get him to talk. She had decided to tell him that she was in serious debt and Reuben didn't know about it. She wanted Sandy to bail her out without Reuben knowing about it—at least for the moment, when he was so concerned about how the trial was going. I have to say that she gave it her best shot. She was very convincing when she told Sandy how much trouble she was in, how badly she needed the money, how hard things would be for her if she had to tell Reuben about it now. Sandy asked her if $50,000 would do the trick, and that's when it started to go bad.

I think Naomi was thrown for a minute. She needed to get an offer (or admission) of a lot more than $50,000. She hesitated for a minute and then said that $50,000 would help but only a little. She *really* needed a lot more than that. I was watching Atkins' face, and in that second, I could see that he sensed that something was wrong. The color drained from his face, and his tone got a little more formal. From then on whatever Naomi said, he just kept saying that $50,000 was all he could do.

As Naomi and I were leaving the office he asked me if I had a minute to spare. It was just him and me in his office. He shut the door and sat down heavily, and said, "Diz, I think she was wearing a wire." Of course I lied. I said no way. I had been with her all morning, stuff like that. He didn't argue with me, but he was no fool, and I knew that he knew. I didn't know how bad things had become, though, till I went back later to see Sandy about the money for the bribe.

Everyone in Reuben's organization was realizing now that it was time to cut losses. When it was clear that the bribe wasn't going to happen, I went back to Sandy Atkins (this is after the meeting with Naomi) and told him we needed the money back. For obvious reasons, he didn't have it all lying around, but I was surprised when he started stalling. Nobody that high in Reuben's organization would have tried to pull something like that when Reuben was riding high. I told him, "Look. You can keep $100,000 for yourself, but we've got to have the money back." He said to give him a month or so. The way things were at the moment, the FBI watching everyone so closely, I said I could understand and live with that. But when I came back in a month's time he put me off again, which was a big mistake. Not long afterwards the FBI pulled me in. They said that if they wanted to they could connect me with the bribe and cause me a lot of trouble. But, they said, they weren't interested in me. It was Atkins they wanted and they asked me to testify against him. The way things were, I said I would testify against Sandy "like yesterday!" And I did.

Since the FBI were so on top of the bribe attempt that never actually happened, I started to get a little worried about Judge White, who in spite of his name was a black judge who I had a lot of respect for. I had no idea how far the bribe business had gone before it was called off, and I didn't want Judge White to get pulled into it because I thought he was basically a good man. I didn't want to risk causing any more trouble by talking to Judge White directly, so I went to see the Reverend Otis Moss at his church in Cleveland. I was sure I could trust him, so I told him what was going on, about my fears for Judge White, and especially about rumors I had heard about the FBI maybe having a search warrant for Judge White's office. I didn't want him to be blindsided. Reverend Moss said he would take care of it and a few days later there was a message on my answering machine from Judge White. It was brief: All he said was, "Thank you, Diz, I am aware of this."

That's how crazy it was in those last years. Everyone spying on everyone, nobody trusting anybody. All of us waiting for the axe to fall. Of course under these circumstances, the defections continued in Reuben's organization. The one that got to me the most was Braverman.

From early on, Ron Braverman had been Reuben Sturman's fair-haired boy. He rose quickly in the ranks of the people Reuben trusted most, and a lot of people thought Reuben favored Braverman over his own son. Over the years, Reuben trusted Ron with more and more of the business, putting a lot of it in Braverman's name (to avoid paying taxes on the profits himself). Eventually he put the Doc Johnson Company in Braverman's name. (Doc Johnson was the trade name for most of the adult products Reuben sold and the source of a huge amount of money each year.) As it got nearer to the end for Reuben and he needed more and more money for court costs, he went to Braverman and told him he needed the Doc Johnson Company—and the revenue it produced—in his own name now. Braverman wouldn't do it. He told Reuben, "It's not your company, it's mine." I was there when it happened, and I looked at Reuben, waiting for him to cut the crap and put Braverman in his place. But Reuben said nothing, and we left soon after that.

I was stunned by Reuben's response and angry on his behalf. Braverman and I had not gotten along since an incident that had happened not long after Reuben married Naomi. Braverman learned that Naomi was sometimes doing cocaine, and he got the word to Reuben anonymously. I was the one who told Reuben that it was Braverman who ratted Naomi out, and when Braverman found out that I had outed him, he had it in for me from then on. The feeling was mutual, and I was furious now about the way he had seemed to defy Reuben, almost literally blow him off. I kept waiting for Reuben to say something, but he didn't. Finally, I said, "What do you think we ought to do about Braverman?" I was muscle for Reuben, and, honestly, at that point I would have done anything he told me to do. I was trying to guide him to give me my orders. I waited. He didn't say anything right away, and then finally all he said was, "I'll take care of it." The way he said it, I knew the matter was closed. There was nothing more I could do.

The end was near at that point. It wasn't long before Reuben was convicted. He managed to stay out of prison for a couple of years during the appeal process, but when it was over he was sent to the minimum-security prison. As I look back on it, his brief escape was a sad little thing. Reuben Sturman, who gave lavish parties at the Cannes Film Festival, hiding out under an assumed name. Naomi and I knew where he was, and we used to take the baby and visit him. Naomi paid for everything in cash, sometimes big bills, and I've always suspected that that was how the government figured out where he was. It was over. Reuben died in prison, and eventually after he died, Naomi married Ron Braverman. As for me, after a pretty amazing run of fourteen years, I was on my own again.

TRYING TO RECONNECT

Things didn't come to an end all at once. When Reuben was in the minimum-security prison, I was still working for him just like I always had. I was still a bodyguard for Naomi and the baby. However, when he was sent to the maximum security prison, we all knew that at his age, it was over, and the people who were now managing what was left of his business empire started going off on their own. I was not one of them, and I have to say it sometimes made me angry.

The way Reuben worked things was always to put his various operations in other people's names. They of course paid him huge percentages of the profits under the table, but as far as the IRS knew, none of the money went to Reuben. The nominal owners of the businesses also made big profits, which they kept. This system was one of the reasons the government had such a hard time getting the goods on Reuben, and while the money was rolling in, it was a win-win operation for everyone concerned—except the government. When Reuben went to prison, the smaller fish running the individual stores and operations still had them, and they continued to be good moneymakers.

Over the years I had repeatedly asked Reuben if I could have one of these operations for myself, but he would never agree to it. I talked with Naomi about it once, and she said, "He'll never let you go off on your own, Diz. You are his protection. He depends on you too much." I was, of course, flattered and had always appreciated Reuben's confidence in me. He told me things that could have put him away for good if I had ever wanted to rat him out or sell the information. But I knew I had Reuben's complete trust, and he knew he had my complete loyalty. You can't live on loyalty, though. After Reuben went to prison Naomi talked him into approving a few months' severance for me, but that was all.

Friends had warned me, suggesting that if Reuben trusted me so much, why wasn't he paying me top dollar? I never let it get under my skin. While I was with Reuben, I was living a life that most people can only dream about. Maybe I could have asked for more, but I was living better than I had ever imagined I would. However, when it was over, it was over. If anyone was in charge of Reuben's empire, it was Braverman, and he wouldn't give me the time of day. It was 1993. I was sixty-eight years old, and I needed some security. So I went to see what I could find for myself in Cleveland, in the places where I had the most possibilities and contacts before I started working for Reuben.

It wasn't easy, and I didn't expect that it would be. Fourteen years is a long time to be out of the streets and neighborhoods. Any possibility of getting back into the black numbers game was obviously gone. All the people in what used to be my organization had long since moved on. Other people were in charge now. You had to know a lot of people to make it work, and I had been away too long.

There was a time—especially when I worked for Carl Stokes—when I had a lot of connections in the city government. When Carl was the mayor, I could always count on him to find a place for me. But Carl had left the mayor's office over twenty years before (1971). Mike White was the mayor now and although

George Forbes had stopped being City Council president a few years back, he still had a lot of power and influence, and I wasn't tight with either White or Forbes the way I had been with Carl. They knew who I was, but it wasn't the same. Not by a long shot.

I tried Lou Stokes because I knew him much better than I knew White or Forbes. I had done some security work for him on some of his campaigns. (Carl had been worried about Lou's safety a couple of times and had asked me personally to take care of him. He told me I was the only one he trusted for the job.) So I talked with Lou Stokes, but he was a congressman now—till 1999—and in Washington most of the time, so he sent me to other people. The people he sent me to talk to were Mike White and George Forbes.

As I look back, I can see what was happening. I should have seen it sooner. They just kept giving me the runaround. I went to talk with Mayor White but was told to talk with his assistant. The assistant was busy—there was some crisis downtown—and he said to try him again another time. The next time I went back, there was some other problem. He really wanted to help me but couldn't do anything just then. And so it went.

This wasn't the way things used to go for me back in the 1970s and 80s. I didn't like playing by the new rules, and so I tried a more direct approach. One day I saw Mayor White at Lancer's Restaurant at a table with an important union official. I went over and sat down and told the Mayor I was glad to finally catch up with him and then explained what I was looking for. It wasn't much, just a regular city job like the ones I used to have, with a salary I could count on. He seemed annoyed at my butting in and sent me to his assistant once again.

I knew what the assistant was going to do for me, and I got angrier and angrier as the days passed. Not many days later

I was downtown across from City Hall, and I saw the mayor going up the steps. He was separated from his assistant and security guard, who were almost at the top of the steps, and I ran over to have a word with him. I need an answer about this job thing, and I was determined to get one then and there. I think the mayor was embarrassed that this was so public, and he got huffy. He stopped, stuck his finger in my face, and started lecturing me about how I couldn't just stop people [he meant important people like him] on the street. That finger pointing really got to me. Nobody treats me like that, especially in public. I told him to get his god dammed finger out of my face. At my age and with what I'd done and who I'd worked for, I wasn't going to take that shit from anybody. I don't know what might have happened next if the mayor's security guy (a guy I knew and who knew me) hadn't come running down and pulled the mayor away. I laughed about it with the security guy afterwards. He said he saw the mayor waving his finger under my nose and he *knew* what was going to happen next if he didn't get down there fast. We both had a pretty good laugh about it, but I wasn't laughing when I thought about how far away I was from getting even a simple city job.

The one bright spot was Charley Warren. Charley was still selling to his small group of elite, high-paying clients, and I was able to connect back up with him. I started keeping his cocaine shipments for him again, and before long I was making even more a month than I had been before. It was $1500 a month tax-free, and it helped a lot. From that point on I stopped worrying about paying the basic bills. But it wasn't the answer to my problems entirely.

While the government seemed to consider me too small a fish for them to waste a lot of time on, I knew from several sources that they were still keeping an eye on me because of all the years I had worked for Reuben Sturman. I knew the way they thought, too. All my money from Charley Warren was of course off the books. I was still living in my big apartment at Winton Place, and if anybody chose to look into my affairs too closely they would see right away that there was no way my above-board sources of income could cover my expenses living in a place like that. I wasn't too worried about it because I didn't think the government would bother with someone so far down the pecking order. But it was there in the back of my mind, and I continued to look for something above board that I could do.

Dick Jacobs, the former owner of the Cleveland Indians, lived in Winton Place while I was there. I would see him in the elevators every once in a while. I talked to a girl I knew who worked for Jacobs and she encouraged me to ask him for a job because she said she'd heard him say he needed a driver. Not long after that I caught him in the elevator and I asked him about it. He told me to send a letter and a resume to his office, which I did. I never heard from him about it officially, but eventually I ran into him in the elevator again, and he said he couldn't use me. He didn't say why. The girl I knew who worked for him told me later that Jacobs had done some background checking on me, asked around, and that George Forbes had apparently told Jacobs about my connection with Reuben Sturman. He [Forbes] supposedly said that I wasn't the kind of person Dick Jacobs ought to have close to him.

I was extremely frustrated, not least because of the way I felt Forbes and White were treating me—like I was some kind of political liability because of my association with Reuben. Like I was someone they felt they were too good to rub elbows with. I knew things about George Forbes that would have been a big embarrassment for him if the word ever got out. To say the least, his telling anyone that they ought to think twice before having me to work for them was the pot calling the kettle black. But I also knew that spilling the beans about George Forbes wouldn't get me what I wanted, and I felt like I was just butting my head against a wall.

Carl Stokes died in 1996, and, along with practically the entire black community of Cleveland, I went to the funeral. Lou Stokes was at the casket when I went by, and with tears in my eyes, I said, "Lou, I loved him." "I know you did, Diz," he said, "and he thought the world of you." It was an emotional moment that caught me off guard. I admired, respected, and trusted Carl. He understood and valued people like me because he knew the streets and the kind of people I came from, and he didn't look down on me. He didn't think I was some kind of liability.

Around the time of the funeral Lou Stokes called from Washington and asked me if "they were taking care of me," meaning whether I had gotten the work I was looking for. I told him nothing had worked out yet, and he suggested he might be able to get me something out at NASA Glenn, maybe some kind of security work. But he never made the call himself. He gave me the names of some people I needed to talk to, and when I did the guy just sat there, listened to me, and then sent me to an employment agency. I heard later, through the grapevine, that the man I talked to there suggested that I was asking for too much. In fact, I heard that he said, "Diz wants a job where he's the president." It wasn't true. I wasn't asking for the moon. Yes, I had been used to the high life, but all I wanted now was a steady job that paid $11 or $12 an hour. But I obviously wasn't going to get it through the people running the show now, and finally I just gave up trying.

I had the guaranteed money from Charley Warren. In the early days after Reuben went to prison I had done some coaching at

East Tech once again. I was licensed to carry a gun, and eventually picked up some security work at Lancer's Restaurant. The days of Armani suits and Luis Vuitton luggage were long gone, but I had enough, although I still had a problem.

I was still living in my luxury apartment at Winton Place, and a couple of friends took me aside and reminded me that because of my association with Reuben Sturman the government was probably still keeping an eye on me, and if they decided to look closely at the income I declared and the cost of that apartment, I could end up being in real trouble. I suggested moving to—and I named another apartment building—and they said that wouldn't work, either, that I had to be living somewhere that it made sense to the IRS that I could afford.

The result was that I lowered my sights quite a bit and began looking into the kinds of government-subsidized places that catered to senior citizens. Most of the better places had fairly long waiting lists, but Lou Stokes, who was a friend in need, put in a good word for me, and for the last ten years I have been a resident at the Abington Arms, between the end of the Case Western Reserve campus and the beginning of Little Italy on the East Side of Cleveland.

IT AIN'T FOR SISSIES

Bzzzzzzzzzzzzzzzzzzzzzzzzzzzzzzzz

In my apartment at the Abington I hear that sound several times a day. If I'm alone or if I'm with somebody, it doesn't matter. It goes off right on schedule. One minute I may be comfortable in my chair watching Oprah or ESPN and half way to a nap. The next thing I hear is that buzzing and then an automated voice—a recording—that says, "It's time to take your medicine."

It's not a friendly voice or an unfriendly voice. It's a neutral or maybe an "official" voice, like a teacher's who is talking to you about something you have to do but is bored and doesn't know you from Adam. After that first buzz, it waits for a certain number of seconds and then if I haven't come over and pushed the button I'm supposed to, it says it again: "It's time to take your medicine." And it will keep it up until I do what I'm supposed to, just like the seatbelt buzzer in some cars.

All of this is coming from a machine that is about the size and shape of an upside down five-gallon bucket sitting on a table along the wall across from me. On the side facing my chair is a small opening with a button above it that lights up so you can't miss it. When I hear the buzzing, I go over to the machine, press the button and in a second down comes a little paper cup. In it are the pills I'm supposed to be sure and take at that time. Of course I take them because if I don't the teacher will be on my case until I do. And this is on top of the other pills I take that

I keep in one of those plastic boxes full of little compartments for every day of the week and even different parts of every day (morning, afternoon, evening). Then there's the blood sugar tester for my diabetes. This is what it's come to.

When I moved into the Abington Arms, I couldn't kid myself any longer about the fact that I was getting old. I don't mean "older", I mean *old*. Even by the time Reuben went to prison I was not a spring chicken. A friend of mine likes to quote Bette Davis, who is supposed to have said, "Getting old. It ain't for sissies." If that's what she said, she got it right.

I was seventy-one when Carl Stokes died and into my seventies when I moved to the Abington. Under the best of circumstances, when you're in your seventies you're starting to slow down, and I had a lot of baggage. Besides the sports injuries I'd had and the times I'd been shot or cut seriously, I had to deal with the onset of diabetes, and things went from bad to worse from there. I had to have a knee replaced and after the replacement the knee got badly infected. They had to put a rod in it, which meant that I couldn't bend the leg. I had problems with my hip on that side, too. The long and the short of it was that before too long, I had a lot of trouble getting around, and it was—and still is—hard to take. The icing on the cake was incipient Parkinson's.

I know people have had lots of things to say about this subject, but it's always new and unsettling when it's happening to you. My body was getting old and harder and harder to manage. My memory was fine, though, which in some ways just made things worse. I could remember when I could run like the wind—nearly making the Olympics. I could remember when I was strong and athletic enough to nearly make a professional football team. Not that I'm the first person to think it, but its hard to get used to the fact that you can't do the things you used to be able to count on doing. It's hard to accept the fact that things that mean a lot to you are no longer in your control or they're so difficult that you have to think twice before you try to do them. Just a simple for instance: I still occasionally go to the grocery store for myself. But if I have more than one or two plastic bags of food to carry up, I have to make several trips because I'm just not strong enough anymore. I used to be a sprint champion and a heavyweight boxer, and now this.

I have also had to realize and learn to deal with the fact that, simply because of my age and where I'm living, I have gone back into the system again. It's not the juvenile court system, or the foster care system, or the mental health system, but it's the system all the same, and there are ways in which it's not that different from those others. Once you're in it, it takes care of you, but there are rules, and it spends a lot of time telling you what to do.

I have people visit me very week to help me, take care of me, and check up on me. There's someone who comes in once a week to help me keep my apartment clean and in order. There are medical people who come to check on my various conditions. There are even people who come to find out more or less how I am, how I am doing. They're not bad people, and some of them are pretty nice, but they're not friends in the ordinary sense. We don't have common memories or know much about one another's stories. I don't have any contact with them except when they visit me officially. And I found out fairly quickly that I have to be careful how I treat them.

There's a young woman who comes for regular visits. Because it's her job, she gets paid according to the amount of time she spends with me, and I sign off on a time slip to indicate how long she was there each time. There are times when I am glad to see her, and other times when I am occupied with something else and don't need to. I didn't like the idea of sending her away and costing her money by signing her out early, so one time when I felt like I needed the time to myself, I told her she could go but to give me the time sheet and I would sign off giving her credit for a full visit. Somebody found out about it, and I was told that if I did something like that again I would "lose the privilege" of having her come visit. You get into the system, and it's a minefield, but things like that are nothing to the grief my car has caused me.

You might be wondering why I would need a car at my age and with everything that makes it hard for me to get around. If you did, you would not be the first. I have a good friend who not too long ago was listening to my complaints about all the trouble my car has caused me and she finally said, "Diz"—in a tone of voice that reminded me a little of my grandmother when she was losing patience with me—"That car is going to kill you!" I

It's possible. I have been in a battle with the bank that has the loan for years. When I bought the car, it was a tiny bit beyond what I could afford given what I have coming in each month. The guy at the bank I bought it from was a friend, and we worked out a deal that that made it possible for me to make the payments. Then that guy retired. Our deal was verbal, not standard policy, and since that time I have been dealing with voices on telephones that dun me for payment every month because I don't get it to them on their schedule. They don't know me personally, couldn't care less, and they don't, or won't, understand me when I try to explain what my arrangement is supposed to be. I won't bore you with all the details, but I got so angry at getting hassled every month that I got in the car and drove all the way to Cincinnati, where I was told the bank's headquarters were. In my condition, it's not easy or even safe for me to be driving that far, but I thought if I could talk with someone in person, I could straighten things out. Fat chance. When I got there I was told that while it was indeed the bank's headquarters—its main office—the financial stuff like mine was handled by their branch in Seattle. They are still calling me every month. I have talked with my lawyer, and he has talked with the bank people, and he tells me everything is fine. But it seems no one has told the people who keep calling me, and sometimes it makes me want to scream.

Although not everything is as frustrating as the thing with the car, there are a lot of things I have to do now that are harder and more confusing than you would think they should be: Medicare and Medicaid paperwork for example. And it didn't used to be like this. Twenty or thirty years ago, if I had financed a car, it would have been with a bank in Cleveland. If there had been problems, there would have been someone I could go and talk to in person. There's no doubt in my mind that we could have worked it out in an hour or two. The pitches are just coming too fast now, and if the truth be known, my swing has gotten slower.

Over and above the physical things and the system things, it's been hard for me to adjust to the fact that I am living now in a building for "seniors." They're nice, well-meaning people, and I'm sure each one of them has his or her own story, but I don't see myself as a "senior." I've gotten to know some of them, and have made some friends. But with one important exception, they're not the kind of friends that knew you when. They understand what it's like to be this age, and they're certainly sympathetic about physical problems, but they're not people you've shared a history with. Almost all of the people I knew best from the old days have passed, and one of the toughest things I have had to deal with has been being alone so much of the time.

It all boils down to adjusting to the way things are, and that's been a lot harder for me than I thought it was going to be. The younger people who come in to take care of me always ask me how I'm doing. I tell them I'm going a little crazy stuck in my apartment all day. They ask why I don't do something about it? When I try to tell them, they say, "You don't have to stay in your room. You can play bingo. You can go watch TV in the lounge. They have all sorts of activities for the residents here." Easy answers from people who don't have a clue what I'm going through. I've walked through major airports with thousands of dollars glued lightly all over my body and smiled at the security guards as I passed them. I've had good times with beautiful women that make me blush just remembering them. I have heard the wind roaring in my ears and jumped out of an airplane trusting to God Almighty that my parachute would open. I have sighted down the barrel of a gun at people whose eyes got as big as dinner plates when they saw me taking aim. How am I going to have fun playing bingo? Why would I want to sit and watch *Jeopardy* in the lounge at night? When I hear myself say things like that, I'm a little embarrassed. But honestly, that's the way I feel.

For most of my life I have been an active person. If I didn't like the way my life was turning out, an opportunity to do something different and change my luck always seemed to turn up. That's one of the reasons I am so stubborn about keeping my car. It's the last way I have to feel like I have some independence and control. I don't use it much, but I know I always can if I absolutely have to. Although it didn't achieve anything except to make me even more frustrated, my angry drive to the bank's main office in Cincinnati at least made me feel like I was doing something and not just sitting around till the next time they called.

I sit around plenty as it is. I have is a lot of time to think, too, and that hasn't always turned out to be a good thing. For example, sometimes I can't help wondering what if? What if I had grown up in a close, two-parent home and had a stable family? What if my athletic ability had gotten me a scholarship, and I had tried to get into the pros coming out of college—instead of out of the sandlots? What if I hadn't been the only one looking out for me? What if? What if? What if? I don't feel bitterness when I ask questions like these, but I have a lot of time on my hands now, and sometimes I'd just like to know.

The mind is a funny thing, though. Sometimes I will sit in my chair and wish it had all been different, but at other times I feel like I wouldn't have wanted to have it any other way than it was. What if I had had a stable family? Would I have followed my dad to the steel mills in Braddock, Pa? Would I have stayed married to Mary King and worked for years at a low paying job at one of the big auto companies in Detroit? If I had, I don't think I would have had any of the experiences I've just been telling you about. I wouldn't have had the money to spend, the clothes to wear, the cars to drive, the beautiful women in my life. I wouldn't have seen the places I've seen or been taken seriously by powerful men and women. I wouldn't have had the highs you can get when there's danger and big money at stake. In the end, I suppose there's no point in spending too much time on What if? What happened happened. What is, is. All I know is that no matter how I sort through it, I don't come out where Charley Warren did.

Charley had never been one to save his money. When he had it, he spent it, and he spent it well. Some people I've known have plenty of money and want to live the good life, but they don't know how. Charley knew how. Whenever he went places, he went first class. Wherever he stayed, it was always four-star. Whatever he drank was the best you could get. He was generous with his friends, and he appreciated what he had, which is maybe why things ended for him the way they did.

Eventually Charley's money ran out. The IRS had their eye on him for years. They finally called him out on his income tax file. He was claiming an income of $40, 000 a year, and what he was driving, and the how he was living was way out of line with a figure like that. Then it all started to snowball. The numbers went bad on him, and then he lost his cocaine connections. He got behind in his condo payments, and all of a sudden he was at the bottom of a mountain, and there was no way he could see to climb back up. He couldn't live the way he was used to living, and he couldn't adjust to the difference. He started to have health problems, too, and I didn't see him for a while. Then finally he called and asked me to come see him. When I got there, I was startled. He had lost a lot of weight and looked pretty bad. We talked for a little while about things that didn't matter, and then he said, "Diz, you are the best friend I have, but after today I don't want to see you anymore. I don't want you to come over. I don't want you to call."

I was shocked. I didn't say anything, but it must have showed on my face, because he said, "I know what it's like to live well, Diz—the way I used to do—and I refuse to go on living like I'm living now. This isn't living, and I'd rather be dead than poor. Please just let me handle things my own way." Of course I respected his wishes. He was dead within a few months.

I believe I understand exactly why he did what he did. Like Charley, I have known what it's like to go first class. I also know what being poor is like, and being poor and black is grimmer still. I'm not where Charley was when he just decided to pack it in. I have enough to get by, and Charley's way is not my way. I don't mean to criticize him. He did what he thought was best for him. But if my memory sometimes makes me frustrated because it reminds me how much I've changed. I've got plenty of good memories, and I think they're what are keeping me afloat.

MEMORIES

"Diz? Diz Long, is that you? Do you remember me?"

I was in a hospital waiting room. I spend quite a bit of time in waiting rooms now. They remind me of bus stations. They get hard use by people whose minds are somewhere else and who don't stay long. I'm a big man and with my bad leg it's almost impossible to find a place to sit that's comfortable. The waits are usually long, and the other people are seldom chatty. A lot of them have dead eyes and look beaten down by hard lives. I usually assume I'm there to wait my turn, take care of whatever it is I'm there for, and go home. I was genuinely surprised when someone who seemed to know me actually spoke to me.

It took me a minute to place her. It's sometimes hard to recognize people in places you don't expect them to be, especially if you haven't seen them for a long time, but the dime finally dropped. It was a woman roughly my age who I used to know from my days at Lancer's Restaurant After she asked how I was we talked about the old days for a while and then she looked at me hard and said, "Diz, you're the only one left." What she meant was that I was the only one left of a group of friends that used to have a high old time together. I had to think about it for a minute, but I finally realized that she was right.

Everyone was gone but me. That's what stuck in my mind.

Everyone gone but me.

When I got home, and started thinking about it, the particulars began to come back, and after I worked at it for a while, I could see it all in my mind's eye: Lancer's Restaurant in it's prime, a nice crowd having a good time, our table in a back room, Charley Warren, Richard Drake (the son of Little Brother Drake), Billy Pope, a guy we used to call Gorgeous George, and another whose street name was Black Homer. We used to get together at Lancer's and do some cocaine, tell stories and catch up. We were always discreet with the coke. We would pass the little cellophane bag around under the table, tap a pinch on the backs of our hands, then with a quick move zip our hands under our noses and snort it up—and laugh like we were back in high school and getting away with something in study hall. I think the management probably knew what we were doing, certainly the waitresses sometimes did. But nobody who wasn't looking for something would have noticed, and as long as we didn't cause a problem or make a scene, the Lancers people didn't care. We used to get going, talking about the old days, and laugh till the tears ran down our faces. Lancer's was our home bar, we belonged there.

I hadn't thought about those days for years till what she said made me remember them. Of course it wasn't the same as really going back in time, but it had its own attraction. When you start remembering things like that, you usually remember only the good things, the best times. That's what I have found was one of the best things about working on this book. It has had the same effect on me as my friend who reminded of those days at Lancer's. If anything, it's been even better.

Asking and answering questions about my life brought back all sorts of memories I thought were long gone. It was decades since I had even had a thought about what it was like in the neighborhoods in Detroit when I was growing up. But when I got pushed about it, or when I pushed myself, I was surprised by the details that started coming back: the ice man, the rag man, the guy who sold coal, the evenings in the park at the recreation center, Mr. Futch and the boxing lessons. It's like all that stuff was up in my head all these years just waiting for something to happen that would let me get at it.

It's funny how your memory works—or at least mine. It's common now for me to forget everything that happened yesterday, but things that happened fifty or sixty years ago sometimes come back clear as a bell. And once I get my memory going I can never anticipate exactly what the particular details or events will be. I'll never know, for example, why I suddenly remembered things like Richard Dixon from the old cowboy movies saying his famous line, "Remember the Alamo" or how I could have I remembered that when I ran away from Braddock and came back to Detroit, "Light Must Fall—Starring Robert Montgomery" was what was on the marquee at the old Michigan Theater in Detroit. Little details like that just kept coming back once I got the process of remembering started.

Occasionally whole episodes would come back. It's not that I literally relived them, but the memories I did have were so vivid that they affected me emotionally. For example when I started remembering the details from the evening when I was waiting up in the tree so I could catch my girlfriend, Dorothy, cheating on me with Scatter, and when I remembered jumping down and not being able to do anything else because my legs had gone to sleep, I started laughing so hard that tears came. It was the same thing but different kinds of tears when I started remembering things in detail about my grandmother.

My grandmother was everything to me, and she died suddenly and unexpectedly. She was hit by a car, and one of the things I regret most in my life is that I never got the chance to tell her how much her love and support meant to me—and still mean. She knew exactly who I was and she loved me without any reservations or conditions. No matter how much pressure she got from her grown children to get rid of me, she always stood up for me, always took my part. I don't even have a picture of her except in my mind's eye, and therefore the memories that came back clearly in the telling of this story mean a great deal.

I don't know to this day why I remembered particular things *when* I did. Very late in this process of trying to recall the details of my life, I suddenly thought of another woman that I haven't talked about yet. Her name is Latifa, and I first met her back in the 1970s—before I was shot and while I was coaching at East High.

I still remember how it happened. There was this girl—a student at East High—who one day asked me if I had a steady girlfriend. I had had several wives at that point, but at the moment I was divorced from all of them, and I had no girlfriend and so I said, "No." She didn't ask me anything else at the time, and I forgot about it. Then one day there she was again, right before classes were to start, and with her was a young woman---obviously not a student—who was one of the most beautiful women I had ever seen. "Mr. Long," the student said," I want you to meet my mother."

It was the beginning of one of the most lasting relationships of my life—and one of the strangest. The way we felt about each other—almost literally from the beginning—wasn't what was strange. We loved one another from the moment we locked eyes. What was strange was that although my relationship with Latifa has been one of the most important things in my life, we never married and we never will.

The problem was timing. I had just had a string of marriages that for one reason or another had ended badly. I was just getting back into the numbers, and then I got shot, and not too long after that I started working for Reuben Sturman and doing a lot of travelling. And what I'm saying is both that I was a little bit gun shy about marriage and also I wasn't in a position to settle down the way you would want to if you were determined to make a marriage work. And I know that after saying all these things, my not marrying Latifa is to this day the other great regret of my life.

We called ourselves married. We did so for years, and we still do. I gave her the ring that had been my grandmother Tellis' that I inherited after she died. She calls me her husband, and I call her my wife, and we both know what we mean. Several years ago she got legally married to another man, but she has continued to wear the ring I gave her to this day.

Along with the love I always got from my grandmother, the unwavering and unconditional love I have gotten from Latifa is one of the best things that ever happened to me. Most people can count themselves lucky if they have one relationship like that in their lives, and I have been lucky enough to have had two, and telling my story has allowed me to revisit the whole relationship. I can visit it when I want to now.

Being alone, feeling that I'm alone, is probably the hardest thing I have to deal with these days. My memories are what help me the most. Some of them are violent, and some of them are painful, but I am lucky in that the ones I have been able to revisit most often are the good ones. My apartment is small, but it's full of things that help me go back into my past. I have pictures, in one place or another, of all my wives. I have pictures of many of my stepchildren from my various marriages, and I can see most of the pictures from my chair. In my bedroom, I have some of my oldest friends: a picture of Charley Warren on my bedside table, a picture of Naomi Del Gado and little Erica, Reuben's daughter by Naomi.

I'm one of those people for whom, along with pictures, things—physical objects—bring back memories, and I have a lot of things that are meaningful to me nearby. I have the beautiful, soft pair of gloves with the black stitching up the side that my Uncle Chris used to wear when he went dancing at the Greystone Ballroom in Detroit. Under my bed I still have the Louis Vuitton luggage that Reuben got me. I've got the big, .44 magnum I used to carry when I was on the streets. If it could talk, it could tell a lot of stories. I've got a little book of mug shots, like the police used to use. There are more than a few faces in it that I used to know. I've got newspaper clippings from my football days with the Erie Vets. I've got prints and some original art on my walls. I bought it at various times, some in the years I was in California. So I'm alone in some senses but not in others. I've surrounded myself with things that help me think back.

My good memories are with me most of the time. When I watch the Browns and the Cavs, and when they lose I get mad and wish I could coach some sense into them. I wish they had players like the ones I used to hang around with: Jim Brown, Marion Motley, Night Train Lane, and Ollie Matson. I wish I was thirty or forty years younger, and still out on the streets and in the clubs keeping in touch, although I know those days are over. I can still remember and sometimes even replay the good stuff, though. When I do, it makes me realize that I'm lucky to have been able to do all the things I've done. I also think I'm lucky to have had the chance working on this book has given me to take a long look back at my life.

When I was younger I didn't look at my life the way I do now, and I certainly didn't look back at it. How many young people do? I've often thought that if I hadn't made it after I was shot, I never would have. Sometimes you need time and you need distance—and maybe you even need adversity—to help you see what the good things are.

Seeing what the bad things are is easy. On a given day my aches and pains are so bad they're all I can think about. On a bad day the loneliness can be even worse than the physical pain. On a bad day I will spend too much time thinking about what might have been, about how confused I was growing up about even something as basic as who I was and where I belonged. But the process getting this story told and thinking about how I wanted to tell it has given me things to think about that I never would have thought about otherwise. I've learned how to find the good memories: my grandmother, the good times with Harold Robbins, my friendship with Naomi,

Charley Warren, Latifa, and one more I haven't mentioned yet.

Late in my life one of the best friends I had was a woman about my age named Leslie. She also lived in the Abington Arms, and she has been one of the very few people there I have connected with. We became friends quickly, almost instantly, and we used to love to spend time together. It was easy to talk with her and fun because at our time of life we had both done a lot of living and we each knew what the other was talking about. We talked the same language. She was the kind of friend who called every New Year's Eve to wish you well, the kind of friend who loaned you money if you needed it and who visited you in the hospital.

She liked the same kind of old movies I did, and I used to go up to her apartment evenings and we would have a drink and sit up on her bed and watch classic movies into the night. Because she spent a lot of time in her bedroom, she had fixed it up just the way she wanted. She had replaced the standard ceiling light—the same in all the bedrooms at the Abington— with a beautiful chandelier, and she had had the paneling on the sliding track doors on the closet replaced with beautiful full-length sliding mirrors. It made the room seem especially elegant, and I told her so many times, and how much I liked what she'd done.

She passed a few years ago, and not long afterwards a friend of hers came to my apartment with a strange request. He asked me if I would leave my apartment for four or five hours. He wouldn't tell me why. I must have looked pretty skeptical because he asked me did I trust him or not? I said I did, and he said, "Well?" So I left.

I wasn't really worried, but I was certainly curious. I gave him a full five hours and then went back. The door was locked and he was gone. When I stepped inside, I took a quick look around and everything seemed fine. It's a small apartment, and I could see everything from the doorway except inside the bathroom and bedroom. It took me a minute, but I finally went into the bedroom, and that's when I understood.

My apartment and Leslie's had exactly the same floor plan. When she knew her time was up, she made an arrangement with her friend, the one who had come to my apartment. While I was gone, he had installed her beautiful chandelier over my bed and replaced my sliding closet doors with the mirrors from her bedroom. I was deeply moved when I realized what she had done and that she had obviously been planning it for some time. Bad days, good days, it doesn't matter which. I know that someone cared about me every time I go into the room.

I have a lot of things I do to keep myself thinking positive. I visit Charley Warren's grave every couple of months just to touch base with the better memories from old days and ways. He's buried in Lakeview Cemetery, which is pretty close to where I live. I go up to the gravesite and sometimes tell him what's been going on with me. I can still laugh with him. I will maybe say something like, "Well, Charley. Things have been getting pretty bad with me, but look at you. I'm better off than you." And I'll get a good laugh out of it and feel better.

Sometimes when I come back from the cemetery people who don't know a lot about me and my life will ask me where I've been. I'll tell them I have been talking with my good friend Charley Warren. Every once in a while they'll ask me what we talked about, and I will tell them, "Oh, not much. Charley Warren doesn't have much to say these days." Then I'll go on up to my room, and usually I'm smiling to myself.

The little sign I see whenever I ride the elevator at the Abington Arms reads, "Make your life a good life with what you have." When you add it all up, I think I have a lot.

Afterward
by William R. Siebenschuh

I kept in touch with Diz after the interviewing was over and the book written. He's only a block and a half away. I visit irregularly but it averages out to about once a month. We talk on the phone more frequently not least, I think, because the project has given us enough common experience to make us friends and because he knows I am genuinely interested in how he gets on and that I will listen.

Looked at objectively, we are a truly odd pair. The way we grew up could not have been more different. As a child—and from an intact home and family-- I went to the Chicago public schools and proceeded in them from conventional stage to conventional stage without a break or a hitch. In fact, I never really left school in the sense that from the time I started going all day in the first grade till the present I have never been out of it. I just went from sitting at the desks as a student to going to the front of the room as a teacher.

Diz, was separated from his parents when he was two years old, after which he was bounced around from special school, to the Juvenile Detention Center in Detroit, to Boys' Vocational High School in Lansing, to the Boys' Republic in Farmington, from there to foster care in Ypsilanti and not long after that into the service and then into the world. At the time when my biggest worries were things like acne and getting into college, Diz was having to deal with things like a foster mother's boyfriend who attacked him and cut him badly with a flick knife. While I was learning to read books and succeed in the classroom, he was learning to read people and situations and succeed in the streets.

I've worked hard on a timeline for the major events in Diz's life, and some of the contrasts with what was going on with me at the same age and at parallel times in our lives are striking. For example, in 1958, when I was a sophomore in high school trying to get up the nerve to ask a girl out, Diz, already getting into the numbers rackets, was a sometime emcee at the Chatterbox in Cleveland, and was taking Billie Holiday to breakfast after late night performances. In his late teens and early twenties Diz was a good enough athlete to have been invited to try out for professional football teams, box heavyweight, and be nearly sent to the Olympic tryouts as a sprinter. When I was in my early twenties I was in college and soon graduate school, and in my late twenties I became a college professor. Thus, at about the time—the mid 1970's--when I was a young Assistant Professor at Fordham trying my best to do a good job teaching Jane Austen and worried about getting tenure, Diz was cracking heads in Cleveland and eventually shot from ambush and nearly killed by rival numbers people. In the later 1970's and the 1980's while I was grading papers, holding office hours, and going to committee meetings at Case Western Reserve, Diz was riding around Cleveland with Shondor Birns, *adjusting the attitudes* of Reuben Sturman's enemies, keeping cocaine shipments safe for a close friend, and sneaking Sturman's payoff money past the police at La Guardia and Logan airports to give to the New York and Boston "families." In short, it would be hard to imagine two people with more different backgrounds and life experiences. And yet somehow or other we got together and managed to become not only collaborators on this book but friends.

I think the reason was the timing of it all.

As I have mentioned above, Diz has often said that he wished that we had met years ago. However, unless we had met a relatively few years ago, I don't think the book would have happened. Until he was permanently slowed by a combination of Reuben Sturman's arrest and conviction (and therefore the end of his major source of income), old age, illnesses, and the effects of accumulated injuries, my sense is that Diz was too busy living his life to have wanted to take time out to record and rethink it. More to the point, until not many years before Diz and my first meeting, I wouldn't have known the first thing about how to go about helping him. But when we met that day at Mac Donald's, the timing was right. Indeed, it was almost the Perfect Storm.

By then Diz was a man who understood that, while his time was by no means up yet, the days were beginning to be numbered. He badly wanted to get his story told and by that time had begun to give it some thought. By exactly the same time and via the process of co-ghost authoring three different autobiographies while working closely with a colleague who is an expert interviewer and a distinguished scholar, I knew how to evaluate what I was hearing. I knew what the process of trying to help Diz tell his story would involve, and I knew I had a good chance to do it justice. That is to say, by the time we had finished our Big Mac's at that first meeting I think we each knew that the other had something to offer. I believe I convinced Diz that I had enough experience to make it worth taking a chance on me. I know that I felt that I was looking at the opportunity of a lifetime. In one sense, then, it was enlightened self-interest on both sides that got this project off the ground. However, it quickly turned into a good deal more.

I remember once in the early stages of the interviewing process the first time around I came home and became animated telling my wife about some of the more hair-raising things that Diz had told me that day. She looked at me somewhat incredulously and said, "You like this guy, don't you?" The answer was emphatically "Yes!' but I hadn't really thought about it till then. So I thought about it. I did like him. I do like him. I enjoy talking and spending time with him. And I have come to respect him as well.

One of the obvious reasons I like Diz is that as big and scary as he can obviously be, he can also be genuinely likeable. If he wanted to I think he could charm almost anybody. And it makes sense. He wouldn't have spent all those years around rich and powerful people, gaining their confidence, being trusted with their secrets, earning their respect without a lot of personal charm, savvy, and discretion. But by this time in both his life and mine there were several other factors in play. As different as our backgrounds are, there were threads of connection I didn't anticipate.

Diz is only fifteen years older than I am. He grew up in inner city apartments in Detroit, and I grew up in them in Chicago. The public school schoolyards he was describing were the kind of schoolyards I remembered. The dynamic among the school kids was familiar as were his descriptions of the walks to and from school picking up friends along the way. There were still trolleys around when I was young, and we both remembered putting pennies on the tracks as kids (when the grownups weren't around) and carrying away our strangely-shaped treasures after the trolley had lumbered over them. Like Diz, I used to listen to radio drama in the evening—the Lone Ranger, The Shadow. When he talked about running out of the house after dinner on summer nights and staying out---I was able to finish the sentence for him—"till the street lights came on." That was the rule in my house, too.

We had movies in common. I knew all the films he liked to talk about because I saw most of them on early TV, and we both remembered enough details to have a good time whenever we remembered them. It became a common language. I am also old enough to know who all of the big name football players he played with were. I knew them the way a very young fan did in those days, from lying on the floor in front of a radio listening to the exploits of the Chicago football Cardinals' Ollie Matson, or Night Train Lane when he was in town with the Lions to play the Bears. When Diz showed me pictures of himself with players like these I could share in the pleasure he took in remembering and he could tell my appreciation was genuine. I understood why it was important to him, and he knew that I did. We even had surgeries in common. I had full hip replacement surgery a few years before I met Diz, and by that time he had had several. I knew from experience what it was like: The bad first day or so in the hospital, the slow recuperation, the difficulty at first of doing even the simplest things at home, and certainly how hard it must have been for him alone (as I was not) for most of the rehabilitation and recovery period.

I am not by any means trying to say that Diz and I discovered we were soul brothers. Clearly our lives have followed completely different paths. What I am saying is that as we got to know one another through the back and forth of the interviewing process we discovered enough overlap in our experiences to allow for a degree of trust that made communication easy and at times I think genuinely heartfelt. In fact, as we got to know one another better, the fact of the differences between us often became a positive factor because on many occasions I was the learner and he was the teacher, a role he sometimes loved to play.

For example I remember how his eyes widened with surprise when he realized that I didn't know how the numbers game worked. As he was telling me about his involvement with it, I began to ask questions that made it clear I didn't have a clue. "You don't know what I'm talking about, do you?" he said. I said I didn't, and he chuckled. "Everybody knows how the numbers work", he said, and the rest of that session and the next was what you might call Numbers 101—a crash course for me. By the time he had finished patiently explaining things, I was nearly convinced that he was correct about black people being the inventors of the current lottery system.

As the weeks and then months went on Diz introduced me to a lot of new things. The dream interpretation books I mention briefly in chapter 11 are a good example. He was again genuinely surprised that I had never heard of them. "You used to be able to get them in any supermarket, or corner deli", he said. I made a few attempts to see if he was right, but the stores I tried in the black neighborhoods immediately around the university didn't know what I was talking about. However, when I asked my department assistant, a black woman in her early fifties, her face lighted up. She had grown up in the Cleveland area and remembered her parents buying them. "My father used to read them", she said. I looked on the internet and found that you can now get nice paperbound collections of these numbered dream predictions, and I did so. I have one in my office now.

From my point of view the books were a genuine discovery. Consider, for example, this sample entry, the interpretation of a dream that involves furniture. (The three-digit number at the end--here 789--would be the number played if you were using it to help you at the numbers.)

> 6 Furniture—this is generally a good dream, but it depends on the circumstances. Handsome furniture is very fortunate, but naturally this depends on the person who dreams. What is ordinary furniture for a wealthy woman would be sheer folly for a working class woman, or for a business girl earning her own living. It should be just a little better in quality than what you actually possess. A common person dreaming of nice furniture: Much love. A business girl dreaming of nice furniture: will earn own living. 789 (Solar's Book of Dreams, Numbers, & Lucky Days, Fireside: Simon & Schuster, New York, 1985. P. 136)

What did phrases like "a common person" or "a business girl" mean in this context? What would the intended audience have assumed "handsome furniture" looked like? How big was the possibility of "earning one's own living"? I am convinced that it would be worth somebody's time and effort to study these books as cultural documents. Of course that's what an academic like myself would think, and of course I learned quickly that it wasn't the way people used them in Diz's day at all.

When I showed him the book I'd bought, he looked through it quickly and then laughed and said, "Besides just getting a number to bet, we used those dream books for a lot of things. We used to look up all the dreams about sex and women, and we memorized the numbers of the raciest ones. Then if one of us had a hot date that night maybe he would brag a little and say, 'If I'm lucky I'm going to have a 652 this evening.' Or we might kid somebody and ask something like, 'Is it gonna be a 749 for you tonight?' and get a good laugh out of it."

I learned all sorts of things from Diz during the course of the interviewing process. He had been licensed to carry a gun from the time he first did security work for Harold Robbins, and I was genuinely interested in his explanations about what it meant he could do and not do. Things like if you are licensed to carry a concealed weapon you can have it with you in a restaurant but not in a restaurant that also has a bar. (Not knowledge I am ever likely to need to use, but interesting for precisely that reason.) I also learned the rules to a couple of card games I had never heard of—Tonk and Bid Whist. (My department assistant knew right away what I meant and was quite familiar with them.) One day—if I could just have stayed a little longer--Diz and his helper Colleen were going to deal out a few hands so I could get the feel of it. I also picked up quite a bit of black history in the course of our weekly talks after which I would often head straight for the computer to look up some of the names I had just learned: People like John H. Johnson, Dolly Mapp, and Jimmy Smith. And after knowing most of the lyrics from the Fats Domino song, "Blue Monday" since I was in high school, I finally learned from Diz what Blue Monday actually was.

In one sense, then, what I learned late in my life is what professional journalists and free-lance writers usually learn early on: that one of the side benefits of this kind of project is the amount of things you discover along the way. It wasn't just facts and information that I was learning, though. There also was what, for lack of a better phrase, I will call a genuinely human dimension, a kind of sharing of experiences that led to mutual respect. It also led, on my part, to the kind of concern and sympathy that come inevitably when you get to know a person well enough that they let their guard down and tell you about things that matter to them.

The title of chapter 19 is "It Ain't for Sissies" for a reason. It is a famous remark by Bette Davis about getting old. She certainly had it right, and no one knows that any better than Diz Long. As strong and physically gifted as he was for most of his life, the kinds of things that happen to everyone who lives as long as he has have begun happening to him. He's pretty good with the diabetes. Like other diabetics I have known, he knows his own body, and he knows when he needs to do what. The Parkinson's is coming on slowly but it continues to advance and worry him. And his bad leg has caused, and still causes, serious problems. In just the years I've known him, he had to have a major corrective operation on it, and for a while there I didn't think he was going to make it. I went to visit him in the hospital, and when I got home and my wife asked how he was I just shook my head. But he made it. He is nothing if not a survivor and to a surprising degree accepts the physical things that he can't change with little complaint.

There are two things that bother him more than the purely physical problems, and he talked about them repeatedly. The first is how much it weighs on him that he is alone so much of the time. He has family by his various former marriages scattered about here and in the Detroit area. I have met some of them when I have visited him in the hospital at various times. His relations with the ones I have met seem cordial, but they are all much younger and appear to have their separate lives. Diz's day-to-day reality is that he is alone in the Abington Arms, a building full of old people like himself but not like himself because no one has lived the kind of life he has lived. It's hard to share memories without a sufficient amount of common experience, and the old friends with whom he could have talked more freely and expansively are gone.

What bothers him more is his relative powerlessness. He spent much of his early life "in the system"—the juvenile courts and the other related social institutions--where he learned the hard way that it could control him completely if it chose. He learned his lessons, got out, lived for years the kind of life he wanted, and now, after a period of success, freedom, and exuberant living, he's back in the system again. The system this time is Medicare, Medicaid, and I think Social Services. He's lucky to have them, and he knows it. Without them there'd be almost literally nothing. But it's a hard adjustment for him, even so.

One of the reasons it's hard is that because his means are severely limited now it's a constant battle for even the smallest things. For example one day not many months ago I went for a visit and found a crisis brewing. Probably his most important piece of furniture is his motorized Lazy-Boy. What's important about it is that the motorized part is what helps him get up when he needs to. Because the left leg is rigid and immobile, it is extremely difficult for him to get out of the chair without its assistance. What had happened was that the motor and the mechanism that raised and lowered the old chair had completely worn themselves out. The timing couldn't have been worse because Diz was having problems with his wrists, a form of Carpal Tunnel Syndrome, I believe. With the motorized function of the chair now gone, he had to push himself up with his hands and the pain in the wrists as well as the lack of strength made this extremely difficult. Medicare made a certain amount available to him to replace the chair. It was enough to buy a Lazy-Boy but apparently not a motorized one that would raise and lower him electronically. When I walked in on that particular day Colleen was on the phone with store after store trying to find someone who would sell Diz a motorized chair—new or used—that he could afford. He did eventually get a chair that will raise and lower him. It's not as good as the old one, but it works. However, it's always something. As with so many people his age, his life is now one thing like that after another.

It is also extremely hard for someone as physically gifted as Diz was to accept the fact of increasing physical weakness. Even harder to accept is the frequent feeling of being invisible, vulnerable, and unimportant that comes with being old and with not much money. When he gets angry about it, he is often the cause of his own problems, as he would be the first to admit.

One day not long ago he pushed a newspaper clipping towards me, and said, "Take a look at what a stupid thing I did." The clipping was from the police blotter of a local paper. It told the story—no names mentioned—of a man who had been caught carrying a gun in a restaurant and pulled in by the police. Diz had taken the gun in a briefcase, which he had then left behind. His friend took him back to get it and the police were waiting. "It's over now," he said. The police took me home but when I showed them my license to carry a concealed weapon they just let it go."

Why was he carrying the gun? Based on what I've heard him say at various times I can think of two possible answers. The first is that, as big as he is, because of his age and multiple physical problems he feels a need for protection, and perhaps with good reason. I once arrived at the Abington Arms just as a cab was letting Diz out. He was getting back from the grocery store. His hands aren't strong enough now to carry more than one plastic grocery bag at a time, and when I saw he was having difficulty I offered to carry all the bags up in the elevator for him. As we were waiting for the elevator to arrive, Diz started a conversation with another black man who was about his age. The subject was a recent shooting not many blocks away in East Cleveland. A gang of kids apparently joyriding through a neighborhood had shot and killed a person just standing in front of his house. No apparent reason.

The thrust of what Diz and he man were saying was that you always had to be on your guard for things like that. Every time you went out.

That's one possibility.

Another possibility, and it's a guess based on two years of interviewing and visiting Diz, is that it's more than just a personal safety thing. It's who he is, who he has been his whole life. In the old days he was powerful, not powerless. People were afraid of him, not the other way around. It's not that he isn't aware—painfully aware—of his limitations now. But once in a while he forgets—or he just doesn't want to accept fully the way things are. Perhaps the best example of this state of mind is the ongoing drama of the car he feels he needs.

Against literally everyone's advice who knows him (including me), he became obsessed with buying a used car to try to maintain at least a small sense of freedom and independence. "So if I just want to get out and go somewhere. Maybe just drive around, get away from here (the Abington Arms) and think. So I just don't have to stay in this room all the time", is the way he put it to me once. It's completely understandable, but the bad left leg and special shoes he has to wear make it extremely difficult for him to operate the pedals. It's therefore difficult and dangerous for him to try driving, and, given his means, too expensive for him to be paying on a car. But it's become a thing with him. I believe a matter of pride as much as anything else. So he put a down payment on a used car. When there were problems with it and he wanted to exchange it for another, the dealership started giving him grief.

I went to visit him not long after things had come to a head. I could see he was upset and asked what was the matter. He looked up from his chair and said, "Take a good look at me. You'll probably have to visit me in jail the next time." Then he dropped his eyes and said, "I made a *big* mistake." The big mistake was physically threatening the sales person he was dealing with. He said he had lost his temper and threatened to kill him. The dealership took it seriously enough to get a restraining order on Diz, so that when he ignored it and with great difficulty, went in person to the showroom to try to straighten things out, the police were there with guns.

When I last talked with Diz, he had been "bonded out" and was on his own recognizance. He was in a pretty good mood, all things considered, and even looking forward to his day in court. But what he said to me about the whole episode is, I think, the point. He said, "What really makes me angry is this. These things didn't used to happen to me. Nobody would have tried to treat me like that thirty years ago. And if they had, I would have known what to do. I had protection then. When I worked for Reuben and he needed violence, I provided violence. I was never worried about consequences because I knew that if trouble came our way Reuben had high-powered lawyers who would take care of me. But now I'm past the time when I am even able to be violent, and I've got no one to protect me."

My wife and I have some friends who have recently come back from a camera safari in Kruger Park in Kenya. When they were showing us the pictures, I was struck by one of an obviously old male lion. He was drinking at a water hole and seemed in pain. You could see his ribs clearly. The outlines of the sinewy muscles in the forelegs and shoulders were still there, the mane was scruffy but intact, and the drooping head still formidable looking. But the strength was gone. I asked about him, and our friends said the guides told them the lion was on his last legs. An apex predator in charge of a pride in his prime, he was old and extremely vulnerable now. The guide said that if the old lion didn't succumb to some of kind of illness or infection, the hyenas would find him sooner or later and that would be that.

All I could think about was Diz.

In making that comparison I am not attempting to romanticize or sentimentalize the violence in his life or the crime. In all fairness, neither does he. He was not literally an apex predator. (To my way of thinking, the real apex predators today are much further up the food chain, the Madoff's and Enron Executives of the world.) However, in his prime Diz was feared and respected on his home turf, and with good reason. He lived in a world over which he felt he had some control. He wasn't invisible. People knew who he was and what he was. It's not like that anymore, and it's perhaps the hardest adjustment for him to make.

Diz Long is what he is. I said earlier that we had some experiences in common and that I could sometimes finish his sentences. There were many more times when I could not. One of the most striking examples occurred about halfway through the interviewing process the first year. It was when he was describing the trouble he had with his foster mother's boyfriend. After he had told me about the incident in which the man cut him badly with a flick knife, he started a sentence by saying, "I knew then", and without saying anything out loud I silently finished it for him. I was sure he was going to say something like, "I knew then *that I had to get out of there*", run away, or something like that. What he said, quite matter-of-factly was, "I knew then that I would have to kill him."

I didn't see it coming. I guess it was because he was still talking about his youth (although he was a teenager) and because that possibility would never have occurred to me. I thought about it quite a bit, and still could never imagine circumstances in which I could imagine myself saying that. But, I also realized, I was never on my own—as completely on my own—as Diz was. I never had to worry that I wouldn't recognize my mother because I had been away from her so long. I never had to deal with anything like the older boys who tried to assault him in the shower. I never had the temptations that would inevitably have accompanied the physical gifts Diz was blessed with. And at every stage of my early life I had options that weren't available to him. I was highly aware of these differences early in the process and because of them I never judged Diz and the decisions he made in his life. I didn't judge them then, and I don't now.

A few times during the interviewing and drafting process, Diz would get impatient at how long things were taking. He was always careful not so seem critical of me, but one day he smiled archly and said, "You know Harold [Robbins] used to just lock himself in a room for a few days and practically write a whole book." I smiled back and said, "I'm sure that's true, but Harold Robbins was writing fiction. He could just make it all up. What we're doing is remembering, and it takes a lot longer." He laughed and didn't bring it up again. More often, however, he would seem to feel genuinely bad because of what he perceived to be all the work I was doing. "You're doing all that work," he would say, and not getting anything out of it." I could never make him see how wrong he was.

Everything about this project was interesting and fun for me. Listening to him talk about his life opened a door to worlds I could never have experienced in the same way just by reading about them. The friendship that happened was unexpected, too, and all the more rewarding because of it. And it's more than that. I have a younger colleague, James Sheeler, who is a Pulitzer Prize- winning journalist. He does what he calls "immersion journalism" which, in simplest terms means that he spends a lot of time with his subjects, gets to know them and what their life is like extremely well—much like my experience with Diz. I went to a talk of Jim's recently in which he concluded by saying—of the people he writes about—that "When someone gives you the gift of something real you have to respect it." His thought captures exactly what I have come to feel about Diz Long: In spending the time he did telling me his story, telling me the things he told me, he did indeed offer gift of something real. I do respect it and only hope I have been able to do it the justice it deserves.

Cleveland, Ohio

Appendix A: A Brief History of the Negro Leagues
1. The Baseball World before 1890.

While it would be quite a stretch to say that professional baseball in the North was integrated between the end of the Civil War and 1890, quite a number of African-Americans played alongside white athletes on minor league and major league teams during the period. Although the original National Association of Base Ball Players, formed in 1867, had banned black athletes, by the late 1870s several African-American players were active on the rosters of white, minor league teams. Most of these players fell victim to regional prejudices and an unofficial color ban after brief stays with white teams, but some notable exceptions built long and solid careers in white professional baseball. In 1884 the Stillwater, Minnesota club in the Northwestern league signed John W. "Bud" Fowler, an African-American with more than a decade's experience as an itinerate, professional player. Fowler, a second-baseman by preference, played virtually every position on the field for Stillwater, enhancing the reputation that had brought him to the attention of white team owners. Fowler's baseball career continued through the end of the 19th Century, much of it spent on the rosters of minor league clubs in organized baseball. In 1883 former Oberlin College star Moses "Fleetwood" Walker began his professional career with Toledo in the Northwestern League. A more than average hitter, Walker was among baseball's finest catchers almost from the beginning of his career. When the Toledo club joined the American Association in 1884 Walker became the first black player to play with a major league franchise. In 1886 both Walker and Fowler were in the white minor leagues along with two other black stars, George Stovey and Frank Grant. Doubtless, many other black players were playing with teams in the "outlaw" leagues and independent barnstorming clubs. At least in the North and Midwest the best black players found a measure of tolerance, if not acceptance, in white baseball until the end of the 1880s. But in 1890 this situation abruptly changed. As the season of 1890 began there were no black players in the International League, the most prestigious of the minor league circuits. Without making a formal announcement, a gentlemen's agreement had been made which would bar black players from participation for the next fifty-five years. Though black players continued to find work in lesser leagues for a time, within only a few short years no team in organized baseball would accept black players. By the turn of the century the color barrier was firmly in place.

2. Professional Black Baseball Comes To The Fore

While Fowler, Walker, Grant and others were working to find a spot (and keep it) in organized baseball, other black players were pursuing careers with the more than 200 all-black independent teams that performed throughout the country from the early 1880s forward. Eastern teams like the powerful Cuban Giants, Cuban X Giants and Harrisburg Giants played both independently and in loosely organized leagues through the end of the century, and in the early 1900s professional black baseball began to blossom throughout America's heartland and even in the South. The early years of the 20th Century saw an emergence of several powerful black clubs in the Midwest. Teams like the Chicago Giants, Indianapolis ABCs, St. Louis Giants and Kansas City Monarchs rose to prominence and presented a legitimate challenge to the claim of diamond supremacy made by Eastern clubs like the Lincoln Giants in New York, Brooklyn Royal Giants, Cuban Stars and Homestead (Pa.) Grays. In the South, black baseball was flourishing in Birmingham's industrial leagues, and teams like the Nashville Standard Giants and Birmingham Black Barons were establishing solid regional reputations. By the end of World War I black baseball had become, perhaps, the number one entertainment attraction for urban black populations throughout the country. It was at that time that Andrew "Rube" Foster, owner of the Chicago American Giants and black baseball's most influential personality, determined that the time had arrived for a truly organized and stable Negro league. Under Foster's leadership in 1920 the Negro National League was born in Kansas City, fielding eight teams: Chicago American Giants, Chicago Giants, Cuban Stars, Dayton Marcos, Detroit Stars, Indianapolis ABCs, Kansas City Monarchs and St. Louis Giants. In the same year Thomas T. Wilson, owner of the Nashville Elite Giants, organized the Negro Southern League with teams in Nashville, Atlanta, Birmingham, Memphis, Montgomery and New Orleans. Only three years later the Eastern Colored League was formed in 1923 featuring the Hilldale Club, Cuban Stars (East), Brooklyn Royal Giants, Bacharach Giants, Lincoln Giants and Baltimore black Sox.

The Negro National League continued on a sound footing for most of the 1920s, ultimately succumbing to the financial pressures of the Great Depression and dissolving after the 1931 season. The second Negro National League, organized by Pittsburgh bar owner Gus Greenlee, quickly took up where Foster's league left off and became the dominant force in black baseball from 1933 through 1949. The Negro Southern League was in continuous operation from 1920 through the 1940s and held the position as black baseball's only operating major circuit for the 1931 season. In 1937 the Negro American League was launched, bringing into its fold the best clubs in the South and Midwest, and stood as the opposing circuit to Greenlee's Negro National League until the latter league disbanded after the 1949 season. Despite the difficult economic challenges posed to the entire nation by the Depression, the three major Negro League circuits weathered the storm and steadily built what was to become one of the largest and most successful black-owned enterprises in America. The existence and success of these leagues stood as a testament to the determination and resolve of black America to forge ahead in the face of racial segregation and social disadvantage.

3. The Golden Years of Black Baseball

When Gus Greenlee organized the new Negro National League in 1933 it was his firm intention to field the most powerful baseball team in America. He may well have achieved his goal. In 1935 his Pittsburgh Crawfords lineup showcased the talents of no fewer than five future Hall-Of-Famers - Satchel Paige, Josh Gibson, Cool Papa Bell, Judy Johnson and Oscar Charleston.

While the Crawfords were, undoubtedly, black baseball's premier team during the mid-1930s, by the end of the decade Cumberland Posey's Homestead Grays had wrested the title from the Crawfords, winning 9 consecutive Negro National League titles from the late 1930s through the mid-1940s. Featuring former Crawfords stars Gibson and Bell, the Grays augmented their lineup with Hall-Of-Fame talent such as that of power-hitting first baseman Buck Leonard.

Contributing greatly to the ever-growing national popularity of Negro League baseball during the 1930s and 1940s was the East-West All-Star game played annually at Chicago's Comiskey Park. Originally conceived as a promotional tool by Gus Greenlee in 1933, the game quickly became black baseball's most popular attraction and biggest money maker. From the first game forward the East-West classic regularly packed Comiskey Park while showcasing the Negro League's finest talent.

As World War II came to a close and the demands for social justice swelled throughout the country, many felt that it could not be long until baseball's color barrier would come crashing down. Not only had African-Americans proven themselves on the battlefield and seized an indisputable moral claim to an equal share in American life, the stars of the black baseball had proven their skills in venues like the East-West Classic and countless exhibition games against major league stars. The time for integration had come.

4. The Color Barrier Is Broken

Baseball's color barrier cracked on April 18, 1946 when Jackie Robinson, signed to the Dodgers organization by owner Branch Rickey, made his first appearance with the Montreal Royals in the International League. After a single season with Montreal, Robinson joined the parent club and helped propel the Dodgers to a National League pennant. Along the way he also earned National League Rookie of the Year honors. Robinson's success opened the floodgates for a steady stream of black players into organized baseball. Robinson was shortly joined in Brooklyn by Negro League stars Roy Campanella, Joe Black and Don Newcombe, and Larry Doby became the American League's first black star with the Cleveland Indians. By 1952 there were 150 black players in organized baseball, and the "cream of the crop" had been lured from Negro League rosters to the integrated minors and majors. During the four years immediately following Robinson's debut with the Dodgers virtually all of the Negro Leagues' best talent had either left the league for opportunities with integrated teams or had grown too old to attract the attention of major league scouts. With this sudden and dramatic departure of talent black team owners witnessed a financially devastating decline in attendance at Negro League games. The attention of black fans had forever turned to the integrated major leagues, and the handwriting was on the wall for the Negro Leagues.

The Negro National League disbanded after the 1949 season, never to return. After a long and successful run black baseball's senior circuit was no longer a viable commercial enterprise. Though the Negro American League continued on throughout the 1950s, it had lost the bulk of its talent and virtually all of its fan appeal. After a decade of operating as a shadow of its former self, the league closed its doors for good in 1962. (www.negroleaguebaseball.com/ho=istory101.html)

Appendix B: Shondor & Danny

By Fred McGunagle

Both were brutal, cold-blooded murderers. Both were also publicity hounds who courted reporters. The violence they started claimed both their lives. But, in the end, it also destroyed not only the Cleveland Mafia but Mafia families across the nation. Mafioso after Mafioso forsook his blood oath of *omerta* and — from the safety of the federal Witness Protection Program — "ratted" on his colleagues.

Shondor Birns and Danny Greene fascinated Clevelanders for four decades. They were first-name celebrities — "Shondor" and "Danny." Shondor Birns. If you crossed him, Shondor would kill you. If you didn't, he would charm you. Everyone agreed he could have been a successful restaurateur if he had stayed legitimate. Cops and reporters were among those who frequented his popular Alhambra Tavern. Lawyers and legitimate businessmen clamored for a chance to shake the hand of the famous killer.

Danny Greene. Swaggering Danny Greene reveled in his Irish ancestry. He devoured books about Ireland and passed out green pens that wrote in green ink. To his poor neighbors, he was Robin Hood, helping those in trouble and sending around turkeys at Thanksgiving. But he too had a second career, of a sort. To the FBI, he was "Mr. Patrick," a top-level confidential source. In the end, Danny got Shondor, blowing him up on Holy Saturday, the eve of Easter. The Cleveland Mob tried time after time to get Danny. Other Mafia families laughed at it as "the gang that couldn't shoot straight." Greene defied them, calling its members "maggots" on television and daring them to come after him. .Finally they succeeded. Greene, who had lived by the bomb, died by the bomb.

What the Mob didn't know was that it had destroyed the Cleveland Mafia. Within a few years, many of its top leaders were either in prison or the witness protection program. The FBI used them to send Mafia leaders toppling like dominoes from coast to coast.

Going Out with a Bang

It can truly be said of Shondor Birns that nothing in his life so befitted him as his leaving of it. The blast that broke the Holy Saturday silence in 1975 could be heard for blocks. It brought people running to the parking lot behind Christy's Lounge, a go-go bar across the Cuyahoga River from downtown Cleveland. They found the wreckage of a light blue Lincoln Continental Mark IV. Next to the open driver's door lay the upper body of the 68-year-old man the newspapers called Alex "Shondor" Birns. It had been blown through what was now a gaping hole in the roof. Other parts of Birns came down nearby. Parts of the car landed on the steps of St. Malachi Catholic Church 1,000 feet away. Parishioners arriving for the 8 p.m. Easter Vigil Mass could see patches of Birns' clothing in the churchyard trees. St. Malachi Catholic Church Police said the blast was among the most powerful they had ever investigated.

Such a Nice Guy

The story was, naturally, all over the media, as had been Shondor's antics for four decades. In the Cleveland Press, Dick McLaughlin summed up his career: "A muscleman whose specialty was controlling numbers gambling on the East Side, keeping the peace among rival operators and getting a cut from each of them, Birns was a feared man because of his violent reaction to any adversary." But the next paragraph told of a different Shondor:" Yet he was popular, had an engaging personality, was known by many newsmen because he was 'good copy' and was ever ready to buy them a drink (including this reporter)."He was a feared man, but a genial and generous man, holding court almost daily at the Theatrical Lounge where he lunched." There, he was gracious with the lawyers and downtown businessmen who, like Tony Soprano's neighbors, came up to shake the hand of the famous criminal.

He was also willing to lend money and do favors. "I was playing around on my wife," said an unnamed businessman, "and she had a private eye tailing me. I told Shondor about it and he told the private eye, 'I'd appreciate it if you'd leave this man alone.' I never saw the private eye again." His old associates were surprised that he had become so careless in his old age. He had settled into the custom of visiting Christy's every Saturday to chat with the owner and the barmaid and sometimes buy drinks for the regulars. One of his friends seemed to have the explanation: "He told me last week that this was his last month in the rackets. He said he was going to retire, that he had enough money and couldn't spend it all." Police rounded up the usual suspects, but the bombing wound up, like so many bombings in previous months, as an unsolved crime. They had a suspect, another hoodlum who had reason to want Shondor dead, but they couldn't get the goods on him: It was Danny Greene, a would-be Shondor, who envied Birns' control of the rackets. Not to mention his front-page reputation.

Shondor the Apprentice Hood

The newspapers called him Alex "Shondor" Birns, but that was backwards. He was born Szandor Birnstein in 1907 in what was then the Austro-Hungarian Empire but is now Lemesany, Slovak Republic. (Szandor, or Sandor, is Hungarian for Alexander.) Shortly afterward, the family moved to Cleveland and shortened its name. With the arrival of Prohibition, his parents were among the many Clevelanders who went into the bootlegging business. In "*The Rise and Fall of the Cleveland Mafia*," Rick Porrello writes that Birns' mother was killed when the still in their home exploded. He spent his youth in the Jewish Orphan Asylum, where he excelled at athletics and street fighting. He was still a juvenile when he was arrested for car theft in 1925. He served 18 months in the Mansfield Reformatory. .It was not until 1933, after he hooked up with the Maxie Diamond gang, that his career made Page One, and then only in a supporting role. The Cleveland Plain Dealer reported: "Maxie Diamond, 36, one of Cleveland's most notorious gang leaders, narrowly escaped death from underworld bullets last night in what police say is a continuation of the city's dry cleaning racket war. The story listed Birns among those picked up for questioning. He was released, but only after paying $2 for two overdue traffic tickets. Later in the year he was shot from the same passing car. Police called it "continuation of guerilla warfare among policy game racketeers." Among others, they picked up "Alex (Shondor) Birns, 27, reputed E. 55th St.-Woodland racketeer, and five of his alleged henchmen." Birns and three others were charged with manslaughter but were acquitted. Four days later, Birns, along with co-defendant Yale Cohen and attorney Max Lesnick were convicted of bribing a witness. It was, the Plain Dealer said, "one of the few cases on record in which men identified by police as 'gangsters' were convicted of anything." The judge sentenced them to 60 days in the Warrensville Workhouse.

Not long after Birns got out, police arrested 19 people in a melee at the opening of a Euclid Avenue nightclub. Searching through the cars in the parking lot, they found Birns lying on the ground. He had been shot, but was able to walk into the emergency room for treatment. He denied knowing who shot him. Two months later, Rudy Duncan, 42, "ex-pugilist and night club bouncer," took his 11-year-old foster son Stanley to a movie. Afterwards, they walked to a confectionery for ice cream. When they got into their car back in the theater parking lot, two men wearing white cotton gloves walked up alongside, one on each side. With a terrified Stanley crouching in the seat, they fired five bullets into Duncan. Police immediate began a search for Birns. They found him, but they couldn't find evidence to tie him to the murder. He was released. Out on the street, however, the word was getting around: Don't mess with Shondor Birns."

Shondor the Genial Host

Birns' reputation as a brutal, ruthless enforcer made it easy for him to establish lucrative "protection" services. Legal businesses grudgingly paid him as a labor consultant. That meant he and his toughs provided protection from, say, the rocks and firebombs that would be thrown through their storefront windows if they didn't hire him. One job provided more than just profits. He protected what the newspapers called "vice resorts." Rick Porrello relates that "It was quite fun and all the girls liked him. ... Many of Shondor's clients were judges, politicians and ranking police officers. They would be important contacts for Birns in the future, as he would be for them."

In particular, Birns found a niche in the city's "numbers racket," an illegal lottery that the newspapers regularly decried until the state of Ohio went into the same business. Rival operators paid him a cut of their take to protect their territories from rivals, something they previously had to do with bullets and bombs. Peacemaker Shondor got a cut of the take from each. If any were delinquent, he left a calling card that, for instance, destroyed their front porch. They quickly paid up. At the same time, Shondor was building a profitable legitimate business as a restaurateur. His Alhambra Tavern on the East Side became the place to be seen. The genial host oversaw the kitchen and welcomed his guests, who included many police and reporters. Shondor's 1011 Club downtown was another popular nightspot. Of course, convicted felons weren't supposed to be able to get liquor licenses. Birns managed to get around that by disguising his connections to the Alhambra. At one point, he was simply its "public relations director." The Cleveland safety director denounced the deal in which the state okayed Birns' license as "stinking to high heaven of politics." Birns did have a patriotic side. When World War II broke out, he tried to enlist. His draft board was willing, figuring that better he should be shooting Germans. Federal prosecutors felt otherwise. Birns had never become a citizen. He was sent to an internment camp as an illegal alien. There he remained, bitterly protesting he was a loyal American, until 1944. The government tried to deport him to his native country, which by now had become Czechoslovakia. Czechoslovakia wouldn't take him. .After the war, Shondor resumed his old habits. In 1959, he made the mistake of beating up a policeman. He was convicted of assault and battery and sent to the Workhouse for nine months. He practically ran the place. The superintendent was later fired for the liberties he allowed Birns. One, it turned out, was masterminding the bombing of the car of numbers operator Joe Allen in an attempt to shake him down for 25 percent of his operation. Twice the state tried Birns for the crime. A Workhouse guard admitted on the witness stand that he had acted as a go-between in trying to arrange a deal with Allen. The first jury hung. The second acquitted him. He blew kisses to the jury. In a Page One editorial, the Press thundered, "Who Runs This Town — Birns or the Law?" The prosecutors didn't give up. They accused Birns to trying to contact a juror in the second case. He said he had merely asked an Alhambra waitress to see if the juror would be fair to him. Ten of the jurors signed a statement protesting the charge that they had been unduly influenced. Shondor had beaten another rap. It would not be the last.

The King & Shondor

Don King in later life, Donald King would be world-famous as the boxing promoter who hooked up with a young heavyweight named Muhammad Ali. Before that, he would spend four years in prison for literally "stomping" to death a minor numbers racketeer as he lay on the sidewalk, calling out, "How much do I owe you? How much do I owe you?" But now, in 1957, he was "The Kid," just one of the numbers operators competing violently for bettors in Cleveland's ghetto. Except that he defied Shondor Birns.

King was flamboyant — always seen "with a .38 in his belt and a big cigar in his mouth," according to a 1988 Plain Dealer series by Christopher Evans. But he had gotten little attention outside the ghetto, except for the 1954 killing of a rival in what was ruled self-defense. Now he made Page One headlines. A bomb blasted his front porch at 3:45 on a May morning in 1957. King told police: "Shondor was one of the five pistols who bombed me." King explained that he had been one of five numbers operators who each paid Birns $200 a week to make sure that none of their competitors paid odds of more than 500 to 1. King was behind in his payments. He told police he had decided to get out of the racket. Birns was charged with blackmail. "He appeared jovial and confident when he was booked," the Press reported. King was promised 24-hour police protection. In October, though, he was ambushed outside his home. A shotgun blast hit him in the side of the head. Taken to the hospital, he refused to cooperate with police. At the trial, however, King told jurors that a Birns emissary had offered him $10,000 not to testify: "He said if I didn't testify, he would guarantee there would be no more shooting at me or bombing my house and I'd have no reason to be scared no more." The prosecution produced a surprise witness, "a former employee of the rackets." On the stand, the Press reported, "she burst into tears again and again and refused to answer questions as Birns and the other defendants glared at her. Her attorney told the judge she was told that she and her 12-year-old daughter would be killed if she testified." Elijah Abercrombie, a co-defendant, told the jury that police had offered to let him run an unhampered gambling game if he gave them information against Birns. Defense lawyer Fred Garmone called King "a scheming, lying, witness-fixing extortionist himself." The jury deliberated 11 hours. It cleared one defendant and hung on Birns and the others. Once more, he had beaten the rap.

Two years later, somebody took a shot at Birns as he arrived home. He missed. Birns cruised the neighborhood looking for him, but he got away. Police picked up a small-time hood named Clarence "Sonny" Coleman, who owed money to Birns. He was released after questioning. .A short time afterward, Coleman was shot on a neighborhood street shortly after midnight. Three bullets hit him, but he managed to run up to the front porch of a house yelling, "Let me in, baby, let me in! "In the hospital, he told police the shooter was a man in the back seat of a car driven by Shondor Birns. Police went to Birns' home. He answered the door in his pajamas and said he had been asleep. However, the hood of his car was still warm. .Still wearing obviously expensive pajamas, robe and slippers, Birns was brought to the booking window at Central Station. As he walked in, he glanced up and saw reporters waiting alongside the window. .A big smile lighted up his face. "Hi, boys," he called out. .A month later, Coleman told police he had changed his mind. He had only thought it was Birns in the car. Police arrested Coleman as a material witness. He changed his mind again and reluctantly agreed to testify. .At the trial, a neighbor backed Birns' alibi. He said he saw Birns arrive home at 12:07 a.m., about the time of the shooting several miles away. .It took the jurors four hours to reach a verdict: Not guilty. They said they didn't believe the changing testimony of a man who had been a dope peddler and police informant, meaning Coleman. .Police predicted what the Press called "a fresh outbreak of shootings and violence in Cleveland's multi-million-dollar numbers racket.

Bonds and Bullets

On Saturday, July 7, 1963, the wife of financier Mervin L. Gold called police to report her husband missing. .Lily Gold hadn't seen him since 10 the previous night, when he put some papers in an envelope and said he was going to meet Shondor Birns. Mervin L. Gold had a history of shady deals. At the time, he was free on bond on federal charges that he had used $55,000 in stolen Canadian bonds as collateral for two bank loans and had embezzled $42,000 by manipulating funds of the defunct Cosmopolitan Small Business Co. There was widespread speculation that he was being used as a scapegoat to protect prominent people. .On Sunday, Gold's car was found in a wooded area. His body was in the trunk. Coroner Samuel Gerber reported he had been beaten, strangled and shot three times. He estimated time of death as shortly before midnight Friday. .A pickup order went out for Birns, but he was nowhere to be found. .On Monday his car turned up outside a motel in Toledo. He was not around. The motel owner said he had checked in Saturday and sought treatment for an injured right hand. He told the doctor a firecracker caused the injury. On Wednesday morning, Birns called John Kocevar, chief deputy Cuyahoga County sheriff. He arranged to surrender at a meeting spot in suburban Garfield Heights. He told Kocevar,

"I would have surrendered yesterday, but it was a Jewish holiday." Somebody also tipped off the Press; a reporter and photograph were waiting when he arrived. Birns told them, "Thanks for coming, fellows." Birns was taken to Central Station for questioning by the head of the Homicide Unit, Lieutenant Carl Delau (pronounced De Law).Reporters outside the office could hear Birns shouting, "I'd like to talk to you sometime when there are no witnesses around!" Birns said he had an alibi: H was at home with a woman of "fine character." He did not name her, but said she was willing to testify for him. .His bail hearing drew the largest crowd in Criminal Courts since the Sheppard murder five years earlier. Bail was set at $50,000. Birns posted it. .Then, the Plain Dealer reported, "Birns cocked his summer straw hat, waved goodbye to reporters, walked out of the building and down the front steps to where his attorney, James R. Willis, was waiting." Two days later his witness was revealed. She was Allene Leonards, a teacher in the Garfield Heights school system. At 24, she was 33 years younger than Birns. .The Press reported the story told by "the pretty brunette:" She had been with Shondor at a Garfield Heights steakhouse. The owner confirmed it. After drinks, Birns had frog's legs and she had whitefish. The bill with tax was $5. They left at 10 or maybe 10:30. Birns was "his normal, smiling self." Gerber saw a chance to help his newspaper friends — and get some publicity himself — by scheduling an inquest, as he had done in the Sheppard case. "Dr. Gerber Vows Alibi Girl Will Testify in Gold Case," headlined the Plain Dealer. Neighbors told reporters that Miss Leonards was "very nice," but they thought she should go out more often. The Plain Dealer reported that the "demure brunette of medium height" lived in Cleveland with her widowed mother. .She refused to testify and was cited for contempt. At her bond hearing, photographers snapped her on the witness stand with her legs crossed. The Plain Dealer said, "Dressed in a knit beige suit, appliquéd with brown butterflies, and a white sweater, Miss Leonards was very attractive." She again took the Fifth, as did Birns. "Arrest Alibi Girl, Wouldn't Testify," the Plain Dealer headlined. .She resigned her teacher's job. The Internal Revenue Service seized Birns' Cadillac toward the income taxes he still owed. Gold had given his wife some papers to be given to police if anything happened to him. She turned them over. Police also found a tape made by Gold of a phone call between himself and Shondor. Gold said, "Here's what I've done to you. Every last drop is down on 23 sheets of paper, single-spaced — just in case you get the clever idea of being cute." Birns replied, "You ain't going to put me up against the wall!" Nothing came of the papers or tapes. Gradually, the case faded from the public eye. On July 5, 1964, the Plain Dealer reported, "Trail Leading to Gold's Murder Grows Cold." The Press said simply, "Mervin Gold Slain One Year Ago Today."

Birns divorced his wife and married Allene Leonards. Perhaps married life mellowed him. He did little that made the papers for the next few years. .There was a good reason in the period from 1968 and 1971. His old antagonist, the Internal Revenue Service, had him sent to federal prison for lying about his assets. .The Birns who emerged from prison was a less flamboyant Shondor. He told his parole officer, "Kid, I don't break any provision of parole. I'll tell you why. If I go back to jail, I'll die there." Still, he kept his hand in. When longtime Mafia capo John Scalish died, Birns teamed up with the faction backing James Licavoli, known in Mafia circles as Jack White, as the new don. .He was suspected in several bombings, including the one that destroyed the home of an ambitious rival named Danny Greene. Greene said of the bomb: "I'm going to send this back to the old bastard who sent it to me" Thus, Greene was an immediate suspect when Shondor was blown to Kingdom Come on Easter Saturday, 1975.But, as in so many cases when Birns was the suspect, police failed to find evidence to tie him to it.

Danny Greene, Champion of Labor

Like Shondor Birns, Daniel Patrick Greene was an orphan. He was born Nov. 9, 1933, five days after his 20-year-old parents were married. His mother died of complications from the birth. Left with a baby to care for, his father turned him over to Parmadale, a Catholic orphanage. Later he wound up with his grandfather, who sent him to Catholic schools until he was expelled from St. Ignatius High School. At Collinwood High School, he starred in baseball and basketball. Young Danny Greene in his baseball outfit. In 1951, he left school and joined the Marines. There he stood out as a boxer and a marksman — talents that would serve him well in the years ahead. .Greene's military ID photo. He worked at first as a railroad brakeman. In off hours, he read Irish history and novels about Ireland. He fancied himself as one of the "Celtic warriors" of old. He switched to the docks, unloading ships as a longshoreman. Greene was bright and popular with his fellow "dockwallopers." In 1961, when the president of the local was removed by the national office of the International Longshoremen's Association, the national officers picked Greene as interim president. He easily won election on He had the union office painted green with thick green carpeting. In "To Kill the Irishman: The War that Crippled the Mafia," Porrello writes: "He even had the union by-laws reprinted in green ink and used green paper to post announcements on the union bulletin board." In addition, he quickly raised dues 25 percent and pressured members to work "volunteer" hours to provide a "building fund." Those who refused found themselves passed over for work at the morning shapeup. .His contacts with leaders of other unions under investigation brought a visit from Marty McCann, an agent in the FBI Organized Crime Division. Greene became a confidential informant, quietly passing along information that suited his purposes. The FBI called him "Mr. Patrick." The FBI connection would serve him well in the future.

On the Waterfront

Greene called a strike and forced the stevedore companies to agree to a union-controlled hiring hall. He declared: "The hiring hall is a place where Irish kids can get a decent day's wages." In practice, the hiring was right out of "On the Waterfront." Greene's supporters got the good assignments. Others got dirty jobs or none at all. Those who complained were beaten by goons. By 1964, his members had had enough. Some of them got in touch with Sam Marshall of the Plain Dealer. The resulting nine-part series began: *A job shakedown on Cleveland's waterfront is forcing longshoremen to work thousands of hours without pay. Workers are being compelled to give up an estimated $30,000 or more a year, former officers of the International Longshoremen's Local 1317 told the Plain Dealer.* Greene scoffed that the complainers were "all dissidents." But the series quickly brought investigations by the U.S. attorney, the Internal Revenue Service, the Labor Department and the Cuyahoga County prosecutor. It also emboldened the members: 92 of them signed a petition asking the International to remove Greene as president. The ILA quickly sent a team that found, among other things, that Greene had failed to make payments to the union's welfare fund and had planted "bugs" throughout the union hall to record what members were saying about him. The officials immediately stopped payment on all union checks and removed Greene from office. Somebody went further: He fired shots into Greene's home when he was out but his wife was in the house. Greene responded with a bitter letter of resignation. He listed his accomplishments — pay raises, a new union office, the ouster of "winos" and drifters who were replaced with "decent men supporting families." He declared: "After nearly four years of devoting all my energies to get the dock workers of Cleveland a fair shake, I now find my only compensation is headlines in the newspaper and bullets through my windows." Greene was eventually convicted of embezzling $11,500 in union funds and two counts of falsifying records. An appeals court overturned the verdict and federal prosecutors settled for Greene's guilty plea of two misdemeanors involving union records. He was also fined $10,000.Porrello notes: "Perhaps Danny was enjoying some protection from the FBI. He paid only a fraction of the fine and was never imprisoned."

Banned from union activity, Danny Greene had little trouble finding employment. A new industry cried out for "protection." Waste collectors fought for business by beating up, and even bombing, their rivals. A group of operators got together to form the Cleveland Solid Waste Trade Guild. They hired Danny Greene to "keep peace" and make sure nobody undercut their prices. Greene also undertook a job that Shondor Birns was temporarily unable to perform because of a prior engagement: He was serving a three-year federal sentence on a tax charge. Shondor saw in young Danny a man after his own heart. He deputized Danny to fill in for him as enforcer for the numbers operators. In May 1968, Greene found himself back on Page One. He was driving on the East Side when a bomb exploded in his car. The car was demolished.   Greene was thrown nearly 20 feet, but escaped with minor injuries — "the luck of the Irish," he said. He told police he had been minding his own business when somebody in a passing car threw the bomb through his car window. He managed to brush it onto the passenger side before it went off. Police couldn't get any more out of him. "I can't hear you," he told them. "The bomb did something to my ears." He told the Press, "I don't know who did it, but I intend to find out." Actually, he did know who did it. He did it himself. He was taking the bomb to use against a waste hauler when he accidentally set it off .From then on, he hired professionals to do his bombing. One of the waste haulers, Mike Frato, had been a friend of Greene's. Until, that is, he organized a legitimate trade group, the Cuyahoga County Waste Haulers Association. Nearly all the others joined him. The Solid Waste Guild fell apart.

In 1971, Frato's Cadillac was destroyed by a bomb. There was a body inside, but it was that of Art Sneperger, one of Greene's men. Sneperger had been careless with the bomb he was trying to plant. Either that or Greene had pushed the detonator early because he suspected Sneperger of being a police informant. A month later, Frato was shot and killed in his car. Police immediately picked up Greene. He admitted he had killed Frato, but said it was self-defense. He had been jogging in a park when a car pulled up, he said. A man leaned out the window and fired at Greene. It was Frato. Greene dropped to the ground, pulled a pistol from his sweat pants and fired two quick shots. One of them hit Frato in the temple, killing him. Police quickly arrested Greene, but the evidence backed his story that he was acting in self-defense. He was released. Not long after, somebody else shot at Greene in the park. Porrello describes what happened: *But instead of ducking to the ground, Danny pulled out his revolver and started shooting, while running toward his would-be assassin, in complete disregard for his own safety. The tactic worked. The sniper fled and was never positively identified*

In 1973, Robert Doggett, director of Cleveland's Model Cities project, was shot while walking to his office. The multi-million-dollar plan to rebuild the rundown Hough Area had been plagued by scandals. Paging through the police "mug book," Doggett picked out Danny Greene as the man who shot him. The head of the police homicide squad was Lieutenant Edward Kovacic, who lived near Greene and had coached Greene's son in Catholic Youth Organization football. In Kovacic's official capacity, he regularly dropped by Greene's house to grill him about recent crimes. Eventually the two developed a grudging respect for each other. Greene would pass along information about other racketeers, something he was already doing for the FBI.

Kovacic would pass along warnings about rivals out to kill him. Kovacic thought there was something fishy about the Doggett case. He told Greene, "Danny, I'm going to send you to prison, but not for something you didn't do." Sure enough, it turned out the shots had been fired by Gerald Johnson, a former employee of a shady contractor who was seeking a city contract. Johnson's body was found in the Ohio River, an anchor tied to his leg. Johnson's murder went unsolved

Returning to his roots, Greene left his wife and moved back to Collinwood, to a storefront with an apartment above it. The storefront became headquarters for Greene's "consulting" business and a hangout for Greene and a group of young Danny wannabees. He also became the Robin Hood of Collinwood. In a Cleveland Magazine story called "How Danny Greene's Murder Exploded the Godfather Myth," Ned Whelan wrote: "Imagining himself as a feudal baron, he supported a number of destitute Collinwood families, paid tuition to Catholic schools for various children and, like the gangsters of the Twenties, actually had turkeys delivered to needy households on Thanksgiving. "His neighbors, in turn, kept an eye out and warned him if they saw suspicious cars cruising past his apartment. Greene also did something that nobody else would have dared to do. He stiffed Shondor Birns out of $75,000.Greene wanted the money to set up a "cheat spot," a speakeasy and gambling house. Shondor arranged a loan through the Gambino "family" — the New York Mafia. Somehow the money wound up in the hands of Billy Cox, a numbers operator, who used it to make a narcotics buy. Police raided his home, arrested him and seized the narcotics and what was left of the $75,000.

The Gambinos "leaned on" Shondor for their money. Shondor leaned on Greene, but he refused to come through with the money. He said it wasn't his fault that it was lost. Not long after, Greene found a bomb under his car. He took it to Kovacic, the homicide squad leader who was also his neighbor. Kovacic offered him police protection, but he refused. He also refused to hand over the bomb. "I'm going to send this back to the old bastard that sent it to me," he said. He did. On Holy Saturday. In the parking lot of Christy's Lounge. Shondor Birns, Cleveland's most infamous/famous hood, was dead. But there was a new claimant to the throne.

Reportedly, Shondor had left $25,000 with an associate. It was to hire a hit man in case anything happened to Birns. Shortly after Birns died, somebody fired shots at Greene and his girlfriend on the street. He missed. Then, on the morning of May 12, an explosion awakened much of Collinwood. Kovacic heard it while he was eating breakfast and immediately headed for Greene's building. The building was in shambles, but Greene, seemingly miraculously, had only minor injuries. When the second floor fell, he somehow was shielded from the debris by a refrigerator that lodged against a wall. A second bomb, a more powerful one, had failed to explode. Interviewed by the Press, Greene credited his escape to the intercession of St. Jude, whose medal he wore around his neck. The Press story continued: "This is what makes make mad,' Greene said, pointing to the shattered windows and cracked foundations of the nearby buildings." If they wanted to get me, why didn't they come straight at me? But endangering the lives of my friends and neighbors — whoever did this belongs in a cage." Again, Kovacic offered police protection. Again, Greene refused." There's not a bomb big enough to kill Danny Greene," he said. Kovacic had coached Greene's younger son, and he took a paternal interest in Danny Kelly, Greene's older son, who used his mother's maiden name. While he was trying to send Greene to the electric chair, Kovacic had to admire his guts. In a Plain Dealer story called" The Cop and the Kid," Mike Tobin described their cat-and-mouse game: *Over the years, an unusual relationship grew between the two. Since Greene trusted Kovacic, he'd shared information with him. It was a different time, when a cop and a racketeer could meet at a bar and pick each other's brains. When it became clear the mob had Greene in its sights, Kovacic tried to warn him. "Danny, I'm telling you, they are going to kill you," Kovacic said. Time and again, Greene dismissed Kovacic's warnings. So Kovacic — who was married and the father of three boys and three girls — made Greene a promise, one that Greene might not have taken seriously but that the cop never forgot. "Danny, after they kill you, I'll watch your two sons like they were my own. I can't raise girls, but I'll make sure the boys don't get in trouble."*

Mob War

Bombs were exploding across Greater Cleveland. Most of them, it seemed, were either sent by or aimed at Danny Greene. On May 26, 1977, two weeks after the bombing of Greene's house, John Scalish, longtime head of the Cleveland Mafia, died during an operation. His body "was followed to Calvary Cemetery by a seemingly endless procession of black Cadillacs," Ned Whelan wrote in Cleveland Magazine. Scalish's consigliere, Milton "Maishe" Rockman — sometimes called "the Meyer Lansky of Cleveland" — said Scalish had favored James Licavoli as his successor. James LicavoliIt was a strange choice. Licavoli was 71 and had not been active in Cleveland operations for years. Rick Porrello wrote in "To Kill the Irishman": "Although he had amassed a fortune from gambling enterprises, he was little more than a stingy old man, satisfied with living as a bachelor in his tiny Little Italy house with the strings of garlic hanging outside the back door." Licavoli had been called "Blackie" while he was growing up in Collinwood. Now he was known in the Mob as "Jack White," a more ironic reference to his swarthy complexion. He accepted the don's role reluctantly to keep peace in the family, and named Leo "Lips" Moceri as underboss. Leo "Lips" Moceri. Licavoli's ascendance did not sit well with John Nardi, a high-ranking Teamsters official who — like many high-ranking Teamsters — was involved with the Mob. He looked around for allies and found an obvious one: "The Irishman" — Danny Greene.

Greene had been growing his vending machine business. Like waste hauling, it was a rough business. The body of one of Greene's competitors, John Conte, was found in a deserted area. He had been bound, gagged and shot. Police believed he had been killed in Greene's office, but a search of the office failed to turn up evidence. Now Greene went to work on those who stood in Nardi's — and Greene's — way. And the Mob leaders went to work on Nardi and Greene. At least, they tried to. One of the most feared hit men in the Mob was Eugene "The Animal" Ciasullo. In July, he was walking up the steps to his front porch when a bomb hidden in a flowerpot exploded. He survived after a long hospitalization. That Greene and Nardi could do that to a brutal killer like Ciasullo shook up the Mob leaders. In August, at the Feast of the Assumption celebration in Little Italy, Moceri and Nardi got into a bitter argument over splitting proceeds of gambling events. A week later, Moceri's Mercedes was found with a bloody trunk. Moceri was never found. That an underboss had been killed — and without a "sit-down" of leaders — sent tremors through Mafia families around the nation. They put pressure on Licavoli:Kill Greene and Nardi! It was more easily said than done. Once, a detonator failed to explode a bomb in Greene's car. Another bomb was improperly wired. A bomb that would have gotten both Greene and Nardi failed to go off. Another bomb was set up correctly, but the hit men were too far away for their detonator to work. Two killers went to Texas, where Greene was negotiating to buy a cattle ranch. They couldn't find him. Licavoli tried hit man after hit man. He asked Jimmy "The Weasel" Fratianno, a former top official of the California Mafia, for advice."How about Ray Ferritto?" Fratianno suggested. Ferritto was a gambler-burglar-murderer from Erie, Pa. Fratianno's suggestion would be fateful for both Ferritto and himself.

Bomb City, U.S.A.

The Press labeled Cleveland "Bomb City, U.SA."Thirty-six bombs exploded around the city in 1976 alone. Still, Greene and his ally John Nardi survived. Bullets didn't work any better than bombs. Somebody fired six shots at Nardi as he entered his parked car outside the Italian-American Brotherhood Hall in Little Italy. Somehow, all missed Nardi. Meanwhile, the Mob got an almost unbelievable break in April. Geraldine Linhart, a clerk in the Cleveland FBI office for nine years, was having trouble with a lawsuit. Her fiancée, Jeffery Rabinowitz, approached a friend of Anthony "Tony Lib" Liberatore for help. Liberatore was an official of the Teamsters and — like many Teamster leaders — the Mob. For what turned out to be $1,000, plus a $15,000 loan and a false promise to help her with her suit, she managed to copy a list of confidential informants from her blissfully ignorant FBI employers. Among the names Mob leaders were surprised to find on the list: Jackie Presser, who was being groomed to succeed his father, Bill Presser, as head of the Cleveland Teamsters. Also listed was Tony Hughes, the liaison between Presser and Licavoli. They were less surprised to find Danny Greene's name. Jimmy Fratianno held his breath, but he wasn't named. He was on the informant list at the FBI office in San Diego, not Cleveland.

He breathed a sigh of relief and called his FBI contact there to tell him of the leak in Cleveland. Finally, the Mob found a bomb that worked. .Nardi varied his daily routine, parking his Cadillac in various locations. On May 17, though, he left it in the lot outside

Teamsters' headquarters. When he returned, he paid no attention to the Pontiac parked next to it. .Somebody watching from nearby pressed a detonator." The Pontiac disintegrated as it blew up, firing its shrapnel cargo and its roof into the victim," the *Press* reported. "Fragments of metal were found atop roofs of several four-story buildings surrounding the parking lot." Now it was just Danny Greene against the Mob.

Interviewed on television, Greene denied any knowledge of the underworld war. But he added, "If these maggots in this so-called Mafia want to come after me, I'm over here by the Celtic Club. I'm not hard to find." The Mob leaders seethed. They had been made to look foolish in the eyes of Mafia families around the country. .Ray Ferritto's "contract" provided that if he succeeded in killing Greene, he would be "made" — sworn into the Mafia with the oath of *omerta* — and would get a percentage of the rackets in Youngstown and nearby Warren. Pasquale "Butchy" Cisternino and Ronnie "the Crab" Carabbia were assigned to keep a close watch on Greene's office and try to pin down his routine. .Ferritto's first attempts were no more successful than those before him. The closest he came was when he planted a bomb in the bushes around Greene's home and office. He had second thoughts when he realized it might kill a number of Greene's neighbors. He retrieved the bomb. Finally, the Mob got the break it had been looking for: Danny Greene had a loose filling. .In early October, Ferritto got a call from Carabbia. Together they drove to Mosquito Lake, near Warren. The leaders of the Cleveland Mob were waiting on a boat. They had something they wanted Ferritto to hear. It was a wiretap recording of a phone call from Greene's girlfriend to the office of Dr. Alfonso Rossi, a dentist in the Brainard Place Building on Cedar Road in the suburb of Lyndhurst. She made an appointment for 3 p.m. on Oct. 6.Cisternino bought two cars, a maroon Chevy Nova and a blue Plymouth, registering them to fictitious addresses.

He welded a steel bomb compartment to the inside passenger door of the Nova, where it would direct the explosion outward. .On the morning of the sixth, Cisternino assembled the bomb and put it in a shopping bag. While Cisternino stayed behind, monitoring the police radio, Carabbia drove the Nova — the bomb car — to Lyndhurst. Ferritto followed in the Plymouth — the getaway car. Greene was late. They waited nervously. .At 3:20, he arrived in a brown Lincoln, parked and hurried into the building. Carabbia quickly pulled the Nova into the spot next to the Lincoln. He armed the bomb, put it in the steel compartment welded to the door and — a final irony — covered it with a green blanket. .Then he walked to a nearby phone booth and pretended to make a call so he could watch the door of the building...A little after 4, Greene emerged. .Carabbia got into the back seat of the Plymouth, holding the detonator. Ferritto slowly cruised the Plymouth onto Cedar Road. , As Greene reached his car, Carabbia pressed the detonator and Ferritto stepped on the gas "The explosion was thunderous," Whelan would write later. "It sent a red ball of fire into the air, a blinding cloud of flame that for an instant bathed the already sunlit parking lot in a terrifying white light." The bomb tore Greene's back apart. It ripped off all his clothing, except for his brown zip-up boots and black socks. It blew off his left arm, throwing it 100 feet away, the gold ring with five green stones still firmly on a finger. "His Adidas bag was untouched. Police found, among other contents, a 9mm pistol and a holy card with a prayer to the Blessed Virgin Mary. .Ferritto quickly turned onto the nearby I-271 entrance and raced northward. He and Carabbia had done it! They had killed the Irishman! Mafia membership and control of lucrative gambling operations awaited him. .Others were equally overjoyed." That night at a restaurant in Little Italy there was a celebration," Whelan writes. "One man who loathed Greene danced about in a drunken stupor. He pulled out a .38 and shot it wildly into the ceiling. "The Irishman is dead!" he screamed. "The Irishman is dead! The Irishman is dead!!"

(From Cleveland's Killer Celebrities, Part 1, "Shondor & Danny," by Fred McGunagle, www.trutv.com/library/crime/gangsters_outlaws/mob_bosses/birns-Greene/1.html)

Index

Birmingham Black Barons, 147

Black Homer, 305

Blue Monday, 191, 320

Blue Pike, 55

Bond, James, 241

Boone, Debbie, 215

Boone, Pat, 215

Boron, California, prison where Reuben Sturman was sent, 280

Bowe, Riddick, 66

Boys' Republic, 106, 107, 108, 313

Boy's Vocational School, 11, 92—96, 102, 103, 105—107, 168, 313

Braddock, Pennsylvania, 76, 77, 81, 302

Braverman, Ron, 287, 288

Brown, Jim, 25, 176—178, 206, 207, 208, 219, 309

Call & Post, the, 22, 37, 254

Callas, Maria, 18

Camp Le Jeune, North Carolina, 119, 121

Cannes, France, 272, 273, 288

Cardiac Kids, 253

Carlos, Juan, 221

Carnegie Avenue, Cleveland, 19

Carson City, California, 12, 263, 264

Case Institute of Technology, 12, 13

Case Western Reserve University, 13, 12, 168, 187, 208, 295, 314

Charles, Ray, 41, 197

Chatterbox, the, 41, 192-193, 200, 314

Cherry Point Naval Hospital, 121

Ciasullo, Eugene "the animal", muscle for Danny Greene, 250

Chicago American Giants, 147

Chicago, city of, 266, 316

Chicago Football Cardinals, the, 143, 144, 147, 167, 316

Chitlin Strut, 57

287

Minnelli, Liza, 215

Minnelli, Vincent, 215

Mitchell, Bobby, 177

Modell, Art, 208, 253

Montgomery, Robert, starring in Light Must Fall, 81

Moore, Archie, 245

Moore School, the, 89, 90, 168

Morgantown, West Virginia, 43

Moss, the Reverend Otis, 286, 287

Motley, Marion, 145, 309

Negro digest, 172

Negro Leagues, 147

Ness, Eliot, grave, 12

New York, City, 269

New York Football Giants, 149

Nixon, Richard, 267

(Endnotes)

1 *Helter Skelter* is a 1976 TV film based on the 1974 book by prosecutor Vincent Bugliosi and Curt Gentry. . .The movie is based upon the murders committed by the Charle s Manson Family. The best-known victim was actress Sharon Tate. The title was taken from the Beatles' song of the same name. According to the theory put forward by the prosecution, Manson used the term for an anticipated race war, and "healter skelter" [sic] was scrawled in blood on the refrigerator door at the house of one of the victims. (en.wikipedia.org/wiki/HelterSkelter_(1976_Film)

2 **Charles Thomas Fisher** (February 16, 1880-1963) was an American businessman and an automotive pioneer. Born in Norwalk, Ohio, Charles was the second son of Lawrence and Margaret Fisher. The family would grow to include seven boys and four girls. At the turn of the 20th century, eldest son Fred was the first to move to Detroit where an uncle, Albert Fisher, had established Standard Wagon Works during the latter part of the 1880s. A year later Charles Fisher joined his brother as an employee at the C. R. Wilson Company, a manufacturer of horse-drawn carriage bodies who were just beginning to construct bodies for the automobile makers. With the fledgling automobile business about to emerge as a major industry, together with their uncle Albert, on July 23, 1908 Charles and Fred Fisher founded the Fisher Body Company. Soon, they brought their five younger male siblings into the business. Highly successful, the Fishers expanded their operation into Canada, setting up a plant in Walkerville, Ontario and by 1914 their company had grown to become the world's largest

manufacturer of auto bodies. In 1919, the Fisher brothers sold sixty percent of their company to General Motors Corporation (GM). In 1926, Fisher Body Company became a subsidiary division of General Motors when the brothers sold their remaining forty percent and Charles Fisher was appointed a GM Vice-President. (en.wikipedia. org/wiki/Charles T. Fisher.

3 **Olympia Stadium**, better known as the **Detroit Olympia** and nicknamed **The Old Red Barn**, stood at 5920 Grand River Avenue in Detroit, Michigan from 1927 until 1987. It seated close to 15,000. The Olympia opened with a rodeo in September 1927, and shortly thereafter the main tenants of the building, the Detroit Red Wings of the NHL (at the time, known as the Cougars), moved in. The Cougars would play their first game at the Olympia on November 22, and Detroit's Johnny Sheppard would record the first goal scored at the new building. However, the visiting Ottawa Senators defeated the Cougars, 2-1.Besides the Red Wings, the Olympia was also home to the Detroit Olympics International-American Hockey League minor league team in the 1930s, and the NBA's Detroit Pistons from 1957 to 1961. It hosted the NBA All-Star Game in 1959 and the NCAA Frozen Four in 1977 and 1979.The Olympia was also a major venue for boxing through the International Boxing Club, featuring such prominent fights as Jake LaMotta's defeat of Sugar Ray Robinson, and professional wrestling, as well as the Harlem Globetrotters and the Ice Capades. Amongst musical performers to play at the Olympia were The Beatles, Led Zeppelin, Elvis Presley, The Rolling Stones, Frank Sinatra, Pink Floyd, and The Monkees. In the mid-1970s, the Red Wings had seriously considered moving to the suburbs, especially after the Detroit Lions moved to the Pontiac Silverdome in 1975. The neighborhood surrounding the Olympia had been in decline since the 1967 riots, and two murders had occurred within the building's shadow. The team was offered a new arena by the City of

Pontiac, and Red Wings owner Bruce Norris nearly moved the team to the Oakland County suburb. But the City of Detroit responded with the counterproposal of a riverfront arena at one-third of the rent that Pontiac was offering, and the package also included operational control of Cobo Arena and the adjoining parking structures. The Red Wings accepted the offer to move to the new Joe Louis Arena, which was completed 19 days ahead of schedule.[3]On December 15, 1979, just three days after the first event held at Joe Louis Arena, the Red Wings played their final home game at the Olympia, a 4-4 tie against the Quebec Nordiques. The Olympia was included in part of the celebration of the 32nd NHL All-Star Game, which took place at Joe Louis Arena on February 5, 1980. Because a provision in the Wings' lease with the City of Detroit prevented them from operating Olympia Stadium in competition with Joe Louis or Cobo Arenas for events, or selling the building for use as a competitive venue, the building was shuttered for good, and demolished in September 1987.Overhead exit signs erected in the early 1970s along the Jeffries Freeway mentioning Olympia Stadium were taken down around 1980; the signs would be stored in the lower levels of Joe Louis Arena. Currently, the U.S. National Guard's Olympia Armory stands on the site. A historical marker was posted inside the armory commemorating the Olympia. (en.wikipedia.org/wiki/Detroit_Olympia)

4 H.V. Kaltenborn's radio career goes back to April 21, 1921 when he addressed the Brooklyn Chamber of Commerce while speaking from an experimental station in Newark, N.J. Two years later he was regularly heard on the air. He joined CBS in 1930 as a regular weekly news commentator. Kaltenborn was known as a commentator who never read from a script. His "talks" were extemporaneous created from notes he had previously written. His analysis was welcome into homes especially during the war and the time leading up to America's entry into it. He had an international reputation and was able to

speak intelligently about events because he had interviewed many of those involved. From the contacts he developed in his travels and his ability to speak fluent German and French, Kaltenborn seemed chosen for the role he developed at CBS. (otr.com/kaltenborn.shtml)

5 The **Civilian Conservation Corps** (CCC) was a public work relief program for unemployed men, providing vocational training through the performance of useful work related to conservation and development of natural resources in the United States[2] from 1933 to 1942. As part of the New Deal legislation proposed by U.S. President Franklin D. Roosevelt (FDR), the CCC was designed to aid relief of the unemployment resulting from the Great Depression while implementing a general natural resource conservation program on federal, state, county and municipal lands in every U.S. state, including the territories of Alaska, Hawaii, Puerto Rico, and the U.S. Virgin Islands. The CCC became one of the more popular New Deal programs among the general public, providing economic relief, rehabilitation and training for a total of 3 million men. The CCC also provided a comprehensive work program that combined conservation, renewal, awareness and appreciation of the nation's natural resources. (en.wikipedia.org/wiki/Civilian_Conservation_Corps).

6 The **blue pike** was not just a fish to Erie residents during the first half of the 20th Century. The pike was both a dietary staple and a delicacy. For some the fish was a hobby. For some it was an obsession. For others the blue pike was a way of life. The Lake Erie blue pike is long gone, and its tremendous impact on the city of Erie is a faint memory. Nearly 25 years have passed since the species was declared extinct. (fins.actwin.com/nanf/month.9906/msg00167.html).

7 In the first half of this century jazz flourished [in Detroit]. There were dozens of nightclubs and dance halls in Paradise Valley, the famed black entertainment district, that today lies buried beneath the Chrysler expressway. Every night, all night - and quite often well into the next morning - Detroit musicians and out-of-town jazz stars played and jammed together. Many ballrooms dotted the city; but, of all of them, the most beautiful and elegant stood on the corner of Woodward and Canfield - the Graystone Ballroom.

Under bandleader and entrepreneur Jean Goldkette's leadership, the Graystone became one of the best-known ballrooms in the country. In the 1920s, '30s and '40s the likes of the Duke Ellington and Jimmie Lunceford orchestras "battled" Detroit bands such as McKinney's Cotton Pickers and Goldkette's own group, to the delight of dancers and listeners who nightly packed the exciting, romantic place. (lpl. org/div/detjazz/about.html)

8 **Berry Gordy, Jr.** (born November 28, 1929) is an American record producer, and the founder of the Motown record label, as well as its many subsidiaries. Gordy, Jr. (born in Detroit, Michigan) was the seventh of eight children born to the middle class family of Berry Gordy II (a.k.a. Berry Gordy, Sr.) and Bertha Fuller Gordy, who had relocated to Detroit from Milledgeville, Georgia in 1922. Berry Gordy, Jr's older siblings were all prominent black citizens of Detroit. Berry, however, dropped out of high school in the eleventh grade to become a professional boxer in hopes of becoming rich quick, a career he followed until 1950 when he was drafted by the United States Army for the Korean War. After his return from Korea in 1953, he married Thelma Coleman. He developed his interest in music by writing songs and opening the 3-D Record Mart, a record store featuring jazz music. The store was unsuccessful and Gordy sought work at the Lincoln-Mercury plant, but his family connections put him in touch with Al Green (not the singer), owner of the Flame Show Bar talent

club, where he met singer Jackie Wilson. In 1957, Wilson recorded Reet Petite, a song Gordy had co-written with his sister Gwen and writer-producer Billy Davis. It became a modest hit but had more success internationally, especially in the UK where it reached the Top 10 and even later topped the chart on re-issue in 1986. Wilson recorded four more songs co-written by Gordy over the next two years, including "Lonely Teardrops", which topped the R & B charts and got to number 7 in the pop chart. On December 12, 1959, At Miracles leader Smokey Robinson's encouragement, Gordy borrowed an $800 loan from his family to create an R&B label called Tamla Records on December 14, 1959, which produced Marv Johnson's first hit, "Come To Me." This was picked up for national distribution by United Artists Records who also released the artist's more successful follow-up records such as "You Got What It Takes", co-produced and co-written by Gordy. Barrett Strong's "Money (That's What I Want)," after initially appearing on Tamla, charted on Gordy's sister's label Anna Records from February 1960. The Miracles' hit "Shop Around" peaked nationally at #1 on the R&B charts in late 1960 and at #2 on the Billboard pop charts on, January 16, 1961 (#1 Pop, Cash Box), and established Motown as an independent company worthy of notice. Later in 1961, The Marvelettes "Please Mr Postman" made it to the top of both charts.In 1960, Gordy formed Motown Records as a second label, signed an unknown named Mary Wells who became the fledging label's first star with Smokey Robinson's penned hits like "You Beat Me to the Punch", "Two Lovers" and "My Guy". The Tamla and Motown labels was merged into a new company Motown Record Corporation which was incorporated on April 14, 1960.Gordy did not cultivate white artists, although some were signed, such as Nick and the Jaguars, Chris Clark, Rare Earth, The Valadiers, Debbie Dean and Connie Haines. Kiki Dee became the first white female British singer to be signed to the Motown label. He also employed many white workers and managers at the company's headquarters, named Hitsville U.S.A., on Detroit's West Grand Boulevard. He largely promoted African-American artists but carefully controlled their public image, dress, manners and choreography for across-the-board appeal.His gift for identifying and bringing together musical talent, along with the careful management of his artists' public image, made Motown initially a major national and then international success. Over the next decade, he signed such artists as Mary Wells, The Supremes, Marvin Gaye, Jimmy Ruffin, The Temptations, The Four Tops, Gladys Knight & the Pips, The Commodores, The Velvelettes, Martha and the Vandellas, Stevie Wonder and The Jackson 5. (en. wikipedia.org/wiki/Berry_Gordy)

9 **Hitsville U.S.A.**" is the nickname given to Motown Records' first headquarters. Located at 2648 West Grand Blvd. in Detroit, Michigan Hitsville U.S.A., formerly a photographers' studio, was purchased by Motown founder Berry Gordy in 1959, and converted into both the record label's administrative building and recording studio, which was open 22 hours a day (closing from 8 to 10 AM for maintenance). Following mainstream success in the late 1960s and early 1970s, Gordy moved the label to Los Angeles and established the Hitsville West studio in Los Angeles, as a part of his main focus on film production. On borrowed money, former autoworker and songwriter Berry Gordy purchased the home at 2648 W. Grand Blvd. that later became Hitsville U.S.A. All of the early Motown hits by artists such as Smokey Robinson & The Miracles, The Marvelettes, Marvin Gaye, Tammi Terrell, The Temptations, The Supremes, The Isley Brothers, Martha & the Vandellas, The Jackson 5, and The Four Tops, among others, were recorded in the studio at Hitsville, located in the back of the property. (en.wikipedia.org/wiki/Hitsville_U.S.A.)

10 **Kronk Gym** was a boxing gym located in Detroit and led by the famous trainer Emanuel Steward. The gym was run out of the

basement of the oldest recreation center of the City of Detroit. It opened shortly after World War I (~1920) and closed in 2006. Kronk began to earn fame during the late 1970s, when boxers like Hilmer Kenty, Thomas Hearns and Mickey Goodwin trained there. In 1980, Kenty became Kronk's first world champion, and Hearns followed him as world champion months after. In 1983, Kronk fighter Milton McCrory won the WBC's world Welterweight title that had been vacated by Sugar Ray Leonard; Jimmy Paul beat Harry Arroyo for the International Boxing Federation's world Lightweight title in 1985. Duane Thomas, another Kronk fighter, beat John Mugabi for the WBC's world Jr. Middleweight title in 1986. McCrory's brother, Steve McCrory, was also a world champion. (en.wikipedia.org/wiki/Kronk_Gym)

11 **Eddie Futch** spent 66 years in boxing, and during that time, he earned the respect and trust of most people in the sport because of his integrity. He received several awards from the Boxing Writers Association of America over the years, and before his death was to be [Eddie Futch] trained thousands of amateurs and 21 champions; six of those champions were heavyweights: Joe Frazier, Ken Norton, Trevor Berbick, Riddick Bowe, Larry Holmes, and Michael Spinks. It was his desire to help others through boxing. Two of his fighters, Joe Frazier and Ken Norton, were the only ones to defeat Muhammad Ali during his prime years.

12 The history of the **Boy's Vocational School** in Lansing seems to involve its conversion from a reform school for both sexes to a boy's school with greater emphasis on rehabilitation and training. Carol McGinnis in *Michigan Genealogy: Sources and References*, explains that "In order to deal with an increase in juvenile crime and to stop imprisoning children in the Jackson prison, the House of Correction of Juvenile Offenders opened in Lansing in 1855. 'Prior to 1861, youths

of both sexes under 20 years of age were sentenced to it.'35 It was known by several names through the years: "Michigan State Reform School, 1859; Industrial School for Boys, 1893; Boy's Vocational School, 1925; and Boy's Training School, 1961.

(*Michigan Genealogy*, Genealogical Publishing, Baltimore, MD. 2005, p. 1)

13 *Boys Town* (1938) is a biographical drama film based on Father Edward J. Flanagan's work with a group of disadvantaged and delinquent boys in a home that he founded and named "Boys Town". It stars Spencer Tracy as Father Edward J. Flanagan, and Mickey Rooney, Henry Hull, Gene Reynolds, Edward Norris, and Addison Richards. Although the story is largely fictional, it is based upon a real man and a real place. Boys Town is a community outside of Omaha, Nebraska. Father Flanagan believes there is no such thing as a bad boy and spends his life attempting to prove it. He battles indifference, the legal system, and often the boys themselves, to build a sanctuary which he calls Boys Town. The boys have their own government, make their own rules, and dish out their own punishment. One boy, Whitey Marsh (Mickey Rooney) is as much as anyone can handle. His brother is in prison for murder, and Whitey himself is a poolroom shark and sometime hoodlum. Father Flanagan takes him to Boys Town. Whitey runs away three times, the third time because he hears his brother has escaped. Whitey joins his brother, but Father Flanagan rescues Whitey and helps capture the gang in the act of robbery. Whitey and Father Flanagan return to Boys Town. (en.wikipedia. org/wiki/Boys_Town_(film)

14 **Foster care** is the colloquial term used for a system in which a minor who has been made a ward is placed in the private home of a state certified caregiver referred to as a "foster parent". The state via the family court and child protection agency stand in loco parentis

to the minor making all legal decisions, while the foster parent is responsible for the day to day care of said minor. The foster parent is remunerated by the state for their services. Foster care in some countries, such as the USA, is intended to be a short-term situation until a permanent placement can be made. Children may enter foster care via voluntary or involuntary means. Voluntary placement may occur when a biological parent or lawful guardian is unable or unwilling to care for a child. Involuntary placement occurs when a child is removed from their biological parent or lawful guardian due to the risk or actual occurrence of physical or psychological harm. In the United States, foster home licensing requirements vary from state to state but are generally overseen by each state's Department of Social Services or Human Services. In some states, counties have this responsibility. Each state's services are monitored by the federal Department of Health and Human Services through reviews such as Child and Family Services Reviews, Title IV-E Foster Care Eligibility Reviews, Adoption and Foster Care Analysis and Reporting System and Statewide Automated Child Welfare Information System Assessment Reviews. Children found to be unable to function in a foster home may be placed in Residential Treatment Centers (RTCs) or other such group homes. In theory, the focus of treatment in such facilities is to prepare the child for a return to a foster home, to an adoptive home, or to the birth parents when applicable. But two major reviews of the scholarly literature have questioned these facilities' effectiveness. (en.ipedia.org/wiki/Foster_Care)

15 **John Warnock Hinckley, Jr.,** (born May 29, 1955) attempted to assassinate U.S. President Ronald Reagan in Washington, D.C., on March 30, 1981, as the culmination of an effort to impress actress Jodie Foster. He was found not guilty by reason of insanity and has remained under institutional psychiatric care since then. Akin to Howard Hughes's repeated viewings of *Ice Station Zebra* Hinckley

watched the 1976 movie *Taxi Driver* on a continuous loop in which a disturbed protagonist, Travis Bickle, played by Robert DeNiro, plots to assassinate a presidential candidate. Hinckley developed an obsession with actress Jodie Foster, who had played a child prostitute in the film.[2] Hinckley would re-edit the film, removing parts of Cybill Shepherd and mainly focusing on Travis and Iris. His routine was to masturbate furiously during the films climax. As Travis enters Iris's flat, Hinckley an Obsessive compulsive, would try to reach orgasm as soon as Iris says "don't shoot him", something which gave him extreme euphoria. The Bickle character was in turn partially based on the diaries of Arthur Bremer, the attempted assassin of George Wallace. When Foster entered Yale University, Hinckley moved to New Haven, Connecticut for a short time to stalk her, slipping poems and messages under her door and repeatedly contacting her by telephone. Failing to develop any meaningful contact with Foster, Hinckley developed such plots as hijacking an airplane and committing suicide in front of her to gain her attention. Eventually he settled on a scheme to win her over by assassinating the president, with the theory that as a historical figure he would be her equal. To this end, he trailed President Jimmy Carter from state to state, but was arrested in Nashville, Tennessee on a firearms charge. Penniless, he returned home once again, and despite psychiatric treatment for depression, his mental health did not improve. In 1981, he began to target the newly elected president, Ronald Reagan. It was also at this time that he started collecting information on Lee Harvey Oswald, the person charged with John F. Kennedy's assassination, whom he saw as a role model. On March 30, 1981, Hinckley fired a .22 caliber Röhm RG-14 revolver six times at Reagan as he left the Hilton Hotel in Washington, D.C., after addressing an AFL-CIO conference. Hinckley wounded press secretary James Brady, police officer Thomas Delahanty, and Secret Service agent Timothy McCarthy. Hinckley did not directly hit Reagan, but seriously wounded him when a bullet ricocheted off the side of the presidential limousine and hit him in the chest.[4] Hinckley did not attempt to flee and was arrested at the scene. All of the shooting victims survived, although Brady, who was hit in the right side of the head, endured a long recuperation period and remained paralyzed on the left side of his body.(en.wikipedia. org/wiki/John_Hinckley Jr.)

16 The **555th Parachute Infantry Battalion** was an all-black airborne unit of the United States Army during World War II. The unit was activated as a result of a recommendation made in December 1942 by the Advisory Committee on Negro Troop Policies, chaired by the Assistant Secretary of War, John J. McCloy. In approving the committee's recommendation for a black parachute battalion, Chief of Staff General George C. Marshall decided to start with a company, and on February 25, 1943 the 555th Parachute Infantry Company was constituted. On December 19, 1943, Headquarters, Army Ground Forces, authorized the activation of the company as an all-black unit with black officers as well as black enlisted men. All unit members were to be volunteers, with an enlisted cadre to be selected from personnel of the 92d Infantry Division at Fort Huachuca, Arizona. The company was officially activated on December 30, 1943 at Fort Benning, Georgia. After several months of training, the unit moved to Camp Mackall, North Carolina, where it was reorganized and redesignated on November 25, 1944 as Company A of the newly-activated 555th Parachute Infantry Battalion. The battalion did not serve overseas during World War II. However, in May 1945 it was sent to the west coast of the United States to combat forest fires ignited by Japanese balloons carrying incendiary bombs. Although this potentially serious threat did not materialize, the 555th fought numerous other forest fires. Stationed at Pendleton Field, Oregon, with a detachment in Chico, California, unit members courageously participated in dangerous fire-fighting missions throughout the

Pacific Northwest during the summer and fall of 1945, earning the nickname "Smoke Jumpers" in addition to "Triple Nickels."

17 **Joe Louis** was born in Alabama, but lived much of his early years in Detroit. As a successful African American professional in the northern part of the country, Louis was seen by many other Americans as a symbol of the liberated black man. Since becoming a professional heavyweight, Louis amassed a record of 23-0 and was considered invincible heading into his first bout with Schmeling in 1936. Louis' celebrity was particularly important for African Americans of the era, who were not only suffering economically along with the rest of the country, but also were the targets of significant racially-motivated violence particularly in southern states by members of the Ku Klux Klan. By the time of the Louis-Schmeling match, Schmeling was thought of as the final stepping stone to Louis' eventual title bid...Schmeling prepared intently for the bout. [He] had thoroughly studied Louis's style, and believed he had found a weakness. Louis's habit of dropping his left hand low after a jab. The first fight between Louis and Schmeling took place on June 19, 1936, at the famous Yankee Stadium in New York, New York. The referee was the legendary Arthur Donovan, and the stadium's seats were sold out. The bout was scheduled for fifteen rounds. Schmeling had studied Louis' style, and in the days before the fight, he claimed to have found the key to victory; fans thought that he was just trying to raise interest in the fight. Nevertheless, boxing fans still wanted to see the rising star against the famed former world champion. Schmeling spent the first three rounds using his jab, while sneaking his right cross behind his jab. Louis was stunned by his rival's style. In the fourth round, a snapping right landed on Louis' chin, and Louis was sent to the canvas for the first time in his twenty eight professional fights. As the fight progressed, stunned fans and critics alike watched

Schmeling continue to use this style effectively, and Louis apparently had no idea how to solve the puzzle. By round twelve, Schmeling was far ahead on the judges' scorecards. Finally, he landed a right to Louis' body, followed by another right hand, this one to the jaw. Louis fell near his own corner, and was counted out by Donovan. This was Louis' only knockout defeat during his prime. (en.wikipedia.org/wiki/Joe_Louis_Versus_Max_Schmelling#The_First_Fight)

18 **Alvin Nugent "Bo" McMillin** (January 12, 1895 - March 31, 1952) was a Hall-of-Fame college football player, and later successful head coach, who served at both the collegiate and professional levels but who achieved his greatest success at the college level. 1921 was a most remarkable season for McMillin and Centre College. McMillin was a consensus All-American, and his extraordinary effort against Harvard on October 29 cemented his legend. After the loss the year before, McMillin had promised that Centre would beat Harvard in 1921, despite the fact that the Crimson had not lost since 1918. Then, in front of 43,000 fans, McMillin dashed 32 yards for the lone score of a 6-0 Centre victory, breaking Harvard's 25-game winning streak. MIT students who attended the game to cheer against Harvard tore down the goalposts and hoisted McMillin on their shoulders. For decades afterward, this was called "football's upset of the century." Building upon his success as a player, McMillin entered the coaching arena, where he spent the next quarter century compiling a mark of 146-77-13. Using a combination of eloquence and determination, the tee totaling McMillin enjoyed nothing but success at the college level, beginning at Centenary College of Louisiana in 1922. Over a three-year period, McMillin lost only three of 28 games. McMillin's success at Kansas State propelled him into his most noteworthy achievements at Indiana University. For 14 years, beginning in 1934, McMillin helped elevate the nondescript program to new heights, topped by an undefeated season in 1945. That year marked the first time ever that

the Hoosiers had captured the Big Nine Conference. He even enjoyed success at the annual College All-Star game, winning the 1938 and 1946 clashes against the defending NFL champions. Despite having become the school's athletic director and seemingly earning lifetime security with seven years remaining on his most recent contract, the 53-year-old McMillin sought new challenges following the 1947 campaign. He accepted a five-year contract to coach the National Football League's Detroit Lions on February 19, 1948.

19 **Robert Lawrence "Bobby" Layne** (December 19, 1926 – December 1, 1986) was an American football quarterback who played for 15 seasons in the National Football League. He played for the Chicago Bears in 1948, the New York Bulldogs in 1949, the Detroit Lions from 1950–1958, and the Pittsburgh Steelers from 1958–1962. He was drafted by the Bears in the first round of the 1948 NFL Draft. He played college football at Texas. He was inducted into the Pro Football Hall of Fame in 1967 and inducted into the College Football Hall of Fame in 1968. His number, 22, has been retired by the Texas Longhorns and Detroit Lions. (en.wikipedia.org/wiki/Bobby_Layne

20 **Ewell Doak Walker, Jr.** (January 1, 1927 – September 27, 1998) was an American football player who is a member of the Pro Football Hall of Fame. He was a teammate of Bobby Layne in high school and the NFL. He was born in Dallas, Texas and attended Highland Park High School in Dallas where he was a multi-sport athlete. He also attended Greenville High in Hunt County, TX in 1940-41.[citation needed] Both he and future college and National Football League star Bobby Layne were on the Highland Park football team. Walker attended Southern Methodist University (SMU), where he played running back, defensive back, and place kicker. He also threw and caught passes, punted, and returned kicks. He was an All-American and in 1948 won the Heisman Trophy as the best college football player in the

nation, as a junior. Walker's impact on SMU and football in the Dallas area led to the Cotton Bowl being referred to as "The House That Doak Built." Walker was also a member of Phi Delta Theta Fraternity and lettered on the SMU basketball and baseball teams. In 2007, he was ranked #4 on ESPN's list of the top 25 players in college football history.Walker went on to play professional football for the Detroit Lions, where he was once again a teammate with Bobby Layne. Although Walker was only 5'11" and 175 pounds, he was voted All-Pro four times, and he helped lead the Lions to two National Football League championships. He also led the NFL in scoring twice (1950 and 1955) and tallied 534 points in his career (330 on field goals and extra points). In honor of his achievements, the Lions have retired his #37. He is a member of the Pro Football Hall of Fame. (en.wikipedia. org/wiki/Doak_Walker)

21 **Harry Leon "Suitcase" Simpson** (December 3, 1925 - April 3, 1979) was an African American outfielder and first baseman in Major League Baseball who played for a number of teams. He played in the World Series with the New York Yankees in 1957, where they lost. He was born in Atlanta, Georgia and died in Akron, Ohio. He was one of the earliest black player in the American League, playing first with the Cleveland Indians in 1951. Casey Stengel once called him the best defensive right fielder in the American League (Cleveland Indians Official 1952 Sketch Book). That his nickname of "Suitcase" came from his being frequently traded during his playing career is a common misconception. According to the 1951 Cleveland Indians Sketch Book, he was called "Suitcase" by sportswriters after the Toonerville Trolley character, Suitcase Simpson. This is years before his many trades. His real nickname was "Goody" which came from his willingness to run errands and help neighbors in his hometown of Dalton, Georgia. (en.wikipedia.org/wiki/Harry_Simpson)

Al Smith was born on February 7, 1928, in Kirkwood, Missouri, a St. Louis suburb, he grew up a fan of both local big-league teams, the Cardinals and the Browns, and his hero was Cardinals outfielder Joe Medwick. Nicknamed "Fuzzy," Smith was a versatile, multitalented athlete at Douglas High in Webster Groves, Missouri. The MVP of the baseball team, he also starred in football, basketball, and track, and was a Golden Gloves boxing champion in the 160-pound division. Smith scored 33 touchdowns in one football season and was reputed to have scored 10 touchdowns in one game. Upon his graduation in 1946, Smith signed with the Negro American League's Cleveland Buckeyes. Because he was only 17, his mother had to sign his contract. In his first full season with the Buckeyes, in 1947, he shifted from third base to shortstop and batted .285 while leading the league with 27 doubles and 11 triples, and finishing second with 12 home runs. The Buckeyes, managed by Quincy Trouppe, posted a pennant-winning 54-23 record and played in the Negro League World Series (losing to the New York Cubans). Smith changed positions again in 1948, this time to the outfield. That summer, he caught the eye of Cleveland Indians scout Laddie Placek, who had been dispatched to old League Park to evaluate pitcher Sam "Toothpick" Jones. On July 11, Placek signed both Jones and Smith to major-league contracts. Smith was sent to Class A Wilkes-Barre in the Eastern League, becoming the league's first African-American player. Primarily an outfielder, he played six positions as a major leaguer and was a fine defender with a strong arm and good speed. Smith finished with a .272 life-time batting average, hit 164 home runs, and reached base nearly 36 percent of the time. He also made two A.L. All-Star teams and played for two pennant winners (both managed by Al Lopez). He hit a career-best .315 in 1960 and posted his biggest power numbers—28 homers and 93 RBIs—in 1961. (www.chicagobaseballmuseum.org/files/Go-Go-to-Glory-Al-Smith-20091005.pdf)

22 **Ollie Genoa Matson II** (born May 1, 1930 in Trinity, Texas) is a former professional American football running back who played in the National Football League, in 1952 and from 1954 to 1966. He graduated from George Washington High School in San Francisco in 1948.Matson attended the City College of San Francisco prior to transferring to the University of San Francisco. While in school, Matson became a member of Kappa Alpha Psi Fraternity, Inc. In 1951, Matson's senior year at USF, he led the nation in rushing yardage and touchdowns en route to leading the Dons to an undefeated season. He was selected as an All-American and finished ninth in Heisman Trophy balloting that year. Drafted #1 by the Chicago Cardinals, he went on to share 1952 Rookie of the Year honors with Hugh McElhenny of the San Francisco 49ers. During his 14-year career, Matson also played for the Los Angeles Rams (traded by the Cardinals for nine Rams players following the 1958 season), the Detroit Lions and the Philadelphia Eagles, and he was named to the Pro Bowl six times (1952, 1954 to 1958). Matson was inducted to the Pro Football Hall of Fame in 1972, and into the College Football Hall of Fame in 1976. Matson also holds a bronze medal in the 400-meter run and a silver medal for the 4x400-meter relay from the 1952 Summer Olympics held in Helsinki, Finland. (en.wikipedia.org/wiki/NFL_Draft)

Richard "Dick" Lane (April 16, 1928 – January 29, 2002) nicknamed **"Night Train"**, was an American football player, best known as a defensive back for the Detroit Lions. During his rookie season in 1952, Lane established the record for most interceptions in an NFL season He was born in Austin, Texas, and raised by Ella Lane, a woman who found him abandoned as an infant. After graduation from high school, he spent one year in junior college before dropping out and serving four years in the United States Army.In 1952, the 24-year-old Lane showed up at the Los Angeles Rams training camp looking for a job because he disliked his current occupation at an aircraft factory. He was originally trying out for end, but the Rams switched him to defensive back. While with the Rams, he acquired the nickname "Night Train" from a hit record by Buddy Morrow, frequently played by teammate Tom Fears. He initially disliked the nickname, but it grew on him after it gained national attention, first appearing in print describing a tackle in a Rams exhibition game: *Dick "Night Train" Lane derails Charlie "Choo Choo" Justice.* He wore number 81, unusual for a defensive back, because he was initially projected as an end. The ends playing in front of him on the Rams, Fears and Elroy Hirsch, were stars and future Hall of Famers, so coach Joe Stydahar tried Lane at defensive back. Lane also had a fear of flying, so he travelled by train. In his rookie season he set an NFL single season record for interceptions with 14, which stands to this day even though the length of the season at the time was only 12 games (it was later expanded to 14 games in 1961 and 16 in 1978). He was traded to the Chicago Cardinals in 1954 and to the Detroit Lions in 1960 From 1954 to 1963, Lane made the All-Pro team six times and was also selected to seven Pro Bowls. He recorded three interceptions in all but four of his 14 NFL seasons. (en.wikipedia.org/wiki/Dick_Lane_(American_Football)

23 John Constantine "Johnny" Unitas. May 7, 1933 – September 11, 2002), nicknamed the Golden Arm and often called Johnny U, was a professional American football player in the 1950s through the 1970s, spending the majority of his career with the Baltimore Colts. He was a record-setting quarterback, and the National Football League's most valuable player in 1959, 1964 and 1967. His record of throwing a touchdown pass in 47 consecutive games (between 1956-1960) remains unsurpassed as of 2009. He has been listed [1] as one of the greatest NFL quarterbacks of all time. (en.wikipedia.org/wiki/Johnny_Unitas)

24 John Heileman & Mark Halperin, *Game Change* (New York, Harper Collins, 2010) p. 36.

25 The **Bellefaire Orphanage** was a Jewish orphanage in Cleveland Ohio founded in 1868 as an orphanage for children who lost their parents in the Civil War, making it one of the oldest orphanages in the US. It was originally founded by Dr. Seele as the Cleveland Water Cure Establishment in 1848. This "was a combination sanitarium and resort for the treatment of various ailments and diseases through hydropathy" "enjoying regional popularity for nearly 2 decades", before being sold in 1868 to a national Jewish organization, and initially being called the Jewish Orphan Asylum. From 1868 to 1918, the Jewish Orphan Asylum "was the home for 3,581 mostly immigrant eastern European boys and girls. Established originally to serve orphaned and destitute Jewish youngsters from 15 Midwestern and southern states", and "was located on over seven acres of land near Fifty-fifth Street and Woodland Avenue." In 1919, as part of the transformation to a more humane place to live, the name was changed to Jewish Orphan Home. "In 1929 the orphanage was relocated to a thirty-acre site in University Heights, an eastern suburb of Cleveland, where it was built as a cottage-type orphanage and renamed Bellefaire. Bellefaire continued as an orphanage for Jewish children until 1943, when it became a residential treatment center for emotionally disturbed children". (en.wikipedia.org/wiki/Bellefaire Orphanage)

26 **Jackie Presser** (August 6, 1926 – July 9, 1988) was an American labor leader and president of the International Brotherhood of Teamsters from 1983 until his death in 1988. He was closely connected to organized crime, and allegedly became president of the Teamsters based on the approval and support of the Cleveland mafia. From 1972 until his death, he was also an informant for the Federal Bureau

of Investigation concerning mafia influence in the Teamsters union. Presser was born in Cleveland, Ohio, in 1926. His grandfather, a Jewish immigrant from Austria, became a garment worker, and was active in and participated in several strikes led by various garment makers' unions in New York City. Presser's father, William (Bill) Presser, was at the time of Jackie's birth a Teamster organizer. The Pressers were very poor: Bill Presser stuffed newspapers into shoes to block holes in the uppers and strengthen worn-out soles. The family often moved into an apartment at the beginning of the month and out again at the end of the month because the Pressers could not afford the rent. Bill Presser, however, was a protégé of Jimmy Hoffa and quickly rose within the local, regional and international Teamsters ranks. He was elected president of the Ohio Conference of Teamsters and eventually a vice president of the international union. Bill Presser was also intimately connected with the Cleveland mob. (en.wikipedia.org/wiki/Jackie_Presser)

27 **John H. Johnson** was born January 19, 1918, Arkansas City, Arkansas and died August 8, 2005, in his hometown of Chicago, Illinois. Johnson and his family settled in Chicago after visiting that city during the 1933 World's Fair. He later became an honor student at Du Sable High School in Chicago, where he was managing editor of the school paper and business manager of the yearbook. Those experiences influenced his choice of journalism as a career. While studying at the University of Chicago and Northwestern University, Johnson worked for a life insurance company that marketed to African American customers. There he conceived the idea of a magazine for blacks; in 1942 he began publication of *Negro Digest*. Its first issue sold some 3,000 copies, and within a year the monthly circulation was 50,000. From that beginning, Johnson launched *Ebony*, a general-interest magazine catering to an African American audience, in 1945. *Ebony*'s initial pressrun of 25,000 copies was completely sold out. By

the early 21st century it had a circulation of some 1.7 million. Johnson went on to create other black publications, including *Jet* magazine in 1951. His firm, Johnson Publishing Company, later diversified into book publishing, radio broadcasting, insurance, and cosmetics manufacturing. In the 1980s Linda Johnson Rice, his daughter, began assuming management of the company. Johnson was awarded the Presidential Medal of Freedom in 1996. (www.britanica.com/EBchecked/topic/305351/John-H-Johnson)

28 James Nathaniel "Jim" Brown (born February 17, 1936) is an American former professional football player who has also made his mark as an actor. He is best known for his exceptional and record-setting nine-year career as a running back for the NFL Cleveland Browns from 1957 to 1965. In 2002, he was named by *The Sporting News* as the greatest professional football player ever.[1] He is considered to be one of the greatest professional athletes the U.S. has ever produced. Brown was taken in the first round of the 1956 draft by the Cleveland Browns. He departed as the NFL record holder for both single-season (1,863 in 1963) and career rushing (12,312 yards), as well as the all-time leader in rushing touchdowns (106), total touchdowns (126), and all-purpose yards (15,549). He was the first player ever to reach the 100-rushing-touchdowns milestone, and only a few others have done so since, despite the league's expansion to a 16-game season in 1978 (Brown's first four seasons were only 12 games, and his last five were 14 games). Brown also set a record by reaching the 100-touchdown milestone in only 93 games, which stood until LaDainian Tomlinson reached it in 89 games during the 2006 season. Brown holds the record for total seasons leading the NFL in all-purpose yards (5: 1958–1961, 1964), and is the only rusher in NFL history to average over 100 yards per game for a career. Brown was also a superb receiver out of the backfield, catching 262 passes for 2,499 yards and 20 touchdowns. Every season he played,

Brown was voted into the Pro Bowl, and he left the league in style by scoring three touchdowns in his final Pro Bowl game. Perhaps the most amazing feat is that Jim Brown accomplished these records despite never playing past 29 years of age. Brown's 6 games with at least 4 touchdowns remains an NFL record. Brown's 1,863 rushing yards in the 1963 season remain a Cleveland franchise record. It is currently the oldest franchise record for rushing yards out of all 32 NFL teams. While others have compiled more prodigious statistics, when viewing Brown's standing in the game his style of running must be considered along with statistical measures. He was very difficult to tackle (shown by his leading 5.2 yards per carry), often requiring more than one person to bring him down. Brown retired far ahead of the second-leading rusher and remains the league's eighth all-time leading rusher, and is still the Cleveland Browns all-time leading rusher. (en.wikipedia.org/wiki/Jim_Brown)

29 **John Wooten** was born on December 5, 1936 in Riverview, Texas, attended Carlsbad High School in Carlsbad, New Mexico and is a graduate of the University of Colorado in Boulder, Colorado with Bachelor of Science Degree. When the Cleveland Browns selected John Wooten in the 1959 NFL Draft, it proved to be one of the most important drafts in Cleveland Browns history. He played for the Cleveland Browns from 1959-1967 and then the Washington Redskins from 1967-1968 and during the 1960-1963 off seasons he was a junior high school teacher at Addison Junior High School in Cleveland, Ohio. His on-the-field honors include, Associated Press All-Big Seven, All American Honors at Offensive Guard at the University of Colorado in 1958, named to the Chicago Tribune's College All Star Game in 1959, Sporting News NFL All Star Team in 1965, named to the NFL Pro Bowl teams in 1966 and 1967, Cleveland Browns All-Time All Star Team, named to University of Colorado's All Century Football Team, he was inducted into the Texas Black Sports Hall of Fame Inductee

in 2002 and Hall of Fame inductee with the University of Colorado in October 2004, September 2005 Honored Jersey with the University of Colorado and has three World Championships -- Browns -1964, Cowboys - 1977 and Ravens in 2000. (www.fpal.org/wooten.php)

Robert Cornelius Mitchell (born June 6, 1935 in Hot Springs, Arkansas) is a former American football halfback and flanker in the National Football League for the Cleveland Browns and the Washington Redskins. Mitchell was inducted into the Pro Football Hall of Fame in 1983.Mitchell was born in Hot Springs, Arkansas and attended Langston High School. While there, he played football, basketball, track, and was good enough at baseball to be offered a contract with the St. Louis Cardinals.[1]Mitchell was drafted in the seventh round of the 1958 NFL Draft by the Cleveland Browns, where he played as a halfback. He was teamed with Jim Brown to give the Browns one of most successful running back combinations from 1958 through 1961. [4]As a rookie, Mitchell had a 98-yard kickoff return. A year later against Washington, he rushed for 232 yards, including a 90-yard scoring scamper. The same year, he returned a punt 78 yards against the New York Giants. As a Brown, Mitchell accumulated 2297 yards rushing, 1463 yards receiving, 607 yards on punt returns, 1550 yards on kickoff returns, and scored 38 touchdowns. He still holds the Browns' career record for kickoff returns for touchdowns with three. He also holds the team's best rookie rushing average (13.36 in 1958). (en.wikipedia.org/wiki/Bobby Mitchell)

30 **Carl B. Stokes** is best known for being Cleveland's 51st mayor -- the first African-American mayor of a major United States city. He was also a soldier, a lawyer, a member of the Ohio House of Representatives, a broadcaster, a judge, a father, brother to a Congressman, and a US Ambassador.

Stokes began his political career in the Cleveland prosecutor's office. In 1962, he was elected to the Ohio House of Representatives, a job he held for three terms. In 1965, he was narrowly defeated in a bid for mayor of Cleveland. He ran again in 1967 and just beat (he had 50.5%

of the vote) Seth Taft, grandson of President William H. Taft. With his victory, the era of black political power in the US had come of age.

America's First Black Mayor: Stokes inherited a Cleveland that was racially polarized, with virtually all of black Clevelanders (99.5%) living on the east side of the Cuyahoga River, many crowded in older, aging neighborhoods. Stokes increased the city's income tax and won voter approval for schools, housing, the zoo, and other city projects. He also created the "Cleveland Now!" program, a privately funded organization to aid a wide range of community needs. The early enthusiasm of his administration was marred when Cleveland's (largely black) Glenville neighborhood erupted in violence in 1968. When it was learned that the organizers of the riots had received funding from "Cleveland Now!" donations dried up and Stokes' credibility suffered. He chose not to seek a third term. After the Mayor's Office: Broadcaster, Judge, Ambassador: After leaving the mayor's office in 1971, Stokes moved to New York City, where he became the first African-American anchorman in that city in 1972. In 1983 he returned to Cleveland to serve as a municipal judge, a post he held for 11 years. In 1994, President Clinton appointed him U.S. Ambassador to the Republic of the Seychelles. (http://cleveland. about.com/od/famousclevelanders/p/carlstokes.htm)

31 **The Lancer Steakhouse** burned down in December 2009. According to then owner George Dixon "The Lancer is very important to the city and it's always been a symbol in the African American community,". . . "When people came into town, they'd stop at the Lancer -- everyone from politicians to athletes to just the regular guy off the street," he said. "It was a melting pot where everybody rubbed shoulders and talked about the topics of the day. "Fleet and Beulah Slaughter opened The Lancer in 1960. The restaurant became a well-known gathering place for the city's black community leaders and business owners. According to Powell Caesar, lifelong Cleveland resident and black

journalist [The Lancer steakhouse] "was the defacto meeting place for black politicians during the '60s and was 'strategy central' during Carl Stokes' mayoral campaigns." The Rev. Dr. Martin Luther King Jr. was said to stop in The Lancer. Slaughter died in 1975 and the family sold the restaurant to attorney John Carson in 1978. Dixon bought the Lancer in 1986 and it continued to be known as the most prominent black-owned restaurant in the city. "It was a place frequented by hustlers, pimps, numbers runners, numbers racketeers as well as Cleveland's black social elite," Caesar said. "It was all things to all people," Caesar said. "Yet another piece of Cleveland gone, but it certainly won't be forgotten." (from an article by Donna J. Miller, http://blog.Cleveland.com/metro/2009/12/the_Lancer_Steakhouse_destroye.html)

32 **Billie Holiday** was a true artist of her day and rose as a social phenomenon in the 1950s. Her soulful, unique singing voice and her ability to boldly turn any material that she confronted into her own music made her a superstar of her time. Today, Holiday is remembered for her masterpieces, creativity and vivacity, as many of Holiday's songs are as well known today as they were decades ago. Holiday's poignant voice is still considered to be one of the greatest jazz voices of all time. Holiday (born Eleanora Fagan) grew up in jazz talent-rich Baltimore in the 1920s. As a young teenager, Holiday served the beginning part of her so-called "apprenticeship" by singing along with records by Bessie Smith or Louis Armstrong in after-hours jazz clubs. When Holiday's mother, Sadie Fagan, moved to New York in search of a better job, Billie eventually went with her. She made her true singing debut in obscure Harlem nightclubs and borrowed her professional name - Billie Holiday - from screen star Billie Dove. Although she never underwent any technical training and never even so much as learned how to read music, Holiday

quickly became an active participant in what was then one of the most vibrant jazz scenes in the country. She would move from one club to another, working for tips. She would sometimes sing with the accompaniment of a house piano player while other times she would work as part of a group of performers. .At the age of 18 and after gaining more experience than most adult musicians can claim, Holiday was spotted by John Hammond and cut her first record as part of a studio group led by Benny Goodman, who was then just on the verge of public prominence. In 1935 Holiday's career got a big push when she recorded four sides that went on to become hits, including "What a Little Moonlight Can Do" and "Miss Brown to You." This landed her a recording contract of her own, and then, until 1942, she recorded a number of master tracks that would ultimately become an important building block of early American jazz music. Holiday began working with Lester Young in 1936, who pegged her with her now-famous nickname of "Lady Day." When Holiday joined Count Basie in 1937 and then Artie Shaw in 1938, she became one of the very first black women to work with a white orchestra, an impressive accomplishment of her time. .In the 1930s, when Holiday was working with Columbia Records, she was first introduced to the poem "Strange Fruit," an emotional piece about the lynching of a black man. Though Columbia would not allow her to record the piece due to subject matter, Holiday went on to record the song with an alternate label, Commodore, and the song eventually became one of Holiday's classics. It was "Strange Fruit" that eventually prompted Lady Day to continue more of her signature, moving ballads. .Holiday recorded about 100 new recordings on another label, Verve, from 1952 to 1959. Her voice became more rugged and vulnerable on these tracks than earlier in her career. During this period, she toured Europe, and made her final studio recordings for the MGM label in March of 1959.Despite her lack of technical training, Holiday's unique diction, inimitable phrasing and acute dramatic intensity made her the outstanding jazz singer of her day. White gardenias, worn in her hair, became her trademark. "Singing songs like the 'The Man I Love' or 'Porgy' is no more work than sitting down and eating Chinese roast duck, and I love roast duck," she wrote in her autobiography. "I've lived songs like that." Billie Holiday, a musical legend still popular today, died an untimely death at the age of 44. Her emotive voice, innovative techniques and touching songs will forever be remembered and enjoyed. (www.cmgww,com/music/holliday)

33 The Blue Monday Parties at the Rose Room nightclub of the old Majestic Hotel at East 55th and Central were probably the most memorable jam sessions in Cleveland jazz history. The Majestic, Cleveland's African-American hotel during the long period when Negroes were not permitted to stay at the major downtown hotels, played host to a constant stream of black entertainers and sports figures. It was almost automatic that the Majestic would present jazz entertainment. As early as 1931, the hotel had a jazz nightclub called the Furnace Room. Later, the name was changed to the Heat Wave. By the 1950s, the Majestic's nightclub had become the Rose Room. Pianist Duke Jenkins and his group played at the Rose Room from 1952 to 1957."I had the house band there," said Jenkins, "and gosh, all the big names that came through there in that time – Erroll, Garner, Arthur Prysock, Joe Williams, Nancy Wilson!" Jenkins and his group played for dancing and listening six days a week at the Rose Room and attracted large crowds almost every night. But, what most people remember were the jam sessions that were held early Monday mornings. "Every Monday morning from five a.m. until ten o'clock, we had a 'Blue Monday' party," said Jenkins. "You couldn't get near the place. People lined up to get in. You couldn't even get a seat because we had all the celebrities, who were working in different clubs, would come in and perform. It was a show you couldn't pay to see really. All kinds of entertainers -- girl singers, dancers, male

singers, quartets, you name them, like the Ink Spots, those kind of people." Jenkins and his band played Sunday nights and then went up in the hotel to sleep for a couple of hours before getting up to play the early morning jam sessions.

A singer who took part in the Blue Monday Party early morning jam sessions at the Rose Room in the early 1950s was a then-unknown vocalist from Cincinnati, Nancy Wilson. Jenkins said, "People went crazy because she was so good." Later, after she had become nationally famous, Jenkins and his group were playing one night in Columbus. He recalled he was doing one of her songs and had his eyes closed. As he was singing, he heard a voice say, "Would you mind if I sang the second chorus?" When he opened his eyes, Jenkins discovered Nancy Wilson standing in front of him. Of course, she sang the second chorus. The Blue Monday Parties at the Rose Room were only one part of the week-long entertainment at the Majestic Hotel. Jenkins said, "On Tuesday, they had Cha Cha Night and on Thursday, Mambo Night." He said the place was crowded all the time. But, the big attraction for jazz fans were the Blue Monday parties that drew some of the biggest names in jazz, early Monday mornings, jamming with Duke Jenkins' group. While the Majestic was a hotel catering to African-Americans in the black section of Cleveland, the audiences at the Rose Room were both black and white. In fact, Jenkins said most of the local judges came to the Rose Room with their wives. (www. cleveland.oh.us/wmv_news/jazz61.htm)

34 **John Birks "Dizzy" Gillespie** (October 21, 1917 – January 6, 1993) was an American jazz trumpet player, bandleader, singer, and composer. Together with Charlie Parker, he was a major figure in the development of bebop and modern jazz. He taught and influenced many other musicians, including trumpeters Miles Davis, Fats

Navarro, Clifford Brown, Arturo Sandoval, Lee Morgan, and Jon Faddis. In addition to featuring in the epochal moments in bebop, he was instrumental in founding Afro-Cuban jazz, the modern jazz version of what early-jazz pioneer Jelly Roll Morton referred to as the "Spanish Tinge". Gillespie was a trumpet virtuoso and gifted improviser, building on the virtuoso style of Roy Eldridge [but adding layers of harmonic complexity previously unknown in jazz. Dizzy's beret and horn-rimmed spectacles, his scat singing, his bent horn, pouched cheeks and his light-hearted personality were essential in popularizing bebop. (en.wikipedia.org/wiki/dizzy_Gillespie)

35 **The numbers games** have a colorful history in Ohio. Before the creation of the Ohio Lottery in 1973, colorful characters such as Don King and Virgil Ogletree ran number games or "policy racket" games in Cleveland. These illegal numbers games were very similar to the Ohio Lottery's Pick 3 and Pick 4 number except for their higher payouts and their profits accruing to the illegal operators of the numbers games instead of the state. These illegal games were based on random numbers that appeared in newspapers, such as the last digits of stock and bond volumes. "At his height, he (Virgil Ogletree) was one of a handful of Cleveland powers in the numbers games, the black-market predecessor to the Ohio Lottery. Typically taking in $20,000 in bets daily with 40 to 50 runners working for him, he was friendly with fellow numbers magnate and later boxing promoter Don King. 'Don King and the others, they had business,' said Ogletree's longtime lawyer and friend James Willis, who often represented the other major players, too. "But I don't think it was as large as his. Virgil Ogletree made as much money, if not more. . ." (Who Plays the Numbers Games in the Middle of the Day?, Kathryn combs & John A Spry, web.bus.edu/cob/econ/research/papers/bsuecwp200705combs.pdf)

36 **Donald "Don" King** (born August 20, 1931) is an American boxing promoter particularly known for his hairstyle and flamboyant personality. His career highlights include promoting "The Rumble in the Jungle" and the "Thrilla in Manila", as well as orchestrating the ascent of Mike Tyson. King has promoted some of the most prominent names in boxing, including Muhammad Ali, Mike Tyson, George Foreman, Evander Holyfield, Julio César Chávez, Andrew Golota, Félix Trinidad, Roy Jones Jr. and Larry Holmes. Don King was born in Cleveland, Ohio. After dropping out of Kent State University, he ran an illegal bookmaking operation, and was charged for killing two men in separate incidents 13 years apart. The first was determined to be justifiable homicide after it was found that King shot Hillary Brown in the back and killed him while he was attempting to rob one of King's gambling houses. King was convicted of second degree murder for the second killing in 1966 after he was found guilty of stomping to death an employee, Sam Garrett, who owed him $600. In an ex parte meeting with King's attorney, the judge reduced King's conviction to non-negligent manslaughter for which King served just under four years in prison. King entered the boxing world after convincing Muhammad Ali to box in a charity exhibition for a local hospital in Cleveland with the help of singer Lloyd Price. Early on he formed a partnership with a local promoter named Don Elbaum, who already had a stable of fighters in Cleveland and years of experience in boxing. In 1974, King negotiated to promote a heavyweight championship fight between Muhammad Ali and George Foreman in Zaire, popularly known as "The Rumble in the Jungle." The fight between Ali and Foreman was a much-anticipated event. King's rivals all sought to promote the bout, but King was able to secure the then-record $10 million purse through an arrangement with the Zaire government.King solidified his position as one of boxing's preeminent promoters the following year with the third fight between Ali and Joe Frazier in Manila, the capital of the Philippines, which King

deemed the "Thrilla In Manila." Aside from promoting the premier heavyweight fights of the 1970s, King was also busy expanding his boxing empire. Throughout the decade, he compiled an impressive roster of fighters, many of whom would finish their career with Hall of Fame credentials. Fighters like Larry Holmes, Wilfred Benítez, Roberto Durán, Salvador Sánchez, Wilfredo Gómez, and Alexis Argüello would all fight under the Don King Productions promotional banner in the 1970s.For the next two decades, King continued to be among boxing's most successful promoters. Mike Tyson, Evander Holyfield, Julio César Chávez, Aaron Pryor, Bernard Hopkins, Ricardo Lopez, Félix Trinidad, Terry Norris, Carlos Zarate, Azumah Nelson, Andrzej Gołota, Mike McCallum, Gerald McClellan, Meldrick Taylor, Marco Antonio Barrera and Ricardo Mayorga are some of the boxers who chose King to promote many of their biggest fights. Outside of boxing, he also managed the Jacksons' 1984 Victory Tour. King was elected to the Gaming Hall of Fame in 2008. Don King has been a lightning rod for controversy throughout his career. He has been the subject of several lawsuits by boxers he managed who alleged that they were forced to hire King's relatives and cronies. He has faced charges of tax evasion by the IRS. Rumors of jury-tampering have swirled around him. And it also became known that the rights to pay-per-view fights he promoted were awarded to organized crime figures, some of whom may have known King from his book-making days King has been investigated for possible connections with organized crime. During a 1992 Senate investigation King pleaded the Fifth Amendment when questioned about his connection to mobster John Gotti. In public, however, he has responded to mob allegations by calling them racist. (en.wikipedia.org/wiki/Don_King_Boxing_Promoter)

37 **Harold Robbins** was born Harold Rubin in New York City, the son of well-educated Russian and Polish immigrants. His father was a successful pharmacist. Robbins was educated at the George

Washington High School and after leaving off the school he worked at several jobs. According to widely spread, but mostly fabricated biographical anecdotes, he spent his childhood in an orphanage. By the age of twenty, Robbins had made his first million by selling sugar for the wholesale trade. Robbins married at a young age and moved to Hollywood where he worked for Universal Pictures, first as a shipping clerk. Later he became a studio executive. His first book *Never Love a Stranger* (1948) followed the rise of an orphan from the streets of New York creating controversy with its graphic sexuality. In Philadelphia the book was banned. *The Dream Merchants* (1949) was about Hollywood's film industry, from the first stages to the sound era. *The Carpetbaggers* (1961) was an international bestseller, a story of Jonas Cord, whose adventures must have amused Howard Hughes, for at least he did not sue the author. Several other characters were also easily identifiable. From 1957 Robbins worked as a full-time writer. Of his many works perhaps the most acclaimed was *A Stone for Danny Fisher* (1951), a coming-of-age story set in New York in the Depression. The book was turned into a musical under the title *King Creole* (1958), starring Elvis Presley. Other books include *The Betsy* (1971), which centered on a shrewd business-minded racing car driver; the story continued in *The Stallion* (1996). Robbins was married five times. From 1982 he was obliged to use a wheelchair because of hip trouble but he continued writing. According to Lee Server (*Encyclopedia of Pulp Fiction*, 2002), Robbins's later years followed the devices of his own plots. He went broke, lost his wife, and wrote his books in the hope that they "would keep him in lobster and cocaine money." Stories tell how the author was locked in hotel suites without room service, to make him produce a sufficient number of typed pages.. . Several of Robbins's books have been made into films, among them *Never Love A Stranger* (1958), dir. by Robert Stevens, *The Carpetbaggers* (1964), directed by Edward Dmytryk, *The Betsy* (1977), directed by Daniel Petrie, and *Harold Robbins' Body Parts* (1999), produced by

Roger Corman. Harold Robbins died in 1997 (www.kirjasto.sci.fi/robbins.htm)

38 **Jimmy Smith** (December 8, 1928 [birth year is disputed and is often given as 1925] – February 8, 2005) was a jazz musician whose performances on the Hammond B-3 electric organ helped to popularize this instrument. In 2005, Smith was awarded the NEA Jazz Masters Award from the National Endowment for the Arts, the highest honors that the United States bestows upon jazz musicians. Born James Oscar Smith and originally a pianist, Smith switched to organ in 1953 after hearing Wild Bill Davis. He purchased his first Hammond organ, rented a warehouse to practice in and emerged after little more than a year with an exciting new sound which was to completely revolutionize the way in which the instrument could be played. On hearing him playing in a Philadelphia club, Blue Note's Alfred Lion immediately signed him to the label and with his second album, also known as *The Champ*, quickly established Smith as a new star on the jazz scene. He was a prolific recording artist and as a leader, recorded around 40 sessions for Blue Note in just 8 years beginning in 1956. His most notable albums from this period include *The Sermon!, House Party, Home Cookin', Midnight Special, Back at the Chicken Shack* and *Prayer Meetin'*. Smith then signed to Verve Records label in 1962. His first album *Bashin'*, sold well and for the first time set Smith with a big band, led by Oliver Nelson. Further big band collaborations followed, most successfully with Lalo Schifrin for *The Cat* and guitarist Wes Montgomery, with whom he recorded two albums: *The Dynamic Duo* and *Further Adventures of Jimmy and Wes*. Other notable albums from this period include *Blue Bash* and *Organ Grinder's Swing* with Kenny Burrell, *The Boss* with George Benson, *Who's Afraid of Virginia Woolf?, Got My Mojo Working*, and the funky *Root Down*. During the 1950s and 1960s, Smith recorded with

some of the great jazz musicians of the day such as Kenny Burrell, George Benson, Grant Green, Stanley Turrentine, Lee Morgan, Lou Donaldson, Tina Brooks, Jackie McLean, Grady Tate and Donald Bailey. In the 1970s, Smith opened his own supperclub in Los Angeles, California and played there regularly. With Guitarist Paul C Saenz, Larry Paxton, on drums, Freddy Garcia on sax. Smith had a career revival in the 1980s and 1990s, again recording for Blue Note and Verve, and for Milestone and Elektra. Smith also recorded with other artists including Quincy Jones/Frank Sinatra, Michael Jackson, Dee Dee Bridgewater and Joey DeFrancesco. His last major album *Dot Com Blues* (Blue Thumb, 2000), featured many special guests such as Dr. John, B. B. King and Etta James. (en.wikipedia.org/wiki/Jimmy_Smith_(Musician)

39 Born in Austin, Texas, **Dolly Mapp** moved to Cleveland with her family as a baby. She had grown up to be a tall, striking woman who had spent time on the arms of a number of well-known prizefighters. As a young teenager, she hooked up with Larry Bivins, regarded as one of the finest boxers ever to come out of Cleveland Bivins scored 86 victories in a 15-year career that ended in 1955. Although undersized, he contended in both the heavyweight and light heavyweight divisions. He was never a champion, but he defeated eight men who were. In 1944, when she was just 15, Mapp bore Bivins a daughter, Barbara.In the early 1950s, Mapp took up with one of Bivins' longtime rivals, Archie Moore. The men had fought five times, with Moore taking four of them.Moore was another undersized fighter who bounced between the heavyweight and light heavyweight ranks.He knocked out 141 opponents in a career that spanned a remarkable 27 years. He was light heavyweight champion for nearly 10 years, through most of his 40s. He lost his next-to-last fight, in 1962, to the upstart fighter who would become known as Muhammad Ali.After years of hanging around tough-guy boxers, Dolly Mapp was no

shrinking violet. Bright and well-spoken, she earned a reputation as a strong woman who would not back down from a challenge. In 1956, she sued Archie Moore for breach of promise, charging that he had broken a vow to marry her. The suit was eventually dismissed after legal wrangling. She supported herself by renting the first level of her tidy, two-story brick home to itinerant men, and she and her daughter often had female boarders living in the spare bedrooms of their upper unit. Her boarders came from her earthy social circle, centered on the prizefight game and gamblers. Through these associations, Mapp lived on the fringes of the numbers rackets. (www.trutv.com/library/ crime/gangsters_outlaws/cops_others/dolly_Mapp/2.html)

40 One night, seven police officers broke into and searched Dolly Mapp's home in Cleveland, Ohio. The search was prompted by an informant telling them that a suspect in a recent bombing was hiding out there. Mapp's house was searched, and no sign of the suspect was found; however, police did find some literature deemed obscene (the possession of which was a crime). Although the police claimed to have a search warrant, but none was produced. In court, their search was upheld and Dolly Mapp was convicted of the possession of obscene material. The Supreme Court overturned this conviction on the grounds that the search was illegal. The Mapp case incorporated the 4th amendment into the Due Process clause of the 14th amendment and created the "exclusionary rule," which prevents the use of evidence gained by these so-called illegal searches. Opponents of the exclusionary rule argue "the criminal is to go free because the constable has blundered," to which Justice Clark answered "The criminal goes free if he must, but it is the law that sets him free." (// library.thinkquest.org/2760/map.htm)

41 For a fuller account, see Fred McGunagle's *Shondor & Danny* in Appendix B.

42 **BIRNS, ALEX "SHONDOR"** (21 Feb. 1905-29 Mar. 1975), a notorious criminal, was involved in rackets prostitution, theft, assault, and murder from the days of Prohibition until his death. Born to Herman and Illon Birn, the family immigrated to Cleveland from Austria-Hungary in 1907. He grew up on Woodland Ave., an accomplished athlete, quick with his fists, and with a volatile temper. He enjoyed notoriety, treating journalists who labeled him "Public Enemy No. 1" very well. Birns dropped out of school after 10th grade in 1922, enlisting in the Navy in 1923 but being discharged 6 months later because he was underage. He began selling bootleg whiskey. Birns's criminal record was extensive, ranging from vagrancy to murder. He was first arrested, for car theft, in 1925, serving about a year in Mansfield Reformatory. Birns was afterwards arrested a number of times but served little time in jail, having friends among lawyers, judges, and policemen, and buying off or silencing witnesses. Birns operated the Ten-Eleven Club and the Alhambra restaurant, often treating off-duty policemen, lawyers, and journalists. In 1942 he was arrested by U.S. immigration officials as an enemy alien, since he was still a Hungarian citizen; and for years, officials tried to deport Birns; however, no country would accept him. Birns married twice. His first marriage was in 1952. He and his wife, Jane, had one son, Michael (d. 1978). They divorced in 1964 and Birns then married Allene Leonards. In the spring of 1975, Birns was released from a short stay in jail and announced that he was going to go straight, but he was killed by a bomb planted in his automobile. No one was arrested for his murder. (//ech.cwru.edu/ech-cgi/article.pl?id=BAS)

43 **Danny[Greene]** got his start in racketeering as president of the local International Association of Longshoremen. He could have been a highly successful businessman, but it wasn't the life for him. After a shocking expose by the Cleveland Plain Dealer, he was ousted from the docks and fined $10,000 for embezzling union funds. Danny had been forcing longshoremen to unload filthy grain boats and "donate" their paychecks to a union hall "renovation fund." The hall had already been renovated - painted green when Danny took office. Later Danny worked for as an enforcer for local mobsters including Alex "Shondor" Birns, well-known Jewish racketeer. After a dispute over $60,000 Greene refused to repay, Birns had a bomb planted in his car. It was the first in a series of botched attempts on the brash Irishman's life. Danny found the bomb. "Luck of the Irish," he would often say. "I'll return this to the old bastard who sent it to me," Greene promised. Sure enough, a few weeks later Birns was blown out the roof of his car, in two pieces. It was an excellent hit and Danny was proud. Danny's big mistake was the 1976 murder of Leo "Lips" Moceri, the respected and feared new underboss of the Cleveland Mafia, and the bombing of enforcer Eugene "The Animal" Ciasullo. Aging mob boss James Licavoli ordered his henchman to "get rid of the Irishman," but the inexperienced soldiers had no luck. The attempts by the self-proclaimed tough guys were almost comical. Then west coast wise guy Jimmy 'the Weasel" Fratianno recommended a hired killer from Erie. In the end, Danny went out the way he predicted. "When you live by the bomb, you die by the bomb." The Irishman was dead. But the Mafia's celebration was cut short. There was much sloppy work, a few observant witnesses (one of whom was a sketch artist!) and extraordinary investigations by federal, state and local officials. The aftermath of Greene's assassination brought about a mob murder plot against Cleveland Mayor Dennis Kucinich and charges against Mahoning County Sheriff James Traficant for accepting Mafia bribe money. Traficant was acquitted and is now a United States

Congressman. As a direct result of Danny's murder, Jimmy "Weasel" Fratianno defected and co-authored The Last Mafioso and Vengeance Is Mine. His courtroom testimony and that of <u>Angelo Lonardo</u>, called "the highest ranking mobster ever to testify for the government" helped put away mob bosses Anthony "Fat Tony" Salerno of New York's Genovese Mafia family, Anthony "Tony Ducks" Corallo of the Luchesse clan and Carmine Persico of the Colombo family. Federal investigators trace these major mob convictions right back to the murder of Greene. Danny would have been proud. (www.americanmafia.com/Featuere_Articles_6.html)

44 From Cleveland Magazine, August 1978

On the morning of May 26, 1976, the end was near. John T. Scalish, the last great don of the Cleveland Mafia, was taking his biggest gamble yet — a long shot. At stake was his life. But the odds favored death. At 63, Scalish was still very much in control of the city's underworld — still its Godfather. In fact, with his wavy silver-gray hair and piercing smile, he looked more like Brando's Don Corleone than Brando himself. Although ill health had plagued him for nearly 30 years, he suffered stoically, continuing to conduct his routine business affairs after doctors performed a colostomy, showing few signs of the pain that had enveloped his body. But cancer had weakened him and given way to premature hardening of the arteries. Even this once fearless man, who had taken away or spared other men's lives with a mere nod, was helpless to control his own destiny. His physicians told him that only a bypass - a delicate heart operation - could possibly save him. Without it, he had only weeks to go. Even then, they explained, such surgery was extremely chancy for a man in his ravaged condition. But once again, he gambled. Only this time, a more powerful force than John Scalish held the odds. Scalish could afford the finest medical attention, and he got it. A team of Cleveland's best heart specialists labored for hours in the operating room, injecting tubes into his body, cutting and tying the fragile arteries. But ever their skill was not enough. An hour or two after the operation, John Scalish lay in the recovery room and took his last breath. He died as he had lived — quietly, without fanfare. Only his closest family was nearby. Word of the leader's death, however, swept through the underworld, and he was accorded a funeral befitting his position Not one, but three priests, said a solemn Requiem mass, and the body of Scalish was followed to Calvary Cemetery by a seemingly endless procession of black Cadillacs. Even as the last shovels of dirt covered the gold-inlaid casket, the Cleveland underworld was already in turmoil. Perhaps John Scalish was wreaking some kind of revenge on his old enemies, or his weakened condition diverted him from making the one crucial decision a *capo* should make. He did not pick a successor -- one who could keep peace among warring lieutenants and decide, once and for all, who got what and when. That sin of omission, if you will, led to the bloodiest and most tumultuous internecine gang wars here since the savage bootleg brawls some 50 years earlier -- when Scalish, a teenager, was just getting his start in crime. (CLEMAG-ClevelandsMafia.doc.)

45 **Reuben Sturman** (1924-1997) was an American pornographer and businessman from Ohio. Though unknown to most Americans, Sturman ran one of the most successful pornography operations in US history. Time Magazine estimated that Sturman was making around $300 million per year in 1991.Sturman, the son of immigrant Russian Jews, grew up on Cleveland's East Side. He served in the Army Air Corps during World War II and then went on to study at Western Reserve University, graduating in 1948, before starting his own business selling comic books from his car. By the late 1950's his business had swelled to a major wholesale magazine company with affiliates in several American cities. During the 1960s Sturman started selling magazines with sexual content, a product he discovered could

make profits that outmatched anything that could be achieved by selling any kind of comic book. By the late 1960s Sturman was the biggest distributor of adult magazines in the US. The first problems with the authorities started in 1964, when FBI agents raided a Cleveland warehouse, confiscating copies of a magazine entitled *Sex Life of a Cop*. This was the start of over two decades of legal difficulties. Though his operations were raided and large volumes of magazines were confiscated on numerous occasions, Sturman managed to avoid prosecution by counter-suits, shady business practices and by using at least 20 different aliases to protect his identity. Sturman became increasingly involved in semi-legal or all-out criminal activities during this time and had connections with the Gambino crime family.The American journalist and writer Eric Schlosser described Sturman in a *US News & World Report* article in 1997:*To his defenders in the sex industry, Sturman was a marketing genius and a champion of free speech, an entrepreneur whose toughness, intelligence, and boundless self-confidence were responsible for his successes. But to anti-porn activists and Justice Department officials, Sturman was the head of a vast criminal organization whose companies enjoyed an unfair competitive advantage: protection and support from the highest levels of the Cosa Nostra.*It was Sturman's refusal to pay any form of tax that finally brought him down. In 1989, Sturman was convicted of tax evasion and sentenced to 10 years in jail and $2.5 million in fines. Another charge, this time for the interstate transportation of obscene material, resulted in a plea bargain for Sturman, but he was later caught trying to bribe a juror and was sentenced to 19 additional years for extortion. He briefly escaped prison in Boron, California, but was reapprehended in Anaheim. He died in a federal prison in Lexington, Kentucky on October 27, 1997. (www.artandpopularculture.com/Reuben_Sturman)

46 **Larry Claxton Flynt, Jr.** (born November 1, 1942) is an American publisher and the head of Larry Flynt Publications (LFP). In 2003,

Arena magazine listed him at the top of the "50 Most Powerful People in Porn" list. He is paralyzed from the waist down due to injuries sustained in a 1978 assassination attempt. In March 1972, Flynt created the *Hustler Newsletter*, a four-page, black-and-white publication about his clubs. This item became so popular with his customers that by May 1972 he expanded the *Hustler Newsletter* to 16 pages, then to 32 pages in August 1973. As a result of the 1973 oil crisis, the American economy went into recession. Revenues of Hustler Clubs declined, and Flynt had to either refinance his debts or declare bankruptcy. He decided to turn the *Hustler Newsletter* into a sexually explicit magazine with national distribution. He paid the start-up costs of the new magazine by deferring payment of sales taxes his clubs owed on their activities. In July 1974, the first issue of *Hustler* was published. In November 1974, Hustler showed the first "pink-shots," or photos of open vulvas. Flynt had to fight to publish each issue, as many people, including some at his distribution company, found the magazine too explicit and threatened to remove it from the market. Shortly thereafter, Flynt was approached by a paparazzo who had taken nude pictures of former First Lady Jacqueline Kennedy Onassis while she was sunbathing on vacation in 1971. He purchased them for $18,000 and published them in the August 1975 issue. That issue attracted widespread attention, and 1 million copies were sold within a few days. Now a millionaire, Flynt bought a $375,000 mansion ($1.4 million in 2009 dollars) On March 6, 1978, during a legal battle (see below) related to obscenity in Gwinnett County, Georgia, Flynt and his local lawyer Gene Reeves Jr. were shot in an ambush near the county courthouse in Lawrenceville. The shooting left him in a wheelchair, with permanent spinal cord damage. White supremacist serial killer Joseph Paul Franklin confessed to the shootings, claiming he was outraged by an interracial photo shoot in *Hustler*. Franklin, who is currently on death row for unrelated murder charges, has never been brought to trial for the attempted killing. He had a one-year flirtation with evangelical Christianity, converted in 1977 by evangelist Ruth Carter Stapleton, the sister of President Jimmy Carter. He became "born again" and stated he had a vision from God while flying with Stapleton in his jet. He continued to publish his magazine, however, vowing to "hustle for God." He has since declared himself an atheist. (e,.wikipedia.org/wiki/Larry_Flynt)

www.ingramcontent.com/pod-product-compliance
Lightning Source LLC
Chambersburg PA
CBHW022001090426
42741CB00007B/849